KING OF SPRINKLER LANE
A Charmed Life

Michael R. Gardner

Copyright © 2014 Michael R. Gardner.

All rights reserved. No part of this book may be reproduced, stored, or transmitted by any means—whether auditory, graphic, mechanical, or electronic—without written permission of both publisher and author, except in the case of brief excerpts used in critical articles and reviews. Unauthorized reproduction of any part of this work is illegal and is punishable by law.

ISBN: 978-1-4834-1230-6 (sc)
ISBN: 978-1-4834-1229-0 (e)

Because of the dynamic nature of the Internet, any web addresses or links contained in this book may have changed since publication and may no longer be valid. The views expressed in this work are solely those of the author and do not necessarily reflect the views of the publisher, and the publisher hereby disclaims any responsibility for them.

Any people depicted in stock imagery provided by Thinkstock are models, and such images are being used for illustrative purposes only.
Certain stock imagery © Thinkstock.

Lulu Publishing Services rev. date: 08/21/2014

CONTENTS

Dedication ix
Prologue xi

The Early Years

4104 Military Road 1
The Cow Pasture Escape 3
The Beach 6
    12th and Simpson
    The 5 lb Flounder
    The Little Black Dog
    The Closet at 12th and Simpson
    My First Hurricane
The Whiskey Bottle Caper 13
The Sugar Daddy – Camel Cigarettes Sting 16
Two Irish Angels: A Nun and A Bootlegger 19
Janitor of D'Alberts Jewelers 21
Peoples Drug Store 22
The Big House 23
J. Edgar Hoover…and LBJ 25
My Mother's Knuckle Sandwich 28
"Flipping the Bird" at Sister Maria Theresa 31
"First Holy Communion" – on BS' Playground 33

The Transformation Begins

Gonzaga High School 36
Impeachment at Gonzaga 40
Life As a Haberdasher 45

New York, New York 53
"Senioritis" and Mrs. Shippens... 55
The Two Martini Lunch at "21". 58
A "Guilt-Free" Georgetown Experience...................................... 60
Tessie's Nose Dive 61
On the High Seas with the U.S. Coast Guard 64
Horses and Mice... 72
Timberlawn: Another Home Away From Home 76
    The Timberlawn Family
    The Black Car Chase
    The Shriver Horse Show for the Mentally Retarded
    Mickey and the Blizzard of 1965
    The Caroline
    Bobby's Big Sister
    Eunice Kennedy Shriver's Legacy
Domino Rebels 91
Busted at the French Embassy... 93
Dino – the Canine Matchmaker 96
From DC Kid to Washington Man.. 97

PRESIDENTIAL POLITICS

Democrats for Nixon (DFN) 112
    The Slush Fund
    Big John Connally in Person
    Sarge – McGovern and Connally
    The Manila Envelop Episode
    Connally and Rocky
    The Hatchet Man at Large
    Nixon and the 30 Rabbis
    The Democrats for Nixon – Texas Hoe-down
    Election Night – 1972
The Connally Trial... 132

INTERESTING TIMES

Theresa and Cary Grant – at the White House 143
The Reagan Years 145
Jim Brady - My Hero 149
Nairobi and Hollywood 152
Israel, the Vatican, the Soviet Union and the USTTI in Nairobi. 168
The Allure of Chauffeured Government Cars 176
The Vacation From Hell 177
Hampton Court, Rupert and the Mikimoto Pearls 197
Carpe Diem and Michelangelo's Sistine Chapel 201
Getting to Know Harry 203

Conclusion 209
Epilogue 211
Acknowledgement 213

DEDICATION

This book is dedicated to my great aunt, Theresa "Tessie" Bennett Bradley. One of thirteen Irish immigrant siblings who came to Philadelphia in the early 1900's, Tessie had an aggressive *joie de vi-vre*. Tessie was also my "self-esteem mentor" and she empowered me to think anything was possible.

PROLOGUE

I initially wrote this book for my grandchildren. I want them to believe - as I do - that anything is possible in life if you've got the right attitude. I also hope that these stories of the historical events and the people I have encountered in my life so far will encourage parents and grandparents who are dealing with an underachieving, iconoclastic child like me.

These following stories are all true. The events are real, and the people are real - except when - in a very few cases - I believed anonymity was necessary and appropriate. These stories have demanded some self-examination on my part as I have worked to write this book. As part of the reflective process, I realize that I knew very early in life that I could make people laugh, and I knew that I could convince friends to follow me in my adventures. As a child, these characteristics sometimes endeared me to people and sometimes got me into trouble. It took some tough lessons in high school and beyond to help me learn how to channel these assets to achieve my goals.

At a very young age, I understood and valued loyalty, and this has turned out to be one of the defining traits of my life. I also knew at a young age that I wanted a professional career and - having worked hard at so many jobs as a child and teenager - I also knew that I wanted to be financially successful. But from my earliest memory, having fun was always a top priority – even when the fun I generated added to some misguided results.

And I was lucky. Not all people are, but I was. As my "stories" confirm, it was a heavy dose of Irish luck that took me on adventures and connected me with some remarkable people far removed from my early childhood row house in the very middle class, neighborhood of Northwest Washington, circa 1940 and 1950.

Besides being lucky, I was blessed. I had devoted parents who never gave up on me, even when I frequently challenged authority and failed, up to my teen years, to take my academic responsibilities seriously. And I was blessed throughout life with countless Jesuits who helped me develop academically and emotionally. But my greatest blessing was marrying a woman who was and remains wise, loyal, fun and the source of unconditional love.

Good luck together with my ample blessings have resulted in a very charmed and exciting life for this King of Sprinkler Lane.

THE EARLY YEARS

4104 Military Road

As World War II ended, Washington, D.C. was flooded with returning veterans like my Dad, Joe, who wanted to make up for lost time – in every sense. And their energy was infectious. So growing up in D.C. in the 1940s and 1950s was an adventure.

For my first eleven years I lived in a modest brick row house at 4104 Military Road in the Chevy Chase section of Northwest Washington. For my brother Tim (four years older), my sister Sheila (just a year older) and me, Military Road and the networks of back alleys behind it were our common parkland. Since we had only one car that my Father used for work, we walked everywhere – to Blessed Sacrament School off Chevy Chase Circle during the school year and to the nearby Chevy Chase playground each weekday in the summer. Perhaps there were child predators lurking somewhere in those days, but my siblings and our parents were oblivious to any threats. As a result, roaming free through the streets and alleys of Chevy Chase, D.C. was an acceptable and an integral part of my childhood.

As I look back on those days a half century ago, most of my good memories deal with summertime when we were out of school. With the exception of the last two weeks in August when the annual Gardner family pilgrimage to Ocean City, N.J. took place, the three Gardner kids spent each Monday through Friday of the summer at the public Chevy Chase playground just two blocks from our row house on Military Road. We went off each morning at 8:30 a.m. to the Chevy Chase playground with peanut butter and jelly sandwiches, 2 nickels for a coke at lunchtime and mid-afternoon, and our bathing suits for a late afternoon romp in Sprinkler Lane.

The routine for the tuition-free summer camp at the Chevy Chase playground never changed: 9:00 a.m.-11:00 a.m. – arts and crafts with college student counselors; 11:00 a.m.-12:30 p.m. – baseball, basketball or tennis; 12:30 p.m.-1:00 p.m. – lunch; 1:00 p.m.-1:30 p.m. – pretend naps under the shady oak trees; 1:30 p.m. – 4:00 p.m. – arts and craft part II or sports; and at 4:00 p.m., Sprinkler Lane promptly opened for an hour.

Sprinkler Lane was a paved area – thirty yards by forty yards – with three rotating sprinklers that shot ice-cold water into the air! Sprinkler Lane was a concrete paradise.

By mid-afternoon each steamy summer day, we were crabby – and sweaty – from a full day of play in Washington's notoriously hot and humid summers. But at 4 o'clock sharp things got cool; we put on our bathing suits and dashed around Sprinkler Lane like maniacs, before the hot march home at 5:00 p.m.

In mid-August, the Chevy Chase playground and its exhausted college counselors would officially closeout the summer camp program by holding the King and Queen of Sprinkler Lane Contest. Wildly popular in our part of Northwest Washington, the King and Queen were chosen by three women who were D.C. public school teachers. Unlike the Miss America pageant, the Sprinkler Lane contest was strictly a "bathing suit" competition. No hard questions, no essays, no feat of daring – just a walk through Sprinkler Lane in your bathing suit. So, in my fourth summer in 1946 – and for two consecutive years, I entered the King of Sprinkler Lane Contest.

And this is where I may have initially gone off track. I not only won the King of Sprinkler Lane contest in 1946; I won it again in 1947 and incredibly I was crowned in 1948 for the third consecutive time as the King of Sprinkler Lane.

In the 1948 contest, my Queen was Jeanne McManus, a younger neighbor, whose father was a respected professor at Georgetown Law School. A retired sports columnist for the Washington Post, the then Queen Jeanne and I made such a smashing couple that our photo ended up on the front page of the *Washington Evening Star*. This was big time on Military Road – and represented my media high point for the next few decades.

When I was crowned for the third time with the star-studded gold paper crown, the smiling judges announced that they were retiring my crown. I had won it three years in a row – and that was it! I would forever be the ranking King of Sprinkler Lane!

Sometimes I think I peaked in kindergarten.

The Cow Pasture Escape

Because ours was largely an urban life on Military Road, my parents always looked for some bucolic setting for our traditional July 4th picnic. So, on July 4th, 1948 the green, shaded fields of the Georgetown Prep School outside of Washington, D.C., became the venue for the Gardner family's most memorable picnic.

After days of preparation – boiling and deviling eggs, frying chicken legs, making potato salad – we drove out of the city on the two lane Rockville Pike that would take us to the "Prep" – a scenic Jesuit prep school where my Father had taught Math and coached football in the 1930s.

As usual, the very portly Father John "Jerky" Jacklin, S.J. joined us, making the cramped 30-minute ride in our un-air-conditioned two-door Buick a challenging journey. I would complain privately to my parents: "Why does Jerky always have to come?" My Father would quietly say; "Remember, Miguel, the Jesuits fed and educated me – and our home must always be a home away from home for them."

On this particular July 4th, an alumni golf tournament was still going on when we arrived at the Prep's nine-hole course. For safety reasons, establishing our picnic beachhead on the golf links was out; so, my parents moved us to a slightly different picnic venue – an inviting field on the private estate immediately adjacent to the Preps' 5th fairway.

From the Prep's driveway, the other side of the Prep's fifth fairway looked like an ideal, golf-ball-free setting for our family picnic: a lush green pasture, beautiful shade trees, a little stream – and on the other side of the stream, a herd of black and white cows. Who could ask for more?

Parked behind the Prep's St. Mary's Chapel, we unloaded the trunk: the cooler, two picnic baskets, the picnic blanket, the watermelon and, of course, the box of fireworks for our after-dinner display. While the trek from the car, across the 5th fairway was formidable, we were quite prepared to make the sacrifice to have the best July 4th picnic ever!

When we finally got to the fence on the far side of the fairway, we discovered a barbed wire fence adjacent to the white wood fence. My Mother exclaimed in irritation: "Joe, after living here for six years and playing golf here every weekend for the past twelve years, didn't you realize there was a barbed wire fence here?"

She was right of course; you would have thought my Dad would have known – but maybe he never hit any golf balls out of bounds on the fifth hole.

But we were all determined. The long awaited picnic and 4th of July fireworks were only minutes away on the other side of these two fences.

After some careful maneuvering, all six of us – even fat old Father Jerky Jacklin – got over the white fence and through the barbed wire without a nick! Within minutes, we were all set-up; the picnic blanket was spread out under a huge elm, the picnic baskets were unpacked, and most importantly for my parents and "Jerky", the gin and tonics – with pre-sliced limes – were raised.

For my siblings and me, the main attraction – after a few chicken legs – was the herd of cows on the other side of the creek. For city kids, real cows were something only viewed during Saturday afternoon cowboy and Indian matinees.

So, off we went to the stream, to serenade the cows with our own "moo, moo!"

To our surprise, the cows mooed back.

Not only did they moo back, the cows started to walk toward us – and some were walking pretty fast!

As usual, my sister Sheila panicked first, although I will admit to shaky knees myself.

"Mommy, Mommy, the cows are attacking! Mommy help" – Sheila shrilled, and with each piercing scream, the cows became more curious.

At first, my parents and Jerky were unmoved. They now were well into their second gin and tonic, and the cows were safely on the other side of the creek. But they were misguided. The creek wasn't even a stream! In reality, it was more like a puddle.

Unfortunately, the more Sheila screamed, the faster the herd moved. No longer mellow, slow-moving dairy cows, the herd of fifteen black and white cows appeared angry.

When the cows crossed the stream – only thirty yards away from our picnic blanket and our July 4th feast – panic set in. The Gardner family with Jerky went into full retreat!

As we ran – the mooing cows moved with incredible speed towards us. No sooner had we gotten to the barbed wire fence, when the cows made it to our picnic blanket! And there to our horror, the cows trampled our picnic blanket – squashing the deviled eggs, crunching the chicken wings and even snorting through the cup cakes. Everything was ruined, including the box of fireworks when an excited cow relieved herself right on our 4th of July display!

As we ran, Jerky, got snagged on the barbed wire fence – and it was a major snag: his ample rear end was now literally caught on the barbed wire fence. For my siblings and me, seeing Jerky's fat fanny stuck to the barbed wire fence was hysterical. And no matter how hard my Father tried, Jerky's pants could not be freed from the stubborn barbed wire that had ensnared him.

After a hushed discussion, my parents and Jerky made a strategic decision: Jerky would take off his black, Jesuit-issued pants. There was no choice: his pants were stuck, therefore he was stuck, and at any minute, the herd of cattle could charge!

Before Jerky's pants came off, my brother, sister and I were admonished by my Mother to "turn around and don't dare look back this way until I tell you!"

Needless to say, the temptation was too great – at least for me. And the sight of this corpulent Jesuit standing in his white boxer shorts with a herd of black and white cows not 10 feet away on the other side of the barbed wire fence was worth every minute of the eternity I surely was doomed to spend in Hell someday.

That night, on the hot ride back to 4104 Military Road, we all laughed until we cried. Yes – our delicious picnic was trampled and our fireworks were gone, but despite those tragedies, the memories of that special Independence Day lived on for years as we recounted how the Gardner Family – and Jerky – had survived "the great cattle stampede of July 4, 1948."

The Beach

12th and Simpson

Each August my family embarked on our vacation to the sleepy and "dry" Southern Jersey town of Ocean City. And, my memories of our annual two weeks in Ocean City loom larger today than my memories of the other 50 weeks of those early years.

For me, the anchor for my fondest beach memories was a shabby, second floor, walk-up rental apartment at 12th and Simpson on the wrong side of Ocean City's railroad tracks.

Three bedrooms, one bath and a largely unusable living room full of ancient, uncomfortable furniture: our apartment at 12th and Simpson was perfect – at least to me. Located eight long blocks from the Atlantic Ocean, our "flat" was just two blocks from the Bay.

Our daily routine at Ocean City was to leave the flat around 10:00 a.m. and drive to Ocean City's wide, snow-white beach at 24th Street. Armed with our beach towels, blankets, buckets and, of course, our snacks and soft drinks, we looked like a horde of immigrants arriving at Ellis Island.

By 2:00 p.m. or 2:30 p.m. each afternoon, the sun had taken its toll on our sun sensitive Irish American skin, so the lobster-red, beach weary Gardner kids typically retreated to the shade of our apartment. For me, the hyper youngest child, a nap was unthinkable. I had to get to the 12th Street dock to swim solo in the Bay and see what my aged fishing friends had caught.

Even at 5 years old, I would walk – unsupervised – to the Bay at the 12th Street dock. For me, swimming off this public dock was an enormous, self-esteem building adventure; I was certain that none of my friends at the Chevy Chase playground had ever had the guts to swim solo in such a fearsome body of water.

The 5 lb Flounder

After my daily swim off the 12th Street dock, I would join the "locals" for some fishing. These crusty World War I and II Veterans fished day and night from this public dock. Since the nearby Atlantic Ocean fed Ocean City's Bay with high tides full of fresh flounders and plump crabs, my fishing buddies were busy – but never too busy to help me bait my drop line.

One afternoon, I dragged my dad to the 12th Street dock and proudly introduced my Father to my "fishing mentors." That day these guys were unusually sullen – and not as gregarious as they typically were with me. My Dad was a humble and cheerful man with absolutely no pretenses. I see now that my fishing buddies at the 12th Street Pier must have thought he was an uptown guy and clammed up. So, in silence, my Dad and I baited my drop-line and let it fall into the Bay.

And then it happened.

I can still remember the powerful pull on my line immediately after it sank into the Bay. The initial pull was quickly followed by a huge tug – a tug that was so forceful that my fishing buddies saw my line suddenly move away from the pilings. No longer silent, the "locals" started yelling: "Kid – pull it in, pull it in Kid!!" And pull I did – as fast as I could, but it was heavy, really heavy.

Suddenly "it" broke the water – and "it" was a truly enormous flounder. Gray and shimmering in the sun, my catch was flapping up a storm and determined not to be taken from its safe saltwater home in Ocean City's Bay. With a non-stop chorus of encouraging instructions from the locals "to pull it in faster kid," I frantically rewound my drop line.

But then, to my shock, my Dad suddenly said, "Miguel – stop. That fish is a skate – and it's dangerous if it gets on this dock!"

"Dad," I replied in disbelief, "It's a huge flounder. I can't stop now, Dad."

But my seasoned Navy-veteran Father was firm, "Miguel – you can't bring it in! Skates are dangerous, and son, that skate could cut you badly!"

Now, I really had a big dilemma: on the one hand, my buddies – the seedy vets – were screaming for me to pull in the "big one;" but my Dad was saying, "stop, Miguel."

Before I could resolve this moral dilemma – the flounder won; it flipped my hook and slipped silently back into the green waters of the Bay.

I was crestfallen at my lost catch; but as it suddenly became clear, my pain was minor compared to the anger of my fishing buddies.

These guys, who had been so withdrawn when my Dad and I first arrived were now on a verbal roll. "What the hell is the matter with you man?" they yelled at my Dad. "That's the biggest F------- flounder that was ever hooked on this Dock – ever." "Are you crazy man?"

My fishing mentors had obviously had their beers – and they were incensed. This tourist - my Dad - has just broken a cardinal rule of the 12th Street Dock: when you've hooked a flounder, you pull it in – quickly!

In order to spare my Dad any more verbal abuse, I quietly suggested that we leave immediately. So, without any angry words of rebuttal to the "locals," my Father and I rewound the empty fishing line, picked up my bait bucket – and took the longest and slowest walk ever back to 12th and Simpson.

The Little Black Dog

Things move quickly in a five year olds' life. One sunny day Dad and I went to his favorite oyster bar in Somers Point – across the bridge from Ocean City. Founded by Methodist ministers, Ocean City was a "dry town," and no alcohol could be sold anywhere on this Island. In contrast, Somers Point was a jumping vacation spot filled with bars, restaurants and liquor stores that prospered each summer.

On our occasional oyster outings, my Dad had a beer or two as we sat on wooden stools at his favorite outdoor oyster Bar, the Spinacle. To call the Spinacle a "Bar" was pretentious; in reality, this dive was nothing more than a weathered shed that shut down each Labor Day when the tourists headed home. But the oysters at the Spinacle were great, and when we finished our oysters on this particular day, my Dad and I went to the adjacent vegetable stand to buy fresh homegrown Jersey tomatoes and even some gladiolas for my Mother. As we approached the makeshift vegetable stand, I heard a soft yelping coming from a little wire chicken coup not more than 30 yards away.

Off in a quick sprint to the yelping, I discovered four little puppies huddled together in their cluttered and stinky cage.

"Please, please, please – please Dad – the little black one. Dad please, we leave for home in three days – Dad, you and Mom promised us a dog last Christmas. Please Dad!" And then the pout – not tears – and a look of overwhelming sadness.

To my utter surprise and without further discussion, my Dad turned to the vegetable lady and asked, "How much for the little black dog?"

It was miraculous. He really did it. Five minutes later, my fearless Father and I were driving across the bridge into Ocean City – with our tomatoes, our watermelon, our gladiolas – and a five-week-old black puppy on my lap.

Heaven had happened. Nothing in the world could be better than holding that warm little black fur ball in my lap as we approached 12th and Simpson.

I wish I could say the story had a happy ending, but it didn't. No sooner did we walk up the creaky wooden steps to the second floor porch when all hell broke lose! My Mother, who was not a screamer, exploded.

"That scroungry dog is not house broken", she yelled. "We're at the beach in someone else's home; Are you crazy Joe?" My uncompromising Mother then reminded my Dad that, "we were going to get an Irish setter when we move into a bigger house." On and on and on!

Not even the gladiolas that I offered diminished my Mother's relentless protests.

I then took my little black puppy into my parents' bedroom. Snugly settled on the bed, I ignored the heated discussion that raged on in the next room. Unfortunately, my little black puppy peed up a storm right on the pillow! Realizing I had a problem, I called out to my sister "Sheila can you come here for a minute?" When she entered the room, Sheila looked at the wet pillowcase and screamed, "Mommy, Mommy the dog has peed all over the bed. It stinks in here; come quickly. Mommy, Mommy!"

Need I say more? My first "nap" with man's best friend was over, and within ten minutes, the debate also was over: my little black puppy, my Dad and I lost. So over the bridge to Somers Point my apologetic Father went once more with the puppy now on his lap, not mine. I cried for the next two days.

Things did improve. We did move to the big house on Nevada Avenue six years later, and we got – as promised – a spectacular Irish Setter named Finnegan who would become my best friend for the next 12 years.

The Closet at 12th and Simpson

On another sunny August day I was too sunburned – and blistered – to accompany my Mother, her sister Shirley and my siblings to the 24th Street beach. As far as I was concerned, it was okay to miss the ocean for a day;

after all I was home with my trusty Dad and his reclusive friend, "Jerky," the Jesuit priest who got his pants snagged on the fence.

As things worked out, my Dad decided to slip over to the Atlantic City Racetrack for a "few quick bets." Jerky, who apparently didn't care for the ponies, volunteered to keep an eye on me. As a celibate priest, "Jerky" had spent his entire adult life in the childfree environment of an all male Jesuit world at Georgetown University. But I was bored; so, I set out to harass Jerky who was attempting to read his Breviary, the prayer book that Jesuits must read each day as part of their contemplative spiritual journey through life.

While the specifics of my harassment campaign are cloudy today, I knew I had hit a nerve when Jerky threw his Breviary to the floor and chased me onto the front porch. Minutes later I heard Father Jacklin say, "Shit."

I had gone too far. The "S" word out of the mouth of a Jesuit Priest! Then Jerky lost it.

Even though he was overweight with a large potbelly, Jerky sprinted across the living room and actually cornered me in the dining room right next to the closet. Suddenly, Jerky had me with both hands around the neck. "Was this it?" I thought, "Had I finally pushed too hard?"

Fortunately, Jerky was a lot of things but not a child murderer.

Once captured justice was swift. Without a word, Jerky merely opened the dreaded dining room closet door, pushed me inside – and to my incredulous ears, he turned the key and locked me in. The closet was a dark and scary space, cluttered with a vintage vacuum cleaner, a broken lamp, several old suitcases and abundant mothballs.

At first, I pleaded – then cried – then yelled, "Help! Help! Help!" After at least a hundred piercing "helps", silence prevailed.

I finally fell asleep after my crying jag. Hours later, when the sun worshippers returned from a glorious, breezy day at the 24th Street beach, my Mother presumed I was with Dad at the Atlantic City Racetrack. Only after my Father returned from the racetrack, did Jerky mention that "Gardner child #3 was in the closet taking a nap."

When that closet door was unlocked and my shocked parents set me free, I put on an Academy Award winning performance.

Did I cry? - No, this was a "wailing event" – and wail I did. On that day, I also earned my masters degree in Irish guilt as I kept asking my distraught Mother: "How could you leave me alone with Jerky when I have blisters all over my body? How Mommy? How could you do that?"

Before the sun set on "the day of the closet," my Mother took me to the boardwalk, bought me a hamburger, a sarsaparilla, two frozen custards – and even played miniature golf with her brave and blistered child. Best of all, when we returned to 12th and Simpson, I overheard my Mother in a hushed but very firm voice tell Jerky that she would never forgive him for "locking my baby in that closet."

As I fell asleep that night with a very full stomach and with the lingering smell of mothballs in my nostrils, I knew that my Mother was totally on my side.

My First Hurricane

When you live on an Island – particularly a puny little mile wide Island like Ocean City, N.J. – the "locals" get very interested in weather reports during August and September. That's hurricane season in the Atlantic and hurricanes are as unpredictable as the thoroughbred horses at nearby Atlantic City Racetrack.

Among my old fishing buddies at the 12th Street dock, there was constant banter about "that big storm in '38" or "that mean sister in '43." With each hurricane, there were endless and surely embellished stories about the treachery of Mother Nature and the bravery of those who "rode her out."

So I was thrilled one late August in 1950 to overhear my parents discussing the possible arrival of a hurricane named Claudia. While I was only eight, I had heard enough from the "locals" to know that this could be more fun than riding the awesome, sky-high Ferris wheel that dominated the north end of Ocean City's boardwalk.

At first, my parents seemed unusually anxious, and they talked about the prospect of heading home to Washington a few days early to avoid Claudia's possible wrath.

"Give me a break," I thought. We waited all year for our two weeks at Ocean City; and now, our parents were thinking of leaving a few days ahead of time in order to miss a hurricane. The mere mention of that possibility prompted a spontaneous protest from me and even my two older siblings who typically were not as into the pleasures of the beach as I was.

Whether it was our pleas, our tears, or merely my parents' own concerns about "overreacting," we won; we stayed put as Claudia moved north from the Caribbean.

Since the antiquated radio at our apartment was on the blink, my parents' decision to "ride out Claudia" was also flawed; it was based exclusively on the day old weather report in *The Philadelphia Inquirer*.

To confirm the reliability of the Inquirer's prediction that Claudia would not touch land until Long Island, I was dispatched to the 12th Street Dock to consult with my fisherman buddies. Sure enough, they all agreed: "Kid, that storm Claudia is so far out to sea, it may even miss Maine."

As it turned out, Claudia didn't stay out to sea as predicted. Instead, by stealth, Claudia arrived in Ocean City one gray afternoon with the thunder rain, winds, and even waves of seawater in the streets.

When the first winds from Claudia hit, it was a blast; just holding onto the front porch railing was definitely cooler than the ferris wheel on a windy night. But as Claudia's eye grew closer to Ocean City and the winds increased, it got scary.

When nightfall fell and it was totally dark, things seemed oddly still.

Then Claudia hit – full force. And I instantly knew why my fishing buddies reminisced with such awe about the various hurricanes they had lived through.

First of all, there was the noise. The relentless roar of the wind in a full blown hurricane is unbelievable – and the sounds spawned by the wind are amazing. For us, now behind locked doors and windows at the fragile "duplex," the cacophony of sounds included windows shaking loudly in their warped wooden frames; rocking chairs screeching across the front porch like dodgem cars on the boardwalk; and most haunting, the eerie endless whistling sound as the wind eked its way through the six foot "tunnel" that divided our duplex from the equally vulnerable one next door.

Crashing, banging, whistling, wailing – these piercing sounds competed for our attention. Then, the lights went out all over the island of Ocean City, and it really got scary.

Fortunately, my Mother was a candle freak. Each night at dinner in Washington or Ocean City, candles gave off a glow on our dining room table. So, as soon as Claudia knocked the lights out my Mother immediately lit her candles; somehow, with that candlelight, a sense of adventure crowded out some of our fear.

In retrospect, it was more than the candles that helped diminish our fears that night; it was my parents' good cheer and calmness – their steady voices assuring my siblings and me, "that this is a great adventure to tell your friends when we get back to D.C." And sure enough, by making Claudia's direct assault on Ocean City "an adventure," the louder the winds roared the more fun it became, especially since no one was suggesting that we go to bed.

Finally – at about 3:00 a.m., fatigue took over – and we "kids" bedded down in the little room off the tiny kitchen. It was a lumpy but snug bed, and that mini-night of crowded slumber became another part of the "great Claudia adventure."

Inexplicably, no matter how loud the wind roared and no matter how much the house quivered, I knew we would be okay. While my sister, brother and I dozed on and off, my parents stayed up all night talking softly in the adjacent kitchen where my Mother's candles gave off a dim but soothing light.

When the gray day dawned, the wind was gone – and so was Claudia. She was somewhere over Long Island.

The Whiskey Bottle Caper

My first friend who was a girl, Jenny O'Reilly, was a bone-skinny neighbor who lived four doors away on Military Road. When I first met Jenny, she was nine years old, but she was so tiny, she looked five or six. Jenny was a good pal, and we were inseparable, playing daily in the alleys behind Military Road and at the Chevy Chase playground.

Jenny was also tough. She would fly off and punch somebody smack in the nose if they said anything bad about the O'Reillys – something that happened often. That's because Jenny's father, Mr. O'Reilly was the neighborhood drunk.

Even when it was daytime, if Mr. O'Reilly was drinking, the front door would be closed and the shades were lowered. When I'd go to get

Jenny on one of those dark days, Jenny would call from within, "I can't come out today."

Initially puzzled by Jenny's conduct, I complained to my parents. They finally explained that the kindest thing for me to do for Jenny was to leave her alone when the shades were down. "When the O'Reilly's house is locked up," my Mother explained with a pained look, "it means Mr. O'Reilly is drinking again. And Mickey, he's a mean drunk."

At first, I thought my parents were wrong, but in time, I realized that it was best if I just pretended that I didn't hear the yelling or smell the foul odor in the O'Reilly's living room. But as much as I tried to be cool, it was really hard to pretend not to notice the pathetic way Mrs. O'Reilly looked after Mr. O'Reilly had been "sick" at home for a few days.

Somehow, my pretending seemed to work. If Jenny could pretend that everything was okay, so could I.

Then, to my shock, the pretending suddenly stopped.

It was a really hot summer day, and Jenny and I were walking home following a quick run through Sprinkler Lane. Without any warning, Jenny suddenly asked me to help her with "something big." Now – this in itself was "big" because Jenny – and the O'Reillys – never asked anyone for any kind of help.

"Of course," I quickly replied. "Jenny, you're my friend." And then she unloaded.

"Tomorrow afternoon after we come back from the playground, I want you to help me drop all my Father's whiskey bottles down the sewer. Will you do it? It's risky!"

I was stunned. Not only was the very private Jenny talking about the whispered whiskey thing at the O'Reilly's, she was planning an all out war against her Father.

"Wow, are you kidding?" I asked.

"No, I'm not kidding; I'm serious and if you don't want to help me, Mickey Gardner, I'll do it myself!" Jenny was really serious – and as I learned, very, very brave. So I agreed – what else could I do?

Next day, Jenny O'Reilly and I entered the O'Reillys' house unnoticed at 5:30 p.m. – well before Mr. O'Reilly returned home from his printing job. Walking up the stairs to the bedrooms, we successfully slipped by Mrs. O'Reilly who was cooking in a steaming kitchen. Once on the second floor, we entered the hall bathroom; there Jenny pointed in silence to eight pint bottles of whiskey clumsily "hidden" behind the back legs of their ancient bathtub.

We only had four hands between us to carry eight whiskey bottles, so Jenny quickly pulled two pillowcases out of the hall closet; we then quietly loaded our cache before moving silently back down the stairs.

Within seconds, Jenny and I were once again on the O'Reilly's front porch – still unnoticed. Safely outside, I got my instructions: we were going to the corner of Military Road and 41st Street where the public sewer awaited us.

Once we reached the sewer, we were no longer "covert." Emboldened, Jenny was particularly animated – almost gleeful – as she began to empty whiskey bottle after whiskey bottle down the sewer.

After each pint bottle was emptied of its foul smelling tan liquid contents, Jenny would then ceremonially drop the stubby bottle down the sewer – one crash of glass at a time.

While it only took a few minutes for this to be completed, Jenny and I, nonetheless, attracted stares from rush hour motorists who stopped at the intersection of Military Road and 41st Street. We also caught the attention of my gracious next door neighbor, Louise Smith.

Looking down from her porch with great distress on her face, Mrs. Smith called out, in her soft Southern voice: "Jenny – honey, don't you think you should take all of that home, honey?"

But Jenny was determined and just answered "No Ma'am" in a firm, but polite voice, as she kept pouring.

I'd like to say that things got better at the O'Reilly's after that, but they didn't. In fact, when I went to Jenny's house the next morning to get her to walk with me to the playground, the O'Reilly's shades were down. And the next day – and the next day.

When Jenny finally emerged several days later, she said in a hushed voice, "I can't play with you anymore." And that was all she said.

As it turned out, Jenny couldn't play with any of us – nor could her siblings. And in two weeks, as school was starting, a "for rent" sign suddenly appeared on the lawn in front of 4110 Military Road. A few days later, the O'Reilly's were gone.

Michael R. Gardner

The Sugar Daddy – Camel Cigarettes Sting

After classes at Blessed Sacrament, two of my young cronies and I typically crossed Connecticut Avenue at Chevy Chase Circle and meandered home. My fifth grade buddies and I were in no hurry to get home to chores, or worse, homework. So one of our favorite detours was the Chevy Chase Pharmacy, right next to the bus station just yards from the Chevy Chase Circle.

In the early 1950s, the Chevy Chase Pharmacy was one of those jammed-packed multipurpose drug stores that included a lunch counter sandwiched in between shelves containing everything from cosmetics to pet supplies. Navigating these narrow aisles of assorted merchandise was challenging, but that was ok; the pharmacy's clutter provided ample cover for our heist one Friday in the fall of 1951.

Our scam was simple: Tommy L, Jimmy and I would enter the Chevy Chase Pharmacy and sit at the lunch counter where we ordered ice cream sodas. We typically did this on Fridays because we would have saved up our school milk money during the week to finance our "end of the school week" blow out.

Once served, we'd laugh loud enough to prompt frowns from the Chevy Chase matrons who frequented the soda counter. After we created a minor ruckus, we would move in the direction of the checkout counter manned by the elderly – and typically flustered – manager. As we fumbled for change and continued to create a ruckus at the checkout counter, one of us who was not paying the check, would quietly reach behind the distracted checkout man and snatch a pack of Camel cigarettes from the shelf.

On this particular Friday, I altered the plan. While Jimmy was paying the bewildered checkout man, and Tommy L was pocketing the Camels, I slipped a Sugar Daddy into my pocket. The poor old guy totally missed it.

We then headed back out to Connecticut Avenue and promptly escaped into the network of nearby alleys on our way to Military Road. As soon as we were safely in the alley, we lit up – just like our parents did – to relieve the stress of a long week at BS.

No sooner had we taken the first long puff of our pilfered Camels, then we were stunned by a booming male voice: "There you are – you little gangsters!"

Before us stood a giant D.C. police officer in his navy blue uniform, with a shinning silver badge on his shirt and a gun holstered to his belt. He was huge, and he was black and back then, you didn't see many black police officers in Chevy Chase, D.C.

I thought my life was over, and I was only nine!

While Jimmy was cool and kept smoking, Tommy immediately dropped his Camel and started crying. For the first time in my life, I was speechless.

What could we say?

Well, we didn't have to say anything; the arresting Officer did all the talking: "You guys are crooks, and you've shamed your families. And don't tell me this is your first offense. We were waiting for you this Friday."

Next thing I knew, we three gangsters were being taken by foot – single file – by this huge police officer to our respective homes.

Since Tommy lived just a block away on McKinley Street, we marched to his semi-detached row house first. Thank God his was the closest house because Tommy's sobbing had turned into a loud, unnatural wailing that was attracting onlookers. As the cop led the now hysterical Tommy up the two flights of stairs to his front door, Jimmy and I were left – unguarded – on the sidewalk. Unfortunately, I couldn't hear what the officer was saying because now Tommy's saintly Mother was also sobbing while Tommy's heightened wailing reverberated down McKinley Street.

Next we marched to 4104 Military Road – three long blocks away. While Jimmy and I were not handcuffed, it was, nonetheless, clear to passersby (and there were many) that we were under arrest.

"We're all going to jail." I thought. "And I'm only nine."

By the time we reached Military Road, a handful of neighborhood children already had spotted the cop bringing Jimmy and me home. Soon there was a crowd of kids around us. To my horror, my long march home – under arrest – was now becoming a major event as our Military Road neighbors watched from their front porches.

While Jimmy waited at the sidewalk in front of 4104 Military Road, my jailer, with his firm hand on my shoulder, led me on the longest walk of my life to our front door.

Unfortunately, at this critical moment, my sister Sheila spotted me and started screaming at the top of her shrill voice: "Mommy, Mommy – Mickey's been arrested! Hurry, Mommy – the cops have him!"

As we approached the open front door my Mother suddenly appeared.

"Mrs. Gardner, is this your son?"

"Yes, Officer. What has happened?" my Mother asked.

"Well, Mrs. Gardner, we have a very serious problem. Your son and his friends were caught stealing Camel cigarettes and one Sugar Daddy from the Chevy Chase Pharmacy. And Mrs. Gardner, this wasn't the first time."

"Officer, I'm so sorry. Mickey has been a good boy, but this is horrible. What are you going to do, Officer?" my Mother uttered.

"Here it comes," I thought.

"Well, Mrs. Gardner, if it was their first time, maybe he could avoid jail time. But your son and his friends are "repeat offenders," and jail time may be the only way to break this pattern."

As I contemplated the lock up and forced separation from my family – even my annoying sister Sheila, the tears started. Sobbing, I glanced over my shoulder and saw that Jimmy now had a bad case of dry heaves as he awaited his fate.

And then I found my voice. "Mother, please, I'll do anything. Officer, it was just a game – we paid for our sodas; we should have paid for our Camels and I should have paid for my Sugar Daddy. Please. Officer, I'll never smoke again, I promise!"

My genuine remorse must have registered with the arresting officer. After a few more painful minutes of serious negotiations between my Mother and the Officer, this huge cop released me to my Mother's "custody" under very explicit terms: my fellow conspirators and I would have to work at odd jobs until we had paid the owners of the Chevy Chase Pharmacy for four packs of Camels – and jointly contributed $30 to the Salvation Army's Christmas Drive. As far as repayment for the stolen Sugar Daddy, that was my sole responsibility.

So work we did for the next eight weeks – cleaning out garages, washing windows – even sweeping the porches and sidewalks of all our Military Road neighbors.

During this "work release program," I had several conversations with my parents about my repeated "grand larceny." My father's quiet reflections were philosophical and compelling: "Miguel, you must never take advantage of people and that's what stealing is. Those old people at the Chevy Chase Pharmacy work very hard for their customers. When you stole from them, you betrayed their trust."

By contrast, my Mother's words were persuasive in their bluntness: "Mickey, you are too young and too little to smoke – and if you want a Sugar Daddy, pay for it; if you don't have the money, work for it."

Not surprisingly, it took months before the notoriety of "our arrest" faded on Military Road. And even after we three felons paid our fines in full, the embarrassment of that long walk home to 4104 Military Road lingered.

And for me, there was one added benefit. I never smoked a cigarette again.

Two Irish Angels: A Nun and A Bootlegger

My Catholic grade school – Blessed Sacrament – or BS was located on Western Avenue, just a hundred yards from the Chevy Chase Circle. The Circle was significant as it marked the official dividing line between modest Chevy Chase, D.C. and tony Chevy Chase, Maryland.

During my eight years at BS, the dour Sisters of the Holy Cross wore half moon starched white bonnets and full-length heavy black robes secured around the waist by a huge rosary bead belt. Penguin-like, these "Women of God" were largely hidden with only their hands and a limited portion of their faces visible to the 52 students per class that each of these Sisters taught from 9:00 a.m. to 3:10 p.m. every school day. And they did it solo – no teachers' assistants, no parental volunteers, no nothing – day after day.

As my report cards from BS confirm, the pursuit of academic excellence in grade school had little importance to me. In fact, I can rarely remember doing homework, even though I am confident that the no nonsense Sisters of the Holy Cross at Blessed Sacrament assigned homework. Then again, maybe not – why would these overworked Nuns assign homework if you were the only teacher for an out-of-control classroom of 52 kids? Yes, 51 students "matriculated" with me from kindergarten through 8th grade at BS!

Unfortunately, most of the Holy Cross Sisters who taught at Blessed Sacrament during my time there were only high school graduates who had little cultural exposure before entering the Convent at the tender age of 16 or 17. With 52 kids in each class and no assistants, most of these Nuns had to rely on Gestapo tactics to maintain control.

But not Sister John Thomas, my 5th grade teacher from Heaven.

Short, stocky, with a thick Irish brogue and a deep booming laugh, Sister John Thomas was the first of two women besides my Mother who convinced me that I was special, even though I had flunked my way through the first four grades at Blessed Sacrament.

Somehow this cheerful little Nun – as wide as she was tall – found the time amidst her crowded class to personally tutor me through 5th grade. Often, during that year, Sister John Thomas would say: "Michael, don't get your knickers in a knot! You can do it – just concentrate". And she was right: before the year ended, I got my first and only 2nd honors Report Card – all B's except for an "A" for effort.

The other woman who convinced me early in life that I was not a loser, even though I had trouble with math and spelling, was my Mother's Aunt, Theresa (Tessie) Bennett Bradley.

One of the 13 Bennetts who had emigrated to the United States in the early 1900s from Ireland via Liverpool, England, "Tessie" had experienced life from many angles. Even in her 80's, Tessie's eyes twinkled as she delivered her wry comments, comments that brought merriment to the bleakest situation.

Thanksgiving, Easter, graduations, First Communions, confirmations…, Tessie and her two sisters Eva (AKA Nanna) and Aunt Mae took the train down from Philadelphia to celebrate with my family.

The three "Bennett girls," as my Father fondly called them, always arrived decked out with their finest hats and loaded down with boxes of delicious Philadelphia-baked pastries not available in Washington, D.C. Best of all, Tessie and her sisters arrived with stories about their early days as immigrants in New York, a New York where Tessie had been an entrepreneurial bootlegger in the wild days of Prohibition.

During one of Tessie's memorable Easter visits, I was trying to write a book report for my humorless sixth grade teacher, Sister Josephine Martin. Tessie realized I was troubled, especially since my goody-two-shoes older brother Tim had just won a major writing contest at his, and later my high school, Gonzaga.

As I huffed and puffed at the dining room table, Tessie sat down next to me, looked me square in the eye, and said: "The hell with this, kid just relax – and do the best you can. If that old witch – what's that Sister's name – doesn't like it, tough."

She leaned forward – so no one else could hear – and in her gravely voice whispered, "Kid, you've got it – and with it, you can do whatever you want in life. You can end up in the White House or Sing-Sing. It's all up to you."

From that moment on, I knew I could achieve whatever I set out to. After all, Tessie said I could.

Janitor of D'Alberts Jewelers

In sixth grade, I had a severe cash flow problem. Based on my "earned" allowance of 75¢ a week, I simply could not get to all the movies I wanted to see, eat the desired quantity of juicy fruits while at the Avalon Theater, and pay for Sugar Daddys at the Chevy Chase Pharmacy.

So I went looking for a part-time job. After the chief "hair cutter" at the Chevy Chase barbershop on McKinley Street rudely turned me down, I went next door to D'Albert Jewelers.

Since my Mother occasionally took me with her when getting her watch repaired, I already knew Tony and Jimmy D'Albert and the layout at their small jewelry store. Believe me, they needed help. Both brothers were serious smokers, so ashtrays on the glass counters were always full of smelly cigarette butts – and where there are smokers, there's also a lot of ash.

Surveying the dirty counters at D'Alberts Jewelers Store, I made my pitch to Tony D'Albert: "Mr. D'Albert, if you let me, I can come here each day after school – and within an hour, I'll have this place as clean as a whistle."

Tony D'Albert hired me on the spot. Happily for me, they were very generous – and agreed to pay me $5.00 a week.

$5.00 a week may not seem like a lot today, but for an 11 year old in 1953, this was a substantial income. For the next three years, my janitorial wages gave me my desired financial independence. If I wanted to take one of my buddies to the pastry shop at the new Woodies Department Store for one of their double chocolate cupcakes, I could do it. If my library book was overdue, I could pay the fine without jeopardizing my movie money. And best of all, I could build a serious cash reserve for use on the Ocean City Boardwalk when we headed to the Jersey Shore in August.

While Tony and Jimmy D'Albert were nice men, they also were very demanding employers. They insisted that I use undiluted ammonia to clean out the ashtrays and brillo pads to clean the toilets. So I learned very early in life that it was far better to be the boss, than the janitor!

Peoples Drug Store

In the 1940's and 1950's Washington, D.C. was a wonderful, friendly, and a very green town. But it was an apartheid city – just as segregated in the 1950's as Richmond or Atlanta.

My first realization that something was not right between white and black people occurred one day at a Peoples Drug Store at the corner of 15th and H Streets, just a few short blocks away from the White House.

The Peoples Drug Store was next to a medical building that housed the Gardner Family's doctors – who – out of their deep affection for my Dad – took care of our family "free." I now realize how generous this gesture was to my Father who had been a teacher, coach and mentor to so many professionals that I would meet during my early life in Washington.

Peoples had a special significance for my siblings and me: it was the "payoff location" for the bribery that my Mother shamelessly engaged in each time we went to our very crabby dentist, Dr. Kennedy.

Whenever we had to visit Dr. Kennedy, my Mother offered a simple bribe: if we behaved stoically during our Novocaine-less dental visits, my Mother would take us immediately to Peoples where we could order anything we wanted from the soda jerk.

In those pre-McDonald's days, the numerous Peoples Drug Stores scattered throughout Northwest Washington were famous for their ice cream floats.

On this particular summer day, we successfully restrained ourselves at Dr. Kennedy's, and immediately went with my Mother for the pay-off at the Peoples' lunch counter. Since we arrived after lunchtime, it was not very crowded as we sat at the counter, gleeful at the prospect of our impending floats.

After we ordered, I noticed that there were all these black people standing in a crowded area at the end of the lunch counter. They were eating with one hand while using the other hand to balance dishes that held their sandwiches, French-fries, and pieces of pie. They were standing up and eating even though there were plenty of empty seats at the lunch counter.

Puzzled, I asked my Mother: "Mom, why are they all standing? Why don't they sit here at the counter?"

My Mom, who was usually pretty cool, immediately leaned down and whispered very firmly, "Shhh!"

Well "shhh" wouldn't do for this Gardner – so I asked her a little louder: "Mother, why are all those black people standing up over there eating their lunch?"

That was it. I had crossed a line, and when that happened, my Mother employed – by stealth – her nearly lethal "pinch" to the tender skin on the inside of the upper arm. It had an instantaneous impact: I immediately shut up and ate the rest of my hot fudge chocolate sundae in silence.

Later, when we were back home, my Mother explained, "Negroes are not allowed to sit down and eat their lunches at the Peoples' lunch counters." When I said that this was silly, my Mother explained – with obvious discomfort – "that this is simply the way it was in Washington and in much of the United States."

The Big House

At the end of my sixth grade at BS, my parents gathered my sister Sheila, brother Tim and me together to announce that the Gardner family was moving to our "own house" at 5311 Nevada Avenue in Northwest, Washington, D.C. "The Big House" on Nevada Avenue was just a half-mile away, but in many ways, it was a million miles up and away from our rented row house at 4104 Military Road.

The "Big House" was huge to me – and certainly a far cry from our cramped quarters on Military Road. Importantly, our new home had large front and back yards – and two side yards, both bigger than our combined front and back yards on Military Road. Inside this stand-alone, five-bedroom brick house, there were luxuries never dreamed of on Military

Road – a working fireplace in the living room, a spacious entrance hall and a gigantic basement large enough for a ping-pong table.

Emotionally, it was an enormous adjustment to move to Nevada Avenue. For my first 11 years on this earth, 4104 Military Road had been the center of my fun universe. Now that universe was on "the other side of Connecticut Avenue."

Moving to Nevada Avenue also complicated my play and work habits; what had been a five minute walk from Military Road to the Chevy Chase playground now became a good 30 minute mile and a half hike. And I could no longer merely "pop by" D'Alberts Jewelers to perform my janitorial services on my way home from BS; I now had to take a major detour – a real pain, particularly when the weather was bad.

But just three weeks after we moved to Nevada Avenue, any downside from leaving Military Road was completely outweighed by the arrival of a frisky, eight-week old Irish setter puppy named Finnegan. My parents had finally delivered on two huge promises that had been pending for years: we got our own house – and at last, we got that puppy I had lobbied for since I could babble.

A soft, gangly orange ball of fur, Finnegan would tear non-stop for 10-15 minutes around the enormous back yard on Nevada Avenue. Then he would just collapse and fall sound asleep for an hour or two; and then suddenly, this Irish setter puppy would go off on another sprint.

As he grew from a gangly puppy, Finnegan became a full-bodied Irish setter with feathers that flowed elegantly from his front legs and tail. But as noble as this dog appeared, Finnegan had a stubborn independence never seen in any of our subsequent family dogs – 13 at last count!

An un-neutered male Irish setter, Finnegan also was a notorious roamer. As inexperienced first time dog owners, my parents did not fully appreciate the fact that you shouldn't just open the door and say, "Okay be a good boy" when Finnegan wanted to go out. So for 12 years, Finnegan roamed, often missing for several days at a time.

On one of his excursions, Finnegan managed to find love on the other side of Chain Bridge in McLean, VA – an amazing and dangerous feat that stunned our family and the bewildered dog lover who briefly took in our four-legged vagabond.

Since the house on Nevada Avenue was too far away from my buddies at the Chevy Chase playground, Finnegan became my trusted pal when I returned home from BS and my janitorial duties. Most afternoons, Finnegan and I would take a long walk in nearby Rock Creek Park.

And before my daily walks with Finnegan, my devoted Mother would have my favorite "snack" waiting: two Hostess Cream Filled cupcakes and a tall glass of milk. The trouble was – as confirmed by my 6th grade photos – little Mickey was not growing any taller but was getting rounder each day.

On one particularly memorable walk, Finnegan was tearing around the open field at the nearby Carnegie Institution. When I summoned Finnegan with a firm "come" he obeyed and "came" full gallop – and couldn't stop.

Bang! He hit my right leg head first causing a distinct "crack" to echo in my ears. And, as my Aunt Tessie would say, I sailed, "Ass over tin cups."

From that "crack" I knew instantly that something was broken – and I was right. Finnegan's hardhead was fine, but my right knee was shattered.

Relegated to crutches for eight weeks, I gained 10 pounds. But happily, once I was ambulatory again, the daily Finnegan-Mickey hikes resumed in Rock Creek Park. And when they resumed Finnegan never again left my side on our walks. Somehow, he knew that we shouldn't have any more collisions.

During the sometimes rocky years of high school, college and even my brief service in the U.S. Coast Guard Reserves, no matter how much "trouble" I might get into, Finnegan remained loyal.

President Harry Truman was right when he said, "If you want a true friend in Washington, get a dog."

J. Edgar Hoover…and LBJ

Growing up in upper Northwest Washington in the 1940's and 1950's was like growing up in a small town within the Capital City. Totally white in racial makeup, we lived in an insular residential conclave that was home to many of the politicians who shaped America's political agenda during the early decades of the Cold War.

With no subway to bring in "outsiders" – and only a sleepy bus line providing public transportation on the major tree lined streets, Chevy Chase, D.C. was an ideal refuge for politicians who often provided fodder for some of those best selling, tell-all books of the 1980's and 1990's.

The neighborhood around our house on Nevada Avenue provided the residential anonymity that important politicians sought. Senator Joe McCarthy, a man who became a controversial anti-communist leader and ended up a broken-down political hack, lived just a block away. Ike's Press Secretary James Haggerty lived nearby in a modest house on Reno Road, a house I remember being surrounded by very grim reporters when President Eisenhower suffered his heart attack in September 1955. And then there was just up the hill off Linnean Avenue: FBI Director J. Edgar Hoover at 4936 30th Place, and Senate Majority Leader Lyndon Baines Johnson, lived just three doors across the street at 4921 30th Place.

While I never knew "the Johnsons from Texas" as they were called by folks in Chevy Chase, D.C., I did have a fair amount of contact during a ten-year period with the FBI's top man.

I first met "Mr. Hoover" when I was 11 on July 4th. After the cow pasture debacle in 1948, my parents chose an alternative for our July 4th celebrations – an all-day outing with Steve and Helen Barabas at the rustic Charles Town West Virginia Racetrack. Going to "the track" was a favorite pastime of my father and Steve Barabas. For me, just watching them handicap the horses was always humorous. Somehow, the more intense their analysis, the more losers they picked.

At 11, I was a pretty good handicapper. Instead of relying on the Racing Form, I'd follow my Great Aunt Tessie's advice: "Kid, just look the horses in the eye – and when you see that special magic, bet on that horse." With a $2 per race subsidy from my parents and Tessie's formula, I always won some cash at the Racetrack.

On this particular 4th of July, I had an incredible string of five wins in the first five races. It was phenomenal. Even the waiters in the clubhouse were asking me, "Who do you like in the next race, kid?" When word spread throughout the Club House, J. Edgar Hoover himself left his box on the finish line to congratulate me.

While my father was already acquainted with Director Hoover, I had never met him. Coming to our table, the squat and bug-eyed Hoover was a formidable presence. So, when the Director asked me to watch the next race in his box, I was thrilled. A fist full of greenbacks from my five straight wins, and now a seat on the finish line with FBI Director J. Edgar Hoover.

Once in the box with the Director and his friend Clyde Tolson, I planted myself for a long stay. I wasn't going anywhere for the final three races. Never at a loss for words, I told Mr. Hoover about my Aunt Tessie's theory on how to pick the winning horse. I also told him about Finnegan and our upcoming trip to Ocean City. And Mr. Hoover seemed genuinely interested as we watched "the ponies cross the finish line."

Based on that encounter, the Director became a friend – to Finnegan and me. When he passed our house on Nevada Avenue as he returned from work, Mr. Hoover would occasionally spot Finnegan and me in the front yard, and instruct his driver to pull over. Every time I took Finnegan over to Mr. Hoover's car, he always had the same greeting: "My, that's a handsome Setter." Then he would ask me how my classes were going.

Since Mr. Hoover's house was just a five-minute walk away, I would use any pretense for Finnegan and me to visit. So when the Holy Cross Sisters at BS launched their fall and spring fund raising campaigns, I was at his house on the very next Sunday morning to sell him and Mr. Tolson raffle tickets. Fortunately for me and the Sisters at BS, even though the Director was not a Catholic, he always bought four books of ten, an enormous $40 contribution in those days.

On one of my semi-annual Sunday morning sell-a-thons in 1954, Mr. Hoover suggested that I could also peddle my raffle tickets to a neighbor who was visiting. At the prospect of an additional sale, Finnegan and I followed Mr. Hoover downstairs to the recreation room to meet his neighbor. And there he was: this really big man with enormous hands who squeezed too hard when he shook hands with me.

After introducing me to his huge neighbor, Mr. Hoover lobbied his friend to "open his wallet" for the benefit of the Blessed Sacrament Grade School and me. "Lyndon, it's a good cause, and Mickey, our friend from the racetrack – wants to win the prize for selling the most tickets."

Unfortunately, Lyndon turned out to be as cheap as he was tall. No matter how much the FBI Director needled his friend he wouldn't even buy a single one-dollar raffle ticket to benefit Blessed Sacrament School.

At our dinner table that night, I told my parents about my latest visit to Mr. Hoover's house and how the neighbor wouldn't even buy one ticket. That's when my father explained that the neighbor was Senate Majority Leader Lyndon Baines Johnson, a man my father said was then the most powerful man in the Senate. But since I had not yet blossomed into the political junkie I would become, I was unimpressed by my accidental – and unproductive – encounter with him.

In 1958, as a junior at Gonzaga, I conducted my first ever interview with Director Hoover for the Gonzaga High School weekly newspaper. My interview with the FBI Director was so "newsworthy" that it got me my one – and only – byline. And, for the record, on my numerous, unscheduled visits to his home, I never saw J. Edgar in a dress!

My Mother's Knuckle Sandwich

While my Mother was a loving, full-time Mom and housewife – she was also a skilled disciplinarian who expected good conduct from her three children.

Being her third – and "most precious" final child – I enjoyed some leeway on the misconduct front; however, even for me, my Mother had her limits.

My Mother had mastered two non-verbal disciplinary tools, and she resorted to them whenever her children really misbehaved. She had developed a world-class pinch and a mean "knuckle sandwich" consisting of a stinging jab from the middle knuckle of her bony, right hand.

As a hyper youngster who thrived on going right to the edge, I learned early in life to spot the warning signs when my Mother was about to resort to "the pinch" or her "knuckle sandwich." But one night, circa 1954, my radar system was on the blink.

On this particular evening, "Father Ed" Jacklin, S.J. (Jerky's brother) and Father "Doc" Edmund Bunn, S.J., were our guests. "Doc Bunn", a gentle and stout little man, was then president of Georgetown University. He and the Jacklin brothers were among a score of Jesuits who routinely came to our house each Sunday night for my Mother's roast beef dinners.

When my Father's various Jesuit friends were visiting, the three Gardner children were expected to remain "interested" in the dinner conversation. Only when coffee and after dinner drinks were served, could we ask to be excused. This mandatory attendance at the dinner table was a problem at times since Sunday night was the last possible window to frantically complete weekend homework.

That night, my sister Sheila and I apparently had little homework to do because, once excused, we headed to our bedrooms and mischief.

We decided to "play chase with Finnegan." The game was simple: Finnegan had a squirrel fixation, and when you said: "Finnegan, where's the squirrel?" the dog went ballistic. He would literally tear from one bedroom to another, barking madly as we – the tormentors – ran from window to window pointing to the fictitious squirrels outside.

Since my sister's and my bedrooms were directly over the dining room, it was not surprising that my Mother suddenly appeared following Finnegan's initial charge. With control, she firmly told us: "Cut it out. It sounds like a herd of buffalo are running around up here, so do your homework – and if you're finished, go to bed."

But we were still bored.

So, once again, we said it: "Where's the squirrel?" On cue, Finnegan went wild – now joining us as we jumped between the twin beds in my room.

Predictably, Mother appeared again – and this time she wasn't kidding: "Okay – you're both grounded; forget about going anywhere fun for the next two weekends. Now lights out. I've had it!"

The door slammed, and silence filled the second floor of our house. At that point, my brother Tim stuck his head in my room where a breathless Finnegan was sprawled out on my bed. My always perfect older brother was gleeful: "Your ass is really in trouble now," he laughed.

Unfortunately, Sheila and I were still bored – and if you've already been grounded for two weekends, the threat of being grounded again didn't have much punch.

We said it again: "Finnegan, Finnegan, where's the squirrel?"

Instantaneously, all hell broke loose again as Finnegan leapt from the bed. All 85 pounds landed with a thud on the hardwood floor, causing the chandelier to rattle in the dining room below.

Oblivious to the thunder we were causing in the dining room below, my sister and I were laughing hysterically as Finnegan tore from window to window looking for that elusive squirrel.

Without warning our Mother suddenly flung my bedroom door open. Red-faced, she entered with her right hand elevated in the "Knuckle sandwich" position.

I warned my sister.

As Sheila fled through the side door to the safety of her room, I realized that I was my Mother's sole target. I panicked.

In a flash, I saw the knuckle sandwich coming – aimed directly at my back – her favorite target – since there was little bruising there. Realizing that my only recourse was to secure some cover from the pillows, I quickly jumped on my bed. As I did, I slipped – fell backward – and caught a direct hit: My Mother's knuckle sandwich landed square on my nose!

Dazed at first, I saw stars.

Off in the distance, I heard my Mother saying, "Mickey, Mickey, are you ok? Honey, are you ok?"

Before I could reply, my sister Sheila let out her shrillest scream: "Daddy. Quick - she's killing Mickey. Mummy's killing Mickey – help – Daddy, he's bleeding to death. Help!"

I was, in fact, gushing blood from my nose. My Mother had ruptured a blood vessel in my right nostril – and there was a literal fountain of very red blood spurting from my nose, spraying the white sheets, pillowcases, lampshades, walls – everything within five feet.

Prompted by Sheila's hysterical cries for help, my Father and the two visiting Jesuits abandoned their brandies and crowded through my bedroom door. They were all noticeably stunned by the blood they encountered.

With Sheila still screeching, my very troubled Father asked, "Elva, Elva what happened?"

My Mother didn't answer, and no matter how hard she tried, the bleeding wouldn't stop; as soon as one compress was removed, the gusher would surge anew.

Fortunately, my blood reserve was ample. But when the bleeding simply would not stop, and I was hastily carried to the car for a wild ride to the emergency room at Georgetown University Hospital.

When we entered the ER – two distraught parents, the two Jesuits (one the University's President), and a very bloody and still bleeding child – the scene became totally chaotic.

As soon as the admitting nurse saw me, she yelled, "Stat, stat," and suddenly doctors and nurses were everywhere. At this point, the evening got vague as I was sedated while the right side of my nose was cauterized in order to stop the hemorrhaging.

As we drove back to Nevada Avenue from Georgetown's ER, I knew I had my Mother over a barrel. Forget her earlier threats of "groundings"; instead of the brat who spoiled the dinner party, I became the "victim supreme."

And my Mother never, ever delivered another "knuckle sandwich."

"Flipping the Bird" at Sister Maria Theresa

One of my most celebrated – and painful – screw-ups occurred one ill-fated morning in June of 1955 in Blessed Sacrament's new auditorium on Patterson Street.

The Principal at Blessed Sacrament, an unsmiling nerdy little Nun named Sister Pascal, was concluding a mid-morning, end-of-school assembly for the sixth, seventh and departing eighth graders. Sister Pascal and the other Holy Cross Sisters on duty, used annoying clickers that would signal when each row was to silently march out to return to the classrooms.

At the end of our seventh year at BS, my classmates and I were feeling pretty cocky. We would soon be eighth graders and own the asphalt playground.

Sitting mid-row between 30 seventh graders, I glanced to my right and noticed that my buddy Joey Malraux was seated at the far end of the row. Joey was a great guy and one of my favorite rebel rousers.

As we waited for Sister Pascal's "click" to command us to silently file up the stairs on our left, Joey leaned forward with an evil smile and flipped me the bird. Joey's gesture caused enough of a commotion from the students around him that Sister Maria Theresa, stationed a few rows back, glided forward to investigate.

In those days, the Sisters' nearly motionless rapid movement was impressive since they wore cumbersome full-length black robes. Dressed all in black with their ridiculous starched, half-moon headdresses, even the tiniest Holy Cross Sister could appear intimidating. And intimidating was an understatement when it came to the six foot tall Sister Maria Theresa.

The stately Sister Maria Theresa moved forward to investigate, but I failed to notice her advance. Thinking the coast was clear, I leaned forward and flipped Joey a full-fisted, bird. Unfortunately, that bird not only made a direct hit on the smiling and blissfully ignorant Joey; it also landed unfettered on Sister Maria Theresa who was now standing over Joey.

Just as my bird was deployed, Sister Pascal's "click, click" sounded for our row to move out. "Thank God", I thought, "we're moving on and Sister Maria Theresa has to direct traffic for the remaining rows."

Wrong.

Before we had climbed the ten stairs out of the auditorium, Sister Maria Theresa had cleared the width of the auditorium and was within striking distance. She caught me as I was mid-way up the stairs. The powerfully built Sister Maria Theresa swung me around and with a firm, wide-open palm, she slapped my face several times.

Nobody moved – and no one was talking. Every student left in the auditorium stood stunned silently watching and wondering.

As much as my plump, red cheeks stung, my number one priority was to keep from shedding a single tear. Remember what Tessie would say in this situation: "Don't give her the satisfaction of seeing you cry." With the moral support of my terrified classmates, I prevailed. No tears!

While I maintained a stiff-upper lip, I couldn't convince Sister Pascal that "I was not flipping the bird at Sister Maria Theresa – but only signaling to Joey Malraux that we'd get together on the playground!" But my lame explanation didn't sell. For the next two and final school days of my seventh grade, I sat in disgrace outside of Sister Pascal's office.

While the punishment really didn't bother me (after all I was able to skip the final classes of seventh grade), I was bothered that I had insulted Sister Maria Theresa. Other than Sister John Thomas in 5th grade, this tall Nun had been a fair and even friendly teacher. But when I went to her at the end of the school year to once again explain that I had not intended to "flip her off" Sister Maria Theresa just blew me off.

When I complained to my Mother on the night of the slapping episode that Sister Maria Theresa was "really a tough cookie," she was totally unsympathetic; "Mickey, you're responsible for your own actions and nobody – not even Joey Malraux – can make you do what you shouldn't do."

"First Holy Communion" – on BS' Playground

Eighth grade at Blessed Sacrament School was an infamous year for me and 38 second graders who received their First Holy Communion one morning on the school's asphalt playground.

Donald Bigannani, another eighth grader, and I had just completed serving 8:30 a.m. Mass one school day in the spring of 1956. As we were snuffing out the Altar candles, we were startled to see that the sacristy safe (a walk in closet) was left open. This was truly a breach of security because Leon, the elderly sacristan, never, ever let his guard down as he helped each priest remove his cassock after Mass and then locked up the chalice and unused communion wafers.

While Donald and I knew that Monsignor Roach had downed all the wine that I had poured into his chalice at Mass, we figured that Leon got a "wee buzz" on from the ample altar wine left over from the three earlier Masses at 6:30 a.m. 7:00 a.m. and 7:30 a.m.

Whether it was Leon's advanced age and/or his consumption of altar wine, Leon had left the sacristy door ajar. As a result, Donald and I had the key to the great unknown: we could once and for all see where all those Holy Communion wafers came from.

So we opened that sacristy door – and entered into the most secret and sacred space of the Blessed Sacrament Church.

There they were in the corner in a large, tin container: thousands and thousands of white Holy Communion wafers!

And the temptation for exploitation was simply too great: we lost it….. and maybe Heaven too.

After a brief hushed exchange, we immediately dug our hands into the tin container – grabbing fistful after fistful of communion hosts and jammed them into our pants pockets.

Once our pockets were full with hundreds of Holy Communion wafers, we left the sacristy's safe – and tripped over each other as we fled through the sacristy's side door to the safety of the adjacent playground.

At this point it was 8:53 a.m. – and the playground was crowded with the school's entire student population as they waited for the 9:00 a.m. school day to began.

So we decided to mimic the priests: we would give Holy Communion to anyone on the playground who was dumb enough to let us.

As fate would have it, the second graders were assigned a small plot of the playground immediately next to the sacristy door.

The 2nd graders were easy prey. They had been preparing for months to receive their real First Holy Communion in just two weeks. During the prior months, they had been lectured repeatedly about the proper way to receive their first Holy Communion; they were so well trained that all Donald and I had to do was hold up one host and the entire 2nd grade was instantly on their knees – with their hands folded.

With precision, Donald and I spread out amongst our devout young flock, hastily giving First Communion to one after another until suddenly a spine-chilling yell erupted from the opposite side of the playground.

That roar – "What are you doing?" – echoes in my ears to this day and I can see a little, gnarled Nun, Sister Gonzaga, hurling herself at full speed toward us. "What? What are you heathens doing? What …what… oh, Jesus, Mary and Joseph – you two are doomed to hell."

Before the little 2nd graders knew what hit them, Donald and I were pulled by our ears back into the sacristy by the little Nun. Sister Gonzaga had suddenly gained the strength of an angel. Once in the sacristy, we emptied our pockets of the remaining communion wafers while Sister Gonzaga roared once again in the still church, "Leon – where are you? We have a crisis."

Her roar worked. A sheepish Leon filled to the gills with altar wine shuffled into the sacristy. At first he looked bewildered, but then Leon smiled, and said: "Boys, how'd you all get those Communion wafers? Altar boys have been trying for 34 years – and you guys did it." Not amused, Sister Gonzaga only wanted Leon to confirm that these were "unblessed hosts" – which he did.

We felt the immediate impact at 10:00 a.m. that morning: Donald and I were permanently thrown out of the Altar Boy's Society. As further punishment for our misconduct, we were suspended and ordered to sit – in total silence – outside of Sister Pascal's office for three days of public shame. We lucked out here because a three-day suspension was just one punishment shy of expulsion, and expulsion could have been very inconvenient for our trying to get into good Catholic high schools.

We became infamous: every child in Blessed Sacrament went home that afternoon – and with shock and horror – blabbed to their parents that Donald Bigannani and Mickey Gardner had given First Holy Communion to the 2nd graders on the playground. And the story took years to die down.

As for my parents, they were disgusted. They told me in no uncertain terms that I had crossed the line. And once again, they reminded me that I had embarrassed myself by my poor judgment.

THE TRANSFORMATION BEGINS

Gonzaga High School

When you've spent your first eight years in school playing and not studying, your chances of getting into a good high school should be severely limited. But not for me.

I was nearly illiterate when I completed 8th grade at Blessed Sacrament but when it came time for me to go to high school, my Father's Jesuit friends were determined that I go to one of the Jesuits' two outstanding prep schools in the D.C. area.

One option was Georgetown Prep, where the fifth fairway had served as the Gardner family's escape route during the July 4th cow stampede of 1948. In sharp contrast to the Prep, Gonzaga High School was the Jesuits' inner city school located just blocks away from D.C.'s Union Station, a concrete campus smack-dab in the heart of Washington's ghetto.

In 1956, one of my Dad's closest Jesuit friends was Father William Ryan, S.J., the stern headmaster of Georgetown Prep. Father Ryan told my Dad one day after a round of golf that; "Mickey will have a full scholarship to the Prep – and we'll even tutor him over the summer before his Freshman Year."

"Summer school tutoring to go to the Prep? No way Dad. All my friends are going to Gonzaga!" was my ungrateful response when my Father informed me about my full scholarship to Georgetown Prep.

Besides this academic act of charity in accepting me to the Prep, a full scholarship was a real financial plus for my hard working Father who was paying full tuitions for my sister Sheila at Georgetown Visitation and for my brother Tim at Georgetown University.

Since Gonzaga's Headmaster Father Anthony McHale, S.J. was not a personal friend of my Father's, there was no prospect of a full scholarship to Gonzaga. More importantly, Gonzaga was then viewed by some as more difficult academically than the Prep – making Gonzaga an even greater challenge from an admission standpoint for a non-student like me.

Incredibly, when faced with this dilemma about high schools for me, my parents, as usual, were totally supportive and unselfish: "Miguel," my Father concluded, "if you really want to go to Gonzaga, then your Mother and I will do everything we possibly can to make your dream come true."

As with many teenagers when choosing a high school, my decision was based in part on the fact that most of my friends were going there. More than anything, however, my determination to attend Gonzaga was rooted in a conversation I overheard between my parents in the spring of 1956.

My parents had just returned from meeting with my 8th grade teacher, Sister Gonzaga. I heard my Mother denounce Sister Gonzaga for advising my parents to send me to a vocational school. Apparently, when my parents asked Sister Gonzaga to give me at least a lukewarm recommendation to Gonzaga, she balked: "I will not – under any circumstances – recommend your son for any Catholic school in this area and certainly not Gonzaga. The best place for Michael Gardner is a well-structured vocational school."

While I knew she didn't like me (especially after the First Communion caper), I never dreamed she'd try to condemn me to a life of unplugging stopped up toilets or changing light bulbs. I was so mad at what I overheard, I burst into my parents' bedroom and declared that I was not going to vocational school, "I'm going to Gonzaga."

My Father and his Jesuit friends did their magic. I went to Gonzaga and there, for the next four years, a group of intellectually tough but nurturing Jesuits put me through a form of academic boot camp – a boot camp that equipped me for the rest of my life.

But before Gonzaga's academic boot camp kicked in, I nearly derailed the whole experience.

It was December of my freshman year, first semester exams had just ended – and as usual, I was a happy-go-lucky guy, blissfully ignorant of my academic peril.

But not for long.

Over Gonzaga's public address system, the Headmaster's voice suddenly intruded. Father McHale barked his command, "Gardner, get to my office – now!"

"Oh my God" I thought, "what's going on? I've been reasonably good lately – why am I being summoned to the headmaster's office?"

On my way down the ancient stairs to Father McHale's office, I tried to steady myself – thinking of my great Aunt Tessie's advice that you should always approach a tough situation with a smile on your face and a confident stride. So I did both.

Father McHale's secretary, a nice, motherly lady named Mrs. Joyner, signaled that I should go in and wait. Although Mrs. Joyner looked somewhat distressed, I remained upbeat; but as I opened the door to Father McHale's office, she whispered, "Good luck." Something bad was up.

Nonetheless, I strode confidently into the office with a smile on my face. Since Father McHale was on the phone with his back to me, I sat down in one of the two empty chairs across from the headmaster's desk.

Trying to appear calm and assured, I even picked up a copy of the Aquilian – the school paper and pretended to read it as Father continued his phone conversation.

After a few minutes, the call ended.

Father McHale began to yell:

"What the fuck are you doing sitting down in my office. Nobody asked you to sit. Now get your fat Irish ass out of my chair – and don't ever, ever sit down in my presence unless I ask you to do so. You are a disgrace, a mess and even though your Father knows every Jesuit in the Maryland Province – you are just two weeks away from being expelled from Gonzaga."

I jumped up, my mind, spinning in overload.

First and foremost, I was trying to process the fact that I was about to be thrown out of Gonzaga – but why?

Secondly, I was in shock that Father McHale just said "Fuck!" – a major league, mortal sin for Catholic boys at that time.

And he said I had a "fat Irish ass." This was definitely not going well!

As I stood trembling, he explained in a no-nonsense manner that I had just flunked four of my six freshman courses. I had – for all intent and purposes – the worst first semester record of any freshman in Gonzaga's 135-year history.

While today, I doubt Father McHale's claim that I was the very worst freshman in Gonzaga's history, I was definitely a poor student, and I certainly deserved to be expelled.

But Father McHale had other plans for me. In an award winning performance, Father McHale went back and forth in a classic one-man, good cop – bad cop routine. While he terrorized me more than I had ever been scared before, he also convinced me that I could make it at Gonzaga if I really worked at it.

"You're an immature clown; you're undisciplined; you go out Friday and Saturday nights – every weekend; your homework is sloppy." He went on and on. "You're a real mess, but you're not dumb, just stupid because of the way you're going through life."

"And let me assure you that I don't care what Jesuit calls me on your behalf; if you're not passing at least five of your six courses at the end of the next semester, you're out of Gonzaga! Do you have that in your immature head?"

"Yes, Father," I whimpered, "I understand."

Before he released me from the most terrifying and life-altering conversation of my young life, Father McHale issued one final demand. I had to agree to immediately cease all social activities on Friday and Saturday nights for the balance of my freshman year. "Nothing Gardner," he reiterated. "No games, No Purple and White dances – nothing until your freshman year is over and you've successfully passed at least five of your courses. Do you understand me?"

I gasped, "Yes, Father, I do."

As oncrous as this final condition was for me, I had no choice. It was either his way or out the door at Gonzaga.

Shattered, humiliated, shaken and terrified, I left Father McHale's office and walked, dazed, past Mrs. Joyner and out into the hallway, now noisy with luncheon recess.

I found my way to the cafeteria where my nosy classmates mobbed me, eager to know my fate. Embarrassed, I blew off their questions. But they knew something big was up. And it was.

That night, after a pained dinner during which my parents kept asking me if I was sick, I told them. Both my parents made it clear that it was totally up to me.

From that point forward, I changed.

For the next five months, without any rancor, each of my six teachers – four young Jesuit scholastics and two elderly Jesuit priests – worked tirelessly with me. With patience and firmness, they did in five months what the poor overworked Holy Cross Sisters at Blessed Sacrament could never accomplish: they taught me how to construct sentences, how to spell, how to focus, and how to study.

By early June, at the end of my first year at Gonzaga, my turnaround was remarkable; my only flunking grade was in math.

When I look back on that "discussion" with Father McHale, I remain impressed with the calculated wisdom of his words. He knew exactly who I was, and he had the concern and skills to turn my life around.

When I passed the D.C. Bar, I wrote Father McHale to thank him for his momentous intervention in my misguided young life. I wanted him to know that his routine had worked.

Impeachment at Gonzaga

My sophomore class trip consisted of a one day bus trip to and from nearby Colonial Williamsburg, VA.

Since Gonzaga had five homeroom sophomore classes totaling more than a hundred sophomores, two huge Greyhound buses were needed for our excursion to Williamsburg. For "crowd control," the two buses were 'policed' by several Jesuit homeroom teachers. My bus was "policed" by our homeroom teacher, Mister Raymond Lelii, S.J.

As an older Jesuit scholastic, Mr. Lelii was not yet an ordained priest but well along the way in the stringent process that then took 13 years to complete. According to school gossip, the short, powerfully built Mr. Lelii was a former Marine who served in the Korean War.

It was also rumored that he had won the "Golden Gloves Boxing Championship" in Washington, D.C. Not only was Mr. Lelii wearing the Roman collar of a Jesuit scholastic, but Mr. Lelii also had the reputation of being able to immediately deck any student who was out-of-line.

Mr. Lelii was also Gonzaga's sole biology teacher. Obsessed with his biology experiments, Mr. Lelii spent all of his free time in a lab that reeked of formaldehyde – and contained hundreds of gross clear glass jars holding the partially dissected remains of countless animals. Oddly, Mr. Lelii was totally at home in his biology lab – much more relaxed working with dead things than with Gonzaga's sophomores.

On the day of our sophomore trip, Mr. Lelii was his typical self: stern and unequivocal in his rigid attitude about student behavior. As our bus exited Gonzaga's parking lot, Mr. Lelii yelled from the front of the bus:

"People – there will be no funny business on this trip. You are to sit quietly in your seat to and from Williamsburg and people, anyone who is out of order, will have me to deal with."

While we were initially subdued, my classmates and I were stir-crazy by the time we got close to Richmond.

Fueling our unrest were those jerks who were on the other bus; each time our bus passed theirs – or their bus passed us, our classmates flipped us off with impunity. Frustrated because the teachers on the other bus were clueless to "the bird attacks" under their very noses, we were repeatedly assaulted – but unable to respond since Mr. Lelii remained vigilant to our slightest move.

During the trip, it also became apparent that our two bus drivers were engaged in their own private "cat and mouse" game.

Somewhere South of Richmond on a dual lane highway, the repeated "bird assaults" from the boys in the other bus had gone unanswered for almost two hours; for me – as the recently elected president of 2E – the situation became intolerable. So, after a brief consultation with my "Kitchen Cabinet," I determined that I had no choice but to respond in order to preserve the honor of 2E.

I waited for Mr. Lelii to gaze out the window as we roared down the highway. Satisfied that he was distracted, I leaned out of the cramped mini-window of our bus as we were passing the offending students. With precision, I flipped several, rapid fire, well-executed "birds" to my cheering classmates as we sped by their bus.

With my head and right arm fully outside the bus window, one of my classmates suddenly gave me a major league push that jolted me further out the window. As a result, all of me – except my legs and rear-end – was now hanging outside the bus window as we were passing the bus carrying the scoundrels from 2A, 2B and 2C.

At that critical juncture – where I could have been decapitated – our bus driver apparently spotted me in his side mirror. Panicked, the driver suddenly hit the brakes! With this second jolt, I was now literally jammed outside the tiny bus window – stuck there only by virtue of my substantial rear end.

After momentary chaos, we screeched to a halt on the highway. Our frazzled driver steered the bus to the shoulder of the road. Since I was firmly stuck and hanging almost upside down out of the bus window, I obviously couldn't see what was going on in the bus; nor could I hear anything because of the roar of trucks and cars that whizzed by.

What I could fully appreciate, however, was pain – real physical pain as someone repeatedly pinched my rear end. Whoever was doing this nonstop pinching, he was good; in fact, the pinching was world class and similar to the deadly stealth pinches perfected by my Mother.

With the top half of my body hanging upside down out of the bus window, I grew impatient with the relentless pinching; so I defended myself. Using my feet that fortunately were still inside the bus, I kicked a wide swath – ignorant, of course, about the identity of the offending, unknown target. And it worked.

Almost instantly, the pinching ceased. Then someone grabbed my legs and pulled and pulled and pulled – until suddenly my hips were unstuck.

Once the top half of my 5-foot 2-inch body was fully inside the bus, I immediately realized that the target of my successful kicking defense had been none other than Mr. Raymond Lelii, S.J., the pincher.

Mr. Lelii yanked me firmly by my left ear lobe and led me to the front of the bus where a visibly shaken Greyhound bus driver stared at me with contempt. In a voice quivering with anger, Mr. Lelii then ordered me to kneel in the aisle next to the driver. "Gardner, you are a disgrace, and you will remain kneeling here at the front of this bus for the balance of this trip."

I was stoic. For the balance of the trip to Williamsburg, I complied with Mr. Lelii's "kneeling" mandate. It wasn't too bad initially as we only had an hour more to go. But when we got to Williamsburg, I started to get annoyed. "Gardner," Mr. Lelii barked, "you've got one head stop and after that, you will kneel here on this bus until the class tour is completed. Do you understand what kneel means Gardner?"

And so it was. While my classmates romped through Williamsburg, I remained on my knees on an empty greyhound bus in the parking lot of the Williamsburg Lodge. When my classmates finally returned several hours later, Mr. Lelii granted me another "head visit" – but no visitation rights to the Lodge cafeteria where my classmates had just eaten dinner.

Like me, my classmates also concluded that Mr. Lelii's treatment of 2E Class President Gardner was cruel and unusual punishment. As they reentered the bus, many of my cronies whispered: "Mick – don't take this shit." "Gardner – Lelii is crazy. We thought he was going to kill you"; "Mickey, this is sooo unfair – you didn't deliberately kick him." "Mick – are you going to let him do this to you?" And on and on.

The more my classmates discreetly expressed their indignation, the more emboldened I grew.

By the time our bus reached the outskirts of Washington, D.C., it was after 9:00 p.m. I had been on my knees in the front of this Greyhound bus for nine of the 12 hours since we drove out of Gonzaga's parking lot. And with every mile on our return trip to D.C., my Irish temper grew.

As we crossed Potomac River and sped past the Jefferson Memorial, it came to me; I would wait until the bus stopped and when the car that would take me home was safely in sight, I would take care of Mr. Raymond Lelii, S. J.

As our bus entered Gonzaga's parking lot, I was relieved to see that my buddy Morgan Lynch's Mother was standing next to her big gray Olds; my safe exit was assured. I knew Mr. Lelii would not dare punch me out in front of parents, so I only had to run and get in the Lynch's car after I settled the score.

Since the other bus had arrived before us, many of my classmates were already milling around the parking lot when our bus pulled up. Happily, my moment for revenge would take place before the entire sophomore class in the parking lot once our bus unloaded.

When our bus came to a stop, Mr. Lelii got out first, followed by the expectant sophomores who now knew, by my facial expression, that I was up to something.

Standing by the open bus door – with only the weary bus driver and me still on board – Mr. Lelii announced in a loud voice: "Gardner – you sorry soul, get off your knees and get off that bus; and plan to see me first thing tomorrow morning."

With raw knees – and a sore bottom from Mr. Lelii's earlier pinching assault – I slowly got up. When I reached the bus' second step I hesitated – and looked Mr. Lelii S. J. right in the eyes.

I then yelled – as loud as I could: "Mr. Lelii, you're a son of a bitch, and you can kiss my ass in Macy's window."

As my words rang out, I ran like hell! And I didn't look back until I was safely in the back seat of Mrs. Lynch's big old gray Oldsmobile.

From the deafening silence of my friends in the car as Mrs. Lynch drove out of Gonzaga's parking lot, I knew immediately that my attack on Mr. Lelii had stunned my classmates.

By the time I got home, I was beginning to panic. When my Father greeted me with: "Hello Miguel, how was your trip?" – I was temporarily speechless.

Realizing that I was in real trouble, I fessed up – but only to my Father who listened quietly. While I tried to portray myself as the innocent victim of the trip (pushed out the window and merely defending myself against an unknown, crazed pincher), I did admit to calling Mr. Lelii an inappropriate name.

When I concluded my confession, my Father just nodded. After a painful pause, he said in a quiet tone: "Miguel, you've obviously shown very poor judgment, and I don't think this event is going to go away easily. As your Mother and I have told you before, you're accountable for your own conduct. I just hope it doesn't cost you your dream of graduating from Gonzaga."

With that warning, my Father folded his newspaper and quietly went to bed.

The thought that I could be expelled nearly paralyzed me as it raced through my stupid Irish brain. Too panicked to sleep, I saw the sun rise as I waited terrified for dawn and the start of the school day.

Without eating breakfast, I hitchhiked to Gonzaga. As I walked into the stark cafeteria, I was greeted not with cheers but with looks of incredulity from the entire student population. Word had spread fast.

By the time the class bell rang, my anxiety level was high; nonetheless, I walked – with feigned confidence – to my homeroom classroom, 2E. Mr. Lelii was standing at his desk looking quite unperturbed.

As we took our assigned seats, the Headmaster's voice came over the scratchy intercom system. Terse as usual, Father McHale whizzed through some routine reminders, and then he paused ever so slightly and added:

"Gardner – 2E – is impeached and will spend the next three days on his knees – in disgrace – on the stage of the auditorium. Now Gardner – go."

That was it – I was "impeached." But what was "impeachment?" What did it mean? "Impeach" was a word I had never heard before. This was 15 years before Watergate.

While Mr. Lelii smiled, I remained puzzled. In panic, I turned to the nice kid next to me, a new classmate who had emigrated from Hungary following the 1956 uprising, and asked, "Gabor, what does impeach mean?"

I'll never forget the sad look on Gabor's face as he told me, painfully: "Meekie – you are no longer our class President."

I was both crushed and relieved: crushed that my classmates' vote of confidence that I cherished so much had been ripped away, but relieved because I had once again survived "expulsion" from Gonzaga. As far as the humiliation of kneeling three school days on the stage as students hurried from class to class – that was no problem. It was losing the presidency of 2E that really hurt.

From that moment forward, Gonzaga was never the same for me. In time, however, a constructive lesson came out of my impeachment – I learned to control my temper.

Life As a Haberdasher

For old time Washingtonians in the 1950s and 1960s, there was one – and only one – quality men's clothing store: the Georgetown University Shop. Located at 36th and N Street just a block off the manicured lawns of Georgetown University's main campus, the "GU Shop" was the shop for well-heeled parents and grandparents.

The Gardner kids frequented the GU Shop because its owners, Steve and Helen Barabas, were my parents' best friends. And because of that deep family friendship, I worked at the GU Shop from Christmas of 1950, until my graduation from Georgetown in June of 1964.

At eight years of age – with Christmas fast approaching – I was in serious need of extra spending money. When the Barabases learned one early December night in 1950 of my cash flow distress, Helen Barabas volunteered that "our crew at the GU Shop needed help with Christmas wrapping; so, Mickey why don't you try it over the school break?" When Helen said the pay would be $1 an hour, I was thrilled.

Two weeks later, I began my 14 year stint as a part-time wrapper, runner, stock room boy, salesman and ultimately, backup cashier!

Initially working only over the Christmas breaks and then part-time three days a week while at Georgetown, the GU Shop became much more important to me than a paycheck; it also was a really fun place to work, full of a rich variety of humorous characters, all except the unsmiling store manager, Ted McAllister.

When I began my Christmas wrapping duties, the GU Shop's "crew" was a diverse one. There were Angelo and Vince, recent imports from Naples, who were the tireless and irreverent tailors in the back room. There was the always smiling Eulla, a huge black lady from the Caribbean who made the funniest asides about "that fruitcake McAllister." In the office, there was "Railbird" Ethel Dwyer, the able backup office manager whose dry sense of humor left us in stitches. And, of course, there was Theodore "Ted" McAllister, the supercilious store manager, who spoke with a British accent, though born and raised in New Jersey.

As I look back on my days at the GU Shop, I am embarrassed by my 14 year campaign to make Ted McAllister's life miserable. Sadly for Ted, as much as he wanted to fire me, as a young member of the owner's extended family, I was immune from anything harsher than Ted's piercing dirty looks and his deep sighs of frustration. Unfortunately for Ted, the more he reacted to my antics, the more I wanted to harass him.

Two incidents standout to this day. The first occurred when I was 15 years old, shortly after my new best friend and co-worker, Patrick Lennon came to work at the GU Shop.

When we first met wrapping Christmas packages in the basement of the GU Shop, Patrick was a freshman boarding student at Georgetown Prep in Rockville, Maryland, and I was a sophomore at Gonzaga. Patrick, whose Father was the President of the five-star Homestead Hotel in Hot Spring, Virginia, was the embodiment of Irish charm and humor. Six feet tall at 14, Patrick was an athletic young man who had stoically overcome several early physical challenges to become a teenage scratch golfer. A smile was never missing from his face, and "having fun" was Patrick's top priority. We bonded instantly!

Patrick and I shared a myriad of chores during his first frantic Christmas rush at the GU Shop, chores that ranged from restocking the shelves to wrapping Christmas packages to occasionally helping the upscale customers who crowded into the GU Shop, to see and be seen. While the chaotic workday typically had us running in different directions, Patrick and I always took the last two 30 minute lunch slots – 2:15 p.m. to 2:45 p.m.

While 30 minutes was hardly enough time to catch-up on the day's gossip and our nighttime plans, Patrick and I packed a lot of talk and refreshments into our lunch break. Each workday, we "treated ourselves" to lunch at Teehans, a greasy bar-restaurant dive just four doors from the GU Shop on 36th street. Besides being close by and cheap, Teehans' was ideal because they sold 15 cent mini draft Budweiser beers. Importantly, age was irrelevant at Teehans. So, each day of our Christmas holiday Patrick, 14, (and looking possibly as old as 16) and I, 15, (but not looking a day over 12) would have a Bud draft with our barely edible hamburgers and fries.

On one particularly hectic day when the Christmas shoppers were being unusually demanding, Patrick and I were feeling especially fatigued, so we lingered over lunch – and took the unprecedented action of having a second Budweiser draft.

During lunch that day, I told Patrick that I was worried because I had to go to Ms. Shippen's black tie Christmas dance that night at the Sulgrave Club, and I didn't know how to Charleston. At that time, there was a temporary resurgence of interest in this dance from the roaring twenties. "Not to worry" Patrick assured me, "I've had dancing lessons for the past two years at the Homestead, and I can show you in a minute."

When we re-entered the GU Shop – 20 minutes late – frantically chewing on our breath-cleaning Clorets, we determined that the coast was clear for my quick Charleston lesson. Steve Barabas was not around, and "Mr. McAllister" was nowhere in sight.

Seizing the moment, my "one minute dance" lesson began in earnest with Patrick singing, "Black Bottom, Black Bottom…." As the giddy six-foot Patrick sang the Black Bottom, he shifted from foot-to-foot, and simultaneously slapped his butt in the tradition of the provocative black bottom dancers from prohibition days. As his pupil, I faced Patrick and made a futile attempt to mimic his gyrations.

Suddenly out of my side vision, I saw McAllister walking down the stairs toward us. Stunned, he stopped and stared in disbelief, and then he roared so that everyone on all three floors of the GU Shop would hear: "Jesus Christ. This has gone too far. How can you run a professional business when these two fucking delinquents are allowed to do the Black Bottom while customers are waiting to be helped?"

Totally ambushed, Patrick and I realized immediately that we had gone too far. We were definitely wrong. But even though I knew it, I was still delighted to watch the normally controlled Ted McAllister totally lose it in front of everyone, including some "very important" customers.

Unfortunately, our boss, the normally taciturn Steve Barabas, was also annoyed. And Steve rarely got annoyed. To this day, I'm not sure whether it was our impromptu Black Bottom lesson that bugged Steve or the public outburst my dancing lesson provoked from the store manager. When "Mr. Barabas" summoned us into his office, we were suddenly very sober and somber. As he closed the office door, Steve gave us a long stern look followed by a barely audible: "Come on you guys – do the damn dancing on your own dime."

That was it. We were not fired – as Ted McAllister hoped and expected – but both Patrick and I had learned that no matter how stressful the Christmas rush, we never came back late again from lunch at Teehans, and we never had more than one 15 cent Bud draft.

And thanks to Patrick, I not only met and married his beautiful sister, I also knew how to dance the Black Bottom with her at our wedding.

The second most memorable assault on my favorite GU Shop target, Mr. Ted McAllister, took place during the Christmas rush of 1961. At that time, Washington was totally obsessed with the Kennedys, and the crew and customers at the GU Shop were no exception. Georgetowners were especially caught up with the excitement of the Kennedys in the White House. After all, the President regularly attended Holy Trinity Church right across 36th Street from the GU Shop, and he was a frequent visitor to his Russian teacher's house just a half a block away. And before moving into the White House, the President and Jackie lived at 3307 N Street, just three blocks from the GU Shop.

We frequently had real live Kennedys shopping at our store, but because of "quality control" rules imposed by Ted McAllister, Patrick and

I had been instructed to alert Ted when any Kennedy or other big name customers showed up. Ted was a shameless social climber, and heaven forbid that an important Washington cave dweller, or a Kennedy family member would be waited on by anyone but Ted!

Since Christmas Eve fell on a Sunday in 1961, all hell broke loose that year on Saturday, December 23, the eve of Christmas Eve, as last minute shoppers swamped the GU Shop. In the early afternoon with shoppers crowded on the main floor, Mrs. Hugh D. Auchincloss, Jackie's mother and the President's mother-in-law, walked in. Suddenly, the first floor of the GU Shop became hushed as the frantic customers stood back and silently stared: Jackie's mother, right here shopping with the masses.

No sooner had the no-nonsense Mrs. Auchincloss walked over to the silk ties than Ted appeared at her side. "Oh, Oh Mrs. Auchincloss, how gooood to see you again. And you're looking so well while most of us are simply exhausted with Christmas preparations."

Polite but distant, Mrs. Auchincloss, with Ted glued to her side, did a fair amount of last minute Christmas shopping: some ties, several cummerbunds, three dress shirts. Then she was gone – at least, that's what Ted thought.

As Mrs. Auchincloss' driver sped away, I decided that I would become Mrs. Hugh D. Auchincloss later that day and personally telephone "Mr. McAllister" with a special, last minute Christmas gift order. And of course, when I called, I could only deal with that charming Mr. Ted McAllister since he – and only he – could possibly take care of my special gift for my son-in-law, the President of the United States.

By 5:00 p.m., the crazy last minute shoppers had picked through the last remnants of the GU Shop's well-stocked inventory. As things settled down, the whole crew was exhausted. Even Ted seemed to lose some gusto; after all, it had been simultaneously thrilling and emotionally draining earlier that day, when Ted took care of the special Christmas needs of Jackie's mother-in-law. "All in a day's work" mused Ted, "but still, soooo significant."

As we moved closer to six o'clock and the official end of the Christmas shopping rush, I told Patrick to stay close to the phone on the first floor.

"Patrick", I whispered, "Watch that horse's ass, Ted, when he takes a phone call that he'll get shortly." Puzzled, Patrick, nonetheless, promised he would take "it all in" – and give me a detailed report.

Since I needed a "secure phone" for my covert plan, I went to a remote phone upstairs in the tailors' backroom. There, with the Italian tailors Angelo and Vince as my puzzled audience, I prepared myself.

And after several deep breaths, I dialed the Shop's main number and suddenly transformed myself into Mrs. Hugh D. Auchincloss!

When Railbird Dwyer answered, "The Georgetown University Shop. How may I help you?" I replied haughtily – with a handkerchief over the phone, "helloooo – this is Mrs. Hugh D. Auchincloss. Could I speak to that young man – Ted something, Ted – well I can't remember his name, but he waited on me earlier today."

Railbird never missed a beat. "Oh, Mrs. Auchincloss, you must mean Ted McAllister, our manager. I'll put him right on." While Railbird was not impressed with big names, this was the mother-in-law of the President of the United States on the phone, so the word went out rapid fire – "Find Ted, its Mrs. Auchincloss!"

Almost instantly, he was on the phone behind the counter, right in the middle of the first floor.

With Ted hyperventilating and speaking in his loud high-pitched, British intoned voice, the weary sales crew realized immediately that Mrs. Hugh D. Auchincloss was on the other end of the phone.

"Oooh, Mrs. Auchincloss, what can I assist you with?"

And was she ever in desperate need of assistance. Mrs. Auchincloss had just realized at 5:40 p.m. on the eve of Christmas Eve, that she needed several additional items for her "old St Nick Christmas Eve luncheon and gift giving ceremony – an age-old tradition held at Merrywood, the Auchincloss' estate across the Potomac River in McLean, Virginia."

"So Mr. McAllister," said I, "could you be kind enough to get me the following items? And, if you don't mind, drop them off at Merrywood tonight."

Be so kind? – From his heightened breathing, I could tell that Ted was trying desperately to regain his composure: "Be so kind? It would by my honor Mrs. Auchincloss to drop your merchandise off this evening!"

Assured that Ted had taken the bait with my high pitched, broad A impersonation of Mrs. Auchincloss, I proceeded to request several items that I knew were either out-of-stock or stored in the most remote corners of the GU Shop's basement.

The first request was an impossible order: three extra large cummerbund and bow tie sets. With glee, I made the request, knowing all were out of stock.

Ted McAllister – sensing that the cummerbund stock had been ravaged by the swarm of earlier Christmas shoppers – was puzzled, and asked "Mrs. Auchincloss, are you sure you need three extra large sets?"

"Yes" I said with a hint of annoyance, "Mr. McAllister, three cummerbund sets – all extra large – two black and one gold."

Five minutes later after his mad tear around the basement, Ted was back on the phone, "I'm so sorry, we are all out of stock, Mrs. Auchincloss."

"Oh my, Mr. McAllister," I said, "What a pity – no, no – that simply won't do."

"Well, Mr. McAllister," a somewhat exasperated Mrs. Auchincloss said, "I also need two white tuxedo shirts – one 17½ by 37, and one 13 by 34."

Anyone who's ever worked in a men's haberdashery knows that a 17½-inch neck size with 37-inch long sleeves is as unlikely to be in stock as the miniature shirt that I also requested with the 13 by 34 inch measurements. While Ted would normally have been condescending about such an odd customer request, store manager McAllister was waiting on the President's mother-in-law. Accordingly, after assuring the Grand Dame of Merrywood that he would check, Ted once again tore down the steep stairs into the Shop cellar where he repeatedly had to climb a stepladder to search for Mrs. Auchincloss' odd shirt requests.

Seven minutes later, a noticeably winded – but ever so apologetic – Ted McAllister was back on the phone, pathetically pleading: "Mrs. Auchincloss, I hope you'll understand, but with the overwhelming Christmas rush, we simply don't have those two evening shirts in stock."

"Well then Mr. McAllister – I hope you can fulfill at least one of my requirements: a white silk evening scarf that I want to give to the President tomorrow. Can you at least do that for me, Mr. McAllister?"

What Ted didn't know was that I had sold the last white silk scarf at approximately 3:45 p.m. that afternoon. I remembered that sale because I had personally wrapped it in bright red Christmas paper – and given it to a nice older woman who thanked me profusely "for finding the very last white silk scarf in all of Washington, D.C."

Blissfully ignorant, Ted assured Mrs. Auchincloss that "I'll be right back with that silk scarf in hand Mrs. Auchincloss. We'll have it wrapped, and I'll personally deliver it to you at Merrywood by 7:00 p.m. tonight."

According to Patrick – who was closely monitoring this wonderful scam as it unfolded, Ted was smiling broadly as he approached the silk scarf counter. But then he looked stricken – and then tearful. As he frantically threw the blue, black and red silk scarves aside, Ted realized, to his horror, that there were no more white silk scarves. "Jesus Christ – where are the fucking white silk scarves? This is simply too much – oh my God!"

Overhearing Ted's outcry while I waited on the phone, I started to feel bad. I knew from my command post one floor above in Angelo's workroom I had to put an end to this charade. After all, it was 6:20 p.m. on the eve of Christmas Eve, and it was time to go home for our own cocktails.

"Mrs. Auchincloss" – a subdued Ted McAllister uttered with a quivering voice – "I have terrible news. I am embarrassed to say that we're totally out of white silk scarves – but Mrs. Auchincloss," he pleaded, "if the President is not going to need it right away, I can guarantee, I'll have a white silk scarf personally in your hands at Merrywood before New Years Eve. Please let me make this up to you Mrs. Auchincloss."

"Oh Mr. McAllister, I am so…" – my voice was starting to change – "Mr. McAllister…" – and then I started to laugh: "Ted, you silly fool, this is not Mrs. Hugh D. Auchincloss. This is Mickey Gardner, and I'm standing with Angelo and Vince one floor above you! So Merry Christmas – you gullible horse's ass!"

Realizing that he had been totally duped, Ted let out a scream that was audible even in the tailors' room: "I'm going to kill that little Irish shit! I'm going to kill him!"

As I left "command center" and started down the stairs to the first floor, I could hear that the entire Shop crew was convulsed with laughter.

But when I reached the first floor, I could not believe my eyes: Ted McAllister, the stern, humorless manager of Shop, was also laughing. With tears streaming down his face, he smiled broadly at me and simply said, "Merry Christmas, you little bastard – you win."

New York, New York

Your first trip alone without parents or siblings is pretty awesome.

For me, my first solo trip at age 14 was to the Big Apple and Broadway in December of 1956.

While my parents had proudly introduced "the kids" to Manhattan five years earlier, I wanted desperately to go back, especially to Times Square where we had seen a statute of George M. Cohan. "George M" – as my Father fondly called him – had become a surrogate Father to my Dad during Joe's teaching days at Georgetown Prep in the 1930s. My Father had been a favorite teacher of the younger George Cohan – and because of that mentoring relationship, the elder Mr. Cohan (one of America's legendary playwrights in the early 1900s) had taken a great interest in young Joe Gardner. Their relationship grew to the point that my Dad had his own bedroom at the Cohan's Fifth Avenue apartment – where night after night, young GU graduate Joe Gardner would have house seat tickets to Broadway's best plays. While my Father was very understated, I loved his stories about those days – the plays, the celebrities and the yet-to-be discovered starlets who frequented the Cohan apartment.

At 14, after my bruising first semester at Gonzaga, I got the parental ok to visit my cousin Barbara McElroy, a newlywed living in the Bronx.

Financing this pre New Year's Eve trip to Manhattan was easy; I was flush after wrapping packages during the frantic Christmas buying frenzy at the Georgetown University Shop. As far as transportation to Manhattan, that was no problem: happily, a friend of my brother Tim offered me a ride to New York where he had planned a post-Christmas visit with his girlfriend. "No problem Tim," this high roller GU senior assured my brother, "I have to be in New York for the big New Year's Eve bash at the Waldorf, so I can give your little brother a ride up."

"What a guy," I thought! So off we went – my brother's magnanimous friend and me with just under $80 for a grand old time in New York City.

On this, my first "parent free" journey to the Big Apple. I learned an important lesson: nothing in life is free! At every tollgate, my brother's "big man on campus friend" would say, "Hey Mick – we need money for the toll." As we approached the Delaware Memorial Bridge, once again he piped up, "Hey Mickey we need a few bucks for the bridge"; then "Hey

Mick – you take care of the New Jersey turnpike!" Finally, "Hey Mick – we need money for the tunnel." No wonder this guy offered Tim's dumb little brother a ride to New York; I financed his stay at the Waldorf.

Once in the Bronx, having been left off at the thruway exit in a non-English speaking neighborhood, I somehow got to my worried cousin's apartment. Detecting my stress, my fun loving cousin Barbara immediately made us martinis. While I had previously sipped a beer and wine on special occasions, my first ever martini was unbelievable – and just the right fix after my rip off journey to New York.

The next day, Broadway was the top priority. I had no idea what was playing on the Great Milky Way, but Barbara insisted on a play called <u>Gypsy</u> starring a woman named Ethel Merman. Even though Barbara told me <u>Gypsy</u> had been sold out for months, she assured me that all I had to do was to go the box office of the Majestic Theater right off Broadway by 6:00 p.m., and if I was persistent, I'd get a seat somehow before the curtain went up at 8:00 p.m.

Trying to appear fearless, I took a bus into the city, found my way to the Majestic Theater on W 44th Street, and prayed that my Irish luck would kick in at the ticket window. Even though it was bitter cold, I remember my awe at the warmth and excitement of Broadway.

All the lights, the marquees, the merriment of the theatergoers, Broadway was intoxicating even without martinis.

And sure enough just as Barbara predicted, when I walked up to the Majestic's ticket window and asked if there was a single ticket anywhere, the wizened little man on the other side of the window said: "Kid, this is your lucky day – an aisle seat in the orchestra just got turned in. So if you're got $28.00 kid, it's all yours."

To this novice theatergoer, I just hit the jackpot. I was going to see my first Broadway play!

I got to my seat; it was on the aisle, fourth row, left side. I was almost sitting on the stage. I must have been awestruck because the older couple sitting on my right – kept asking me "Are you okay?" and "Are your parents seated nearby?"

When the curtain went up, all my nervousness evaporated; it was as if I had known Baby Jane, Gypsy and Momma Rose all of my life. The cast members were so real, particularly Momma Rose (Ethel Merman),whose powerful voice shook the Theater.

While I enjoyed every minute of Gypsy's first act, I was in for a sudden bonanza in the second act. That's when the show suddenly got racy as three unbelievably beautiful, statuesque strippers – all at least a foot taller than me – started coaching the young Gypsy Rose on the fine art of stripping. Today, no teenager in America would blush at the strippers' words and gyrations as they belted out, "You've Gotta Have a Gimmick." But for a 14-year-old Catholic School boy on his first solo theater outing in New York in 1956, this routine was a major – and thoroughly enjoyable – mortal sin waiting to happen.

With every bump and grind, I grew increasingly stressed – and blessed. When the three strippers showed Gypsy Rose what gimmicks they used – including Christmas tree lights on their bazooms – I thought I had died and gone to heaven! Who would ever believe that Broadway could be this fantastic?

At that point in my life, clearly the strippers' tutorial song was the most breathtaking routine of the play. But today, more than fifty years later, the song from Gypsy that has lasting meaning for me was when Ethel Merman belted out the words, "Some people sit on their butts, got the dreams but not the guts. That's ok for some people, for some humdrum people to be, but that's not okay for me!"

Again and again in the years since I saw Ethel Merman in Gypsy, her words that night have reinforced the fundamental message that my father Joe reiterated from the time I was little until his passing in 1968: "Miguel attitude is 90% of the ballgame – if you have big dreams and a determined attitude to make those dreams happen, there's no limit to what you can do with your life."

"Senioritis" and Mrs. Shippens

In Washington, D.C., in the 1960's, one of the most respected institutions was Mrs. Shippens' Dance Class, a "must" for the sons and daughters of the privileged.

For the teenage set, Mrs. Shippens' holiday dances at Thanksgiving, Christmas and Spring Break were social training grounds both on the dance floor and at the small parent-supervised dinner parties that preceded each black tie event. By 8:30 p.m., "everyone who was worth knowing" would have arrived at the Sulgrave Club on Washington's Dupont Circle decked out in their newest frock and tuxedo.

Once inside the grand old Sulgrave Club, every young Shippenite went through a parent-populated receiving line consisting of 10-12 very serious elders on the Shippens Dance Committee. While the parents smiled broadly as they shook each young person's hand, they also leaned forward to smell the little darlings' breath! Drinking prior to Mrs. Shippens was a serious infraction. To make certain that no alcohol-corrupted teen got into her dances, the senior Mrs. Shippens always stood at the end of each receiving line.

I was invited to join Mrs. Shippens during my sophomore year at Gonzaga. Strangely enough, I enjoyed the dances and usually ended up afterwards at some impromptu sherry sipping party in one of Georgetown's grand houses.

By the time of Mrs. Shippens' Christmas Dance in 1959, my senior year at Gonzaga, I was a seasoned Shippenite. I also was suffering from a serious case of "senioritis," an ailment that grips many high school seniors who feel they've already moved "beyond" high school.

So more cocky than usual, I went to Mrs. Shippens on that cold December night after a brief detour at Trader Vic's with my friend Billy White and some girls from Immaculata High School.

In those days, Trader Vic's was the home of exotic Polynesian drinks with gardenias floating on top; more importantly, the Trader Vic's waiters cared nothing about the legal drinking age. Housed in the basement of the Capital Hilton, Trader Vic's policy was simple: you pay, you stay! And we did on that December night – drinking the mind numbing cocktails topped with tropical flowers. I even pinned a rum smelling gardenia on my tuxedo lapel.

At 9:15 p.m., realizing that the Shippens Christmas Dance was well underway, I persuaded Billy to drive me the few blocks up Massachusetts Avenue to the Sulgrave Club. At this point, the pizza and beer that my friends were planning to get at a nearby family restaurant called the Roma were sounding very attractive. But first, I had to at least make an appearance at Mrs. Shippens.

"Ok," my friend Billy said, "We'll wait out front for 20 minutes, but if you're not out by 9:40 p.m., we're out of there. You can take a cab to the Roma."

"No problem," I replied, Three minutes max for the receiving line if there still was one, and 20 minutes dancing in the ballroom was plenty of time.

Bidding my friends a temporary farewell at the Sulgrave Club's massive wrought iron door, I walked confidently into the lobby. Because I was 40 minutes late, I presumed that the receiving line would have "retired to the ballroom" to watch the young people socialize.

Regrettably, as I turned to go up the stairs to the grand ballroom, I saw that I was not so lucky. "No problem," I thought. As Tessie had urged me years earlier: "Just look each of those stiffs in the eyes and give them a firm hand shake."

And that is exactly what I did. If the first few parents in the receiving line got a whiff of my breath or my floral lapel, they didn't react. However, by the time I got to the last father, it was clear that suspicion had formed. And just then I got a good unobstructed look at Mrs. Shippens herself, and the sight wasn't good.

As I gazed at Mrs. Shippens, I was horrified. This stern little rotund woman had dressed herself in a very low cut full-length beige gown. At first, I thought Mrs. Shippens had appropriately covered her ample chest with a wrinkled looking flesh colored lace material. "Definitely not a great look," I thought, "but perhaps appropriate for an 78-year old matron."

But then the full horror of the moment hit me. That wasn't flesh colored lace covering the top portion of Mrs. Shippens body – that was her actual skin. Not only was Mrs. Shippens almost topless; she looked like there were hundreds of little tunnels and tiny canyons running all across her bare chest!

Startled, but not speechless, I shook Mrs. Shippens hand and firmly stated in a very concerned voice: "Mrs. Shippens, that dress is entirely inappropriate for a woman of your age."

Before I could explain to the stunned Mrs. Shippens that my comments were offered in her best interests, two firm hands were suddenly under each of my elbows. Without a word from the two outraged fathers, I was carried down the stairs past the shocked Parents' Host Committee, past the doorman (whom I saluted once again), and out to the circular driveway where my friend Billy White's car was idling.

"Goodnight young man and don't plan on returning to Shippens – ever again!" was all one father uttered through barely open lips!

A week later my parents received a very curt note from the Chairman of the Shippens' Dance Committee. It officially confirmed that I was *persona non grata* and no longer welcome at Mrs. Shippens. That night at dinner, my father's one sentence comment said it all, "Miguel, you have embarrassed yourself once again, and you really had no right to comment on that elderly lady's dress."

The Two Martini Lunch at "21"

As noted earlier, when I was 14, I visited New York City for the first time all by myself. Dropped off at the edge of Spanish Harlem, it was 20º and by the time I made it to my cousin Barbara's little apartment, I was frozen.

Taking one look at me, Barbara said she had the cure – a dry Beefeater's Martini.

Since her husband, a young resident doctor, was on duty until midnight, Barbara felt it was safe to teach me how to make and drink a dry Martini. So even though it was only 4:30 pm on this dark, December afternoon, Barbara reasoned it was already cocktail time in Bermuda, so the Martini tutorial began.

The result: I sipped my first Martini, warmed up immediately – and drank thousands of equally dry Martinis from that day forward.

Six years later when I was a sophomore at Georgetown, I was back in New York City with my girl friend, a stylish Mount Vernon College student, Lynn Shattuck.

On this particular trip, Lynn's father and Schrafft's President, H. Morgan Shattuck, asked Lynn and me to join him at his regular luncheon spot, the famous 21 Club. While I had certainly heard about the fabled 21 Club, I never dreamed I'd lunch at "the 21." "Excited" was an understatement for me as I dressed for lunch: the traditional Georgetown uniform would be just right: a blue blazer with brass GU buttons, white shirt with a red Hermes power tie (my one and only Hermes), gray slacks and loafers.

When we entered the lobby of "the 21" – only tourists call it "the 21Club," Lynn's father was met by a chorus of enthusiastic greetings from scores of people ranging from the hat check girl to familiar CEOs who, like Morgan Shattuck, ate at this restaurant on a regular basis.

After being introduced to scores of Mr. Shattuck's friends, Lynn, her father and I sat down at the Schrafft's table. It was easy to spot since a good sized, miniature Scharfft's truck hung from the ceiling above the table.

Immediately a waiter was at our table asking Mr. Shattuck, "Do you want your regular Mister Shattuck?"

"Yes, Pete, but load it up with olives, not a twist."

Ah, I thought, Mr. Shattuck is a Martini man! My kind of guy.

"Ms. Shattuck, what about you and your friend." Pete asked.

Lynn wisely said, "Ice tea, Pete, thanks."

Full of myself, I responded confidently: "Pete, I'll have a dry Beefeater Martini with olives."

When our drinks arrived I noticed that Mr. Shattuck's Martini had at least four or five olives in it, while mine had the standard two olives. They obviously took good care of Lynn's father.

Lunch was a blur as I tried not to gawk at the room full of celebrities and familiar business leaders, many of whom came over to our table to greet Morgan Shattuck. Midway through our lunch "21 burgers" with special French fries – Pete asked Mr. Shattuck if he wanted another drink.

Mr. Shattuck nodded, and I said, "Make it two, Pete."

As our lunch plates were being cleared away, I realized that my lips were getting numb. The Martinis at the 21 are huge, and I normally only drank alcohol in the evening. Nonetheless, my lips shouldn't be going numb.

Boldly, I sipped on.

When Mr. Shattuck asked Lynn and me about dessert, I could barely answer. "Just…just…just coffee, thank you," I pleaded.

While Lynn and her father ate their chocolate cream pie desserts, I gulped black coffee – three cups in a vain attempt to get my lips to work.

And then Mr. Shattuck smiled and leaned over to me so no one but Lynn and I could hear.

"Mick, try my Martini – its half full, and tell me what you think."

While I was reluctant to put one more drop of gin in my body, I took a sip of Morgan Shattuck's Martini. Then another. Then a third sip.

"Mr. Shattuck, there's no gin in your Martini! It's all water!" I exclaimed.

"You're right Mickey. I only drink one Martini at night when I'm home with Lynn's mother. I've watched too many friends mess up their lives with two martini lunches. So I hope you'll continue to enjoy liquor in moderation and only after the sun sets."

At that, H. Morgan Shattuck got up, kissed his beloved daughter Lynn and shook my hand firmly.

A "Guilt-Free" Georgetown Experience

Most sons of Irish American or Jewish "Mothers" have wrestled with a common and vexing problem: guilt. Mothers from these two ethnic heritages seem particularly adept – early in life – at instilling in their sons a deep sense of guilt. For those of us who were their Mother's "favorite sons," the guilt problem can be even more severe.

As my mother's favorite son, I had amassed a ton of guilt by the fall of 1960 when I entered Georgetown University. Moreover, as a freshman at a school where students partied with vigor, my reckless behavior only exacerbated my tendency to feel "guilty."

But "God works in strange ways" as my 5th grade teacher, Sister John Thomas often proclaimed. For me, meeting Father Royden Davis, S. J. early in my freshman year turned out to be a real miracle.

When I first encountered "Roy" dressed in "civvies" without his Roman Collar, I didn't realize that this middle aged Korean War Veteran was a Jesuit priest.

On our first outing, over beers at Martin's Tavern, Roy was so soft-spoken, I had trouble understanding him. In fact, he whispered. But as I would find out over the next decade, Father Davis' hushed comments were full of profound wisdom.

After I learned he wasn't just "Roy" but a full-fledged Jesuit Priest, I would frequently seek his advice on my "crisis de jour." And even though he was enormously busy with real world challenges – especially when he became Dean of the College at Georgetown – Fr. Davis never once rushed our conversations or gave any indication that he had other more pressing issues on his radar screen.

During one life altering discussion, Father interrupted me in the middle of my anguish. He then looked me firmly in the eyes and in his barely audible voice, said: "Mick – guilt is a wasted emotion."

As a 20-year old Irish-American, I had lived and breathed guilt for the past two decades.

While Father Davis acknowledged the critical need to learn from one's mistakes, he also stressed the overarching need to then move on, secure in the forgiveness of a loving God. According to Father Davis' vision, guilt was not only a wasted emotion, it could get in the way of one's spiritual progress – a vital element for a productive life. It wasn't that you weren't accountable for your actions; you were. But once you accepted responsibility for your misdeeds or omissions, you then had to move on with your life, determined not to make that mistake again.

Years later, I chaired Father Davis' Baker Scholars Program at Georgetown. I would occasionally recount for the new Baker Scholars that profound discussion years earlier in which I was set free from the chronic habit of Irish guilt.

Invariably, Father Davis would say, "Now, now – it's not quite that simple."

Tessie's Nose Dive

Whenever my Mother's three Aunts visited us from Philadelphia, the fun began.

Aunt Mae Bennett Sands was the genteel one of the crowd; married to a British soldier killed in World War I, Aunt Mae was soft-spoken and refined.

Eva Bennett Johnson, Nanna, was the youngest of the three Bennett sisters. A complex woman, she could be simultaneously funny and demanding – and could she ever get on my Dad's nerves during her week-long visits to Washington. When Nanna woke each day and retired each night, she did so with a cigarette in one hand and a cup of strong black coffee or a glass of beer in the other hand.

The third Bennett sister – Theresa "Tessie" Bennett Bradley – was unquestionably my favorite and definitely the most fun. Short, with a spunky walk and a wry smile permanently fixed on her wrinkled face, Tessie, had seen a lot of life in her many years. Her stories about her early years in Liverpool and tales of her subsequent bootlegging days in old Manhattan were so captivating that we begged Tessie to repeat them on each of her many visits to Washington.

The most remarkable thing about Tessie was her pluck. She was always upbeat and always ready with a little sage advice. "Christ, kid – it can't be that bad. Lighten up – laugh, kid."

When the Bennett sisters arrived at our house, there was an unspoken rule that there would be no drinking or swearing by my siblings and me until after our Father had retired. But as soon as he bade everyone "a fair good night," we'd race to the kitchen, grab a beer and start playing poker with Tessie and Nanna as they entertained us with their salty stories. Aunt Mae would never join us during these sessions as she was easily scandalized by the racy tales that her sisters routinely told as the cards were dealt.

As I grew into a college kid, Tessie and Nanna's stories became so celebrated that my friends would literally beg me to invite them over when "the Bennett girls" were visiting. It wasn't the card games or the beer that held the attraction; it was those uproarious stories that Tessie and Nanna would whisper with a twinkle in their worldly eyes.

After an especially late night of poker that topped off my graduation party from Georgetown University in May of 1964, I entered the kitchen on Nevada Avenue the next morning with bloodshot eyes and a very bad headache. As usual, Nanna was "parked" at the kitchen table puffing away on her cigarette between sips of strong black coffee. Unlike her sedentary sister, Tessie was on her typical cleaning tear – standing at the kitchen sink where she was pouring hot water in a pink plastic trashcan.

Incredulous, I asked, "Tessie what are you doing?"

"Don't you worry kid." Tessie replied, "this can smells like cigarette butts, so I'll just rinse it outside."

"Ok, Tessie" I murmured as I poured a cup of coffee and sat down at the kitchen table.

Sitting across from Nanna, I picked up *the Washington Post* and tried to focus. I watched Tessie out of the corner of my eye as she walked out onto the back porch…and then suddenly she wasn't there.

Puzzled – but without any rush, I walked to the screen door – looked out – but no Tessie. I called out guardedly "Tessie, Tessie – where are you?"

"Christ kid, I'm down here," came Tessie's faint reply.

I stepped out onto the back porch – and there she was: Tessie was sitting four feet below me on the grass, her head surrounded by a blooming red rose bush and pieces of the broken trellis. The trellis which served as a makeshift railing had given way when Tessie leaned against it as she rinsed out her pink plastic trashcan.

As I gazed down on my Mother's 84-year old aunt, Tessie Bennett Bradley proudly held up the pink trashcan as if it were a Ming vase.

While I should have been terrified, all I could do was laugh.

Nanna, who heard my howling, became curious and walked over to the porch door to investigate what had me so convulsed. When she realized that I was laughing at her obviously injured, older sister, Nanna's anger was instantaneous. With a nasty knuckle rap on my shoulder, Nanna cursed me: "You damn fool, Tessie needs help and you're standing here laughing."

Terrified, Nanna started yelling frantically: "Help, help! Joe, Elva, come quickly, Tessie's hurt."

My Dad, who must have been dozing on the front porch glider, arrived on the scene somewhat bewildered: "What, what…what are you doing down there Tessie?" He said as he ran on to the back porch.

As I watched my panicked Father rush down the porch stairs to Tessie, I realized the seriousness of the situation and finally got control of myself.

"Tessie," my Father explained, as he knelt beside her, "you shouldn't move at all. I think it's best that you let Elva call the Rescue Squad, so we can get you quickly to Georgetown Hospital."

"Christ, Joe," Tessie promptly replied, – "just get me a shot of Bourbon and a beer and I'll be fine."

Minutes later, that's exactly what Tessie got from my Dad – a full jigger of Old Fitzgerald Bourbon, washed down by a cold Bud.

After a few minutes, she slowly got up and picked the red rose bush from her housecoat. "No broken bones" Tessie assured us, "now, let's get those cards shuffled!"

On the High Seas with the U.S. Coast Guard

Since my family vacationed each summer at Ocean City on the Jersey shore, it was logical for me to pick the United States Coast Guard for my military service in 1964. What could be better than 12 weeks of boot camp at the Coast Guard's base right on the Atlantic Ocean in nearby Cape May, New Jersey? After just 24 hours at the Coast Guards' sprawling base on the outskirts of scenic Cape May, I learned a painful lesson: read the fine print.

When choosing the Coast Guard, I presumed I would have time for an occasional swim in the Atlantic Ocean during the three months of boot camp that began just five days after my graduation from Georgetown. During the 12 long, hot, mosquito infested weeks at the Coast Guard's sun drenched beachfront boot camp, my fellow seamen apprentices and I never once were allowed to swim in the Atlantic Ocean. Despite frequent marches on Cape May's white sandy beaches, with full military gear, I never put my big toe in the Atlantic Ocean. When we did swim, it was always butt naked in the huge indoor pool where we "booties" looked like Yul Brenner clones – bald and shaven clean to prevent a possible lice epidemic.

My second major miscalculation was presuming that I would learn about ships and nautical matters under the nurturing tutelage of seasoned Coast Guard officers. Based on years of seafaring movies, I was sure Coast Guardsmen loved the sea and would want to share their passion with the young recruits. But the entire Cape May drill staff were retired Marine Corps Sergeants who had previously "shaped" dedicated recruits at Parris Island, South Carolina. These chiseled, tattooed men were not only nasty, they were also maniacal and especially hostile to those "fucking college graduate draft dodgers" who obviously had used their college connections to avoid combat duty in the escalating Vietnam War. If you were a recent college graduate in 1964, you were deserving of special treatment – and it was all bad!

Throughout my three-month boot camp experience, my philosophical Father would often write: "Miguel – try to have a sense of humor: it's only 12 weeks (11 weeks, 10 weeks, 9 weeks...) until you'll be at sea on a proud Coast Guard cutter."

So with loving support in daily letters from my parents and friends, I got through my ocean swim-free summer, lost some weight and prepared myself for 12 weeks at sea.

When I was assigned to duty on the 327-foot cutter USCGC Ingraham, I was genuinely excited about the potential learning experience that three months of sea duty represented. After all, the Coast Guard recruiter had assured me that the U.S. Coast Guard Reserve Program "guaranteed an intensive learning experience whereby recruits rotated every two (2) weeks to a new duty station during active duty."

So in the first hour of my first night on the USCGC Ingraham, I learned for the first time how "federal officials" can lie with total impunity.

Upon boarding the Ingraham, tied to a filthy dock in Norfolk, VA, the five new "seamen apprentices" with whom I arrived were told to put our duffel bags next to us and stand at attention. And stand we did – for more than an hour as rag tag members of the Ingraham's 118-man crew ambled by making snide remarks about "the little girl college graduates who just arrived."

After an hour of standing at attention, a huge Coast Guard chief with tattoos blanketing his bulging "Popeye" forearms, strutted up and shouted: "You fucking college assholes – guess where you are spending the next 12 weeks, in the galley."

Before I could object, Popeye – the muscle man continued: "And guess where we're going in three days? Good old Gitmo (short for the Guantanamo Naval Air Base in Guantanamo, Cuba). And guess what, assholes? We're going to be on maneuvers, and you sorry bastards are going to work your fucking asses off on the steam line. Now, get out of my sight until 5:00 a.m. tomorrow."

End of welcoming speech. As we dragged our heavy duffel bags to the enlisted men's sleeping quarters two decks below, we had no idea how bad it would get on the USCGC Ingraham.

First of all, the Ingraham was not air-conditioned, at least not in any of the enlisted men areas – including the galley. And the galley, so cramped that the crew had to eat in shifts – was located right over the engine room. As a result of this engineering fiasco, when under way, the galley would get so hot that you could fry an egg on the galley deck.

Since my Father had drilled into me and my siblings that "attitude was 90% of the ballgame," I tried to view this reversal philosophically.

Unfortunately, any attempt to maintain a good attitude vanished after just one week in Gitmo. The Master of Arms (MA) in charge of the galley turned out to be the same creepy, tattooed chief who welcomed us upon our arrival on the Ingraham. A seasoned "Coastie", this huge man whose name I long ago repressed, was certifiably crazy. And we were his new targets – for 12 long weeks.

After just two weeks on the Ingraham, the crew's relentless hostility to the "six college ass holes" became so intense that we were moved for "safety reasons" to the ship's sickbay. Moving to the Ingraham's sickbay was both good and bad: bad because sickbay only had four bunks – forcing two of the notorious "college six" reservists to rotate sleeping on the sickbay's steel floor; but it was good – really good – because sickbay was located off the main deck with a door that opened directly to the sea. After two weeks in the cramped, un-air-conditioned enlisted men's sleeping quarters with 100 plus hanging hammocks for an equal number of smelly sailors, it was paradise to sleep each night with the fresh sea air blowing into the sickbay.

Once we six college grads were "isolated" in the sickbay, our only meaningful contact with the crew came during mealtimes. To our dismay, mealtimes while a ship was on maneuvers could mean a 14 hour work day. Starting work with the pre-dawn early morning breakfast shift, the lunchtime shift began at 11:00 a.m. and ran to 1:30 p.m. Once we secured the galley after the midday meal, we then prepared for dinner which often could end as late as 11:00 p.m. following evening maneuvers.

Between meals when we often had several boring hours of down time, the tattooed "Popeye" refused to let us read, play cards or nap. "You fuckers are on duty – get it, and the galley floor can never be too clean."

Popeye's cleanliness fetish took on psychopathic proportions one night when we had just "secured the galley" after a long day of Navy-led maneuvers in the huge green-blue Guantanamo Bay. Finally "off duty" at 10:30 p.m., we six reservists were preparing to visit the enlisted men's beer hall located adjacent to the rat-infested dock to which the Ingraham was tied. After a quick shower, we were dressed in fresh whites when Popeye suddenly appeared at the sickbay door and bellowed: "All six of you assholes get back to the galley – now! And bring your fucking toothbrushes."

No amount of guessing could have anticipated what Popeye had in mind for his draft dodgers. As we arrived in the empty galley – now dressed once again in our sweaty dungarees and long-sleeved blue Coast Guard work shirts, Popeye announced: "This fucking deck is fucked up.

So each of you little girls are going to scrub this fucking deck with your toothbrushes, and if you're here until the sun comes up over Guantanamo Bay, tough shit."

That night Popeye actually did the "college six" a big favor. His demands had become so ridiculous that they were almost humorous. Given the overwhelming futility of our lives as galley hands, we all just gave up trying to please – we'd just get along: no mutiny of course, but somehow when the toothbrush episode ended the next morning at 3:10 a.m., we were liberated.

From that point forward, we were also emboldened. John McCawley – one of the college six and a wonderful North Carolina boy who had just graduated from Chapel Hill, decided he would antagonize the crew at the beginning of each meal: instead of ringing the galley bell which officially opened the galley chow line for the hungry sailors lined up at the top of the galley ladder, John would holler the same hog calling "melody" that he learned slopping pigs on his grandparents' farm: "Here pig, here pig, here pig. Soeey, sooeey, sooeey!"

For me, a city boy from Washington, D.C., John's three-times-a-day meal summons was Greek. But it wasn't Greek to many of the Coast Guard enlisted men who had grown up on family farms. They were furious as they climbed down the galley ladder to go through the steaming meal line, the high point of any sailor's day. Despite their curses, John was fearless, and to the delight of his fellow galley hands, he boldly continued his "pig calls" for the duration of our cruise.

From the ludicrous toothbrush incident until the end of our Cuban voyage, we "college sixers" stayed together – 24 hours a day. Emotionally, we also were totally disengaged from the crews' obsession with the Ingraham's maneuver exercises in Guantanamo Bay. To the regular crew, winning an "E" for excellence from the "hard ass Navy team of supervisors" was the top priority of these maneuvers. If the Ingraham was awarded the coveted E which would then be painted on the cutter's towering stack, sailors earned special time off, salary increases, and a whole range of perks. The Ingraham's officer corps also viewed the Navy's award of an "E" as essential to their next promotion – a promotion that, hopefully, would take them off the broken down, circa 1942 USCGC Ingraham.

By contrast, the "E" meant absolutely nothing to the "college six" galley crew. When our Cuban voyage ended in mid-November, we only would have nine more days of active duty to serve in Norfolk, and we'd be free men by December 1. So none of us gave a rat's ass about doing well in the maneuvers or getting a big yellow "E" painted on the ship's stack!

During the Navy's endless supervised maneuvers, the Ingraham occasionally would zigzag violently, forcing galley hands, to hold onto the bolted down tables or railings that circled the galley. This radical zigzagging always took place during "general quarters" when all the portholes in the galley were "secured" (Navy lingo for closed). With all the galley portholes closed and because we were totally isolated from the crew, my fellow reservists and I were completely uninformed about what triggered the zigzagging; we just held on and sweated profusely in the galley.

And "sweating profusely" is a gross understatement. After one hour at "general quarters," with the engines going full blast right below us and the portholes closed, the galley's temperature would soar well past a 100°.

On one particularly hot Cuban afternoon, when we were at "general quarters," the heat in the galley became unbearable. But because we were at "general quarters," we were locked in the "secured" galley! According to the demented Popeye, if we broke "general quarters" by merely opening a hatch or galley door, the ship would flunk that day's entire exercise.

Desperate – with sweat soaking our dungarees and long sleeved work shirts, we "college six" unilaterally decided that getting some air had become a health issue! The question then before us was: "How to get relief from the heat, while simultaneously appearing to preserve the integrity of the Ingraham's general quarters?

With the temperature still rising, John McCawley had a brainstorm.

Unfortunately, our challenge at this point was understanding just what John had in mind. While John could flawlessly do his "here pig, here pig" call three times a day, he had a rather serious stammer, so it took him several stressful minutes to get out his survival plan.

After a series of painful stutters, John's plan finally became clear. Since the door at the top of the galley stairs opened directly onto the main deck, immediately below the Captain's bridge, John proposed that we climb the galley stairs and then very quietly un-hatch the galley door just enough for us to squeeze our sweat drenched bodies out onto the empty main deck.

As far as being spotted after we sneaked onto deck, John reasoned that was unlikely. "Don't worry, you guys, I studied engineering," John assured us, adding that "the angle from the bridge to the remote corner of the main deck below makes it impossible for anybody to see us from the Captain's Bridge." All we had to do was sit – yoga like – with our legs under us, pressed right up against the ship's bulkhead. John had thought of every angle and further explained that "since the Bridge windows were closed due to General Quarters, none of the officers on the Bridge could lean out and look down to see us as we escaped the galley's inferno."

John's plan sounded foolproof.

We climbed the galley ladder. We cracked the galley door just enough to slide out onto the breezy main deck, and then re-secured the galley door. Without a word spoken, we slithered along the deck right below the bridge until we were seated leaning against the bulkhead, facing the turquoise waters of Guantanamo Bay. Since the Ingraham was speeding along at a good pace, we were instantly refreshed by the tropical breezes off the Cuban coast.

Sitting in total silence, we unbuttoned our grimy long sleeve blue shirts. We were finally at peace.

Out of the clear blue Cuban sky, two jets suddenly appeared. In that instant we all knew they were Russian Migs. First Castro had cut the water pipe line to the U.S. Navy Base at Gitmo, and now two Russian Migs were diving out of the sky, aimed right at the Ingraham.

As soon as the Russian jets appeared on the horizon, the Ingraham started to zigzag violently as it attempted – in vain – to escape the pending attack from the rapidly descending Migs.

As terror took hold, John McCawly decided on his own escape strategy.

Without a word, John jumped up – ran to the railing not 10 feet away, and started to climb it in a hasty effort to abandon ship. With his unbuttoned blue shirt flapping in the wind, John McCawley had one leg over the railing and was now just seconds away from jumping into Guantanamo Bay.

As John struggled to get fully over the railing, he looked back at us with terror in his eyes – and screamed: "Je…Je..Jes…Jesus Christ! They're go…go…going to kill us!"

We all leapt to our feet and dashed to John, grabbing his arms, legs, neck – anything to keep him from going overboard. As we desperately held on to John, the two "Russian Migs," with U.S. Navy markings on their tails – screeched overhead, not 25 yards above the Ingraham's bridge.

And then we realized they were Navy fighters conducting the final test of a simulated attack on the USCGC Ingraham.

Suddenly, the zigzagging stopped and the Ingraham became deadly still. Then the announcement blared over the Ingraham's public address system: "All hands, listen up. This is the Captain. General quarters are canceled. The Ingraham has just flunked her final drill. Return at once to your normal duty stations; I repeat, return to your normal duty stations."

We knew instantly what the Captain's stern announcement meant: it meant no big "E" would be painted on the Ingraham's stack. And we also knew that our clever "escape" from the 108° galley was the reason why.

That night, as we stood behind the galley's steamline, the heckling reached a much nastier fever pitch. But by now, we were totally indifferent to the concerns of our crewmates. As far as the terse letter of rebuke from the Captain that was placed in our files, who cared? We would be free men in less than two weeks!

But before we were "free at last," the USCGC Ingraham had to get safely back to its home-port in Norfolk, Virginia.

The night before the Ingraham was scheduled to dock in Norfolk, the full crew was assembled on deck for a "trial run" of our arrival ceremony. As we practiced, I learned for the first time that the Coast Guard – and also the real Navy – typically staged elaborate welcome ceremonies when a ship returned to its homeport after three months at sea. Bands, balloons, and families all decked out in their Sunday best were expected to be on tap for our 10:00 a.m. return the next day. Knowing that local television stations may be on hand, the Ingraham's fastidious Captain sternly admonished the crew to be in top form with pressed dress blues and shined shoes when we stood in formation on the Ingraham's main deck as we docked in less than 14 hours.

After the Captain outlined the agenda for the next day's ceremonies, our predictable Master of Arms, the tattooed Popeye, stuck his bald and empty head into our sickbay hideaway and barked: "Listen up you fucking draft dodgers, you better be spit shined from head to toe tomorrow, or you won't be leaving this boat next week. Assholes!"

The next day – after early galley duty, we put on our dress blues for the big welcome home ceremony. Happily, since we had never rotated out of the galley as promised, the serious responsibilities attendant to the Ingraham's safe docking were "above our pay scale." The only thing we "galley hands" would have to do was stand at attention on the deck as the Ingraham docked.

As we entered Norfolk harbor on schedule at 9:45 a.m. and moved closer to our destination at "Pier 39," we heard the painful sound of a very inexperienced band. The music grew louder and louder as the number "39" came into view on the pier where the Ingraham would dock.

Visible on Pier 39 was a full-fledged uniformed high school band. In addition, red, white and blue balloons were tied to every piling, and there were two groups of cheering family members. The smaller group – more formally dressed – obviously were the loved ones of the Ingraham's officer corps. The much larger – and considerably more boisterous group – were clearly the family and friends of the Ingraham's enlisted crew.

While I had no nautical frame of reference to gauge the appropriate speed for docking a ship, I thought we were going rather fast. But who was I to be concerned?

Suddenly a panicked command rang out.

"Reverse, reverse, reverse," the Captain's screamed over the ship's public address system. Even with my limited nautical experience, I knew instantly that something was wrong. We had gone too wide and too fast in the approach turn.

But it was too late. While the Ingraham's engines grinded into reverse, we kept moving forward at a good clip, now aiming for a direct hit on the uniformed high school band.

The previously poised officers' families sprinted first. They had the good sense to know that you don't dock a Coast Guard cutter by ramming bow first into your berthing pier. When the officers' families broke ranks and ran for dry land, the screeching enlisted men's families also panicked and started running down the long dock. And then – at the last moment before impact – the band fled, knocking over music sheet holders, violin cases and folding chairs.

As we stared in disbelief, a portly teenage tuba player still holding his bulky instrument ran awkwardly down the wooden pier, a split second before the United States Coast Guard Cutter Ingraham tore bow first into pier 39!

For minutes, all we heard were the stark sounds of bending steel combined with the chilling squeaking of torn pilings.

When the noise finally stopped, the Ingraham was sticking straight into Pier 39. We had docked but instead of lying safely adjacent to the dock, we had partially mounted Pier 39.

So much for the U.S. Coast Guard Cutter Ingraham.

Horses and Mice

In the fall of 1960, I met Stephen Benedek, Hungary's 1952 Gold Medal Olympian equestrian. Steve, and his elegant wife Elizabeth, had fled Hungary after the failed Revolt in 1956. Fleeing their homeland literally with the clothes on their back, the Benedeks settled in Washington, D.C. where Steve became Georgetown University's track coach.

And as luck would have it, I became the riding protégé of the great Stephen Benedek.

It all happened quite by chance. My brother Tim, then a senior at Georgetown, and some classmates, determined that they needed to become horsemen. While Steve coached Georgetown University's track team, he also had a riding camp appropriately called "Camp Olympic" in Olney, Maryland – just 40 minutes outside of Washington, D.C.

Wanting to erase the memory of my first terrible pony ride, I decided to join my brother and his friends as they began their riding lessons with the no-nonsense Benedek. And so it was from October, 1960 – after my first month at Georgetown – until I was married seven years later, I rode each Saturday and Sunday at Camp Olympic. I also became part of the Benedeks' wild, always hospitable and incredibly nurturing Hungarian world.

Within weeks of my first painful riding lesson under the relentless "Coach Benedek," I knew – as did my Coach – that I was a natural. Before long, I was jumping five-foot fences and doing basic dressage drills. In May 1961, the supreme compliment came when Steve offered me a summer job as his "top-riding instructor." I couldn't believe my good fortune – getting paid to spend eight hours a day working with horses, teaching riding, and actually riding!

But as I soon found out, working for Steve Benedek was a form of physical boot camp. Steve pushed you to your physical limit – telling you to take that higher jump, and then demanding five more laps around the ring without your stirrups.

During this challenging period of my life as Camp Olympic's Senior Riding Instructor, Steve's steady wife Elizabeth was always there with a gentle word of encouragement when Stephen was particularly demanding. "It's okay Mike, be patient," she would say, "Stephen just wants you to be the best rider that you can be."

While the Benedeks were always supportive, there were times when Camp Olympic's "senior riding instructor" messed up. And "mess up" I did on one ego deflating day during my first summer at Camp Olympic.

As any former camp counselor knows, the counselor must always be mindful that he or she is a "role model." Therefore, you must be brave, firm but kind, and mindful at all times of safety considerations. Finally, a good camp counselor must never, ever use profanity in front of the campers.

For most of my first summer as Camp Olympic's "senior riding instructor," I scrupulously followed these basic commandments for good camp counseling. The children I taught riding to each day were appropriately respectful as I supervised them in the riding ring and in the barn where the campers learned all aspects of horse care. Our campers didn't just get on push button horses and ride for an hour. At Camp Olympic, young riders had to enjoy the full "horse experience" that included grooming and feeding our four legged friends and even mucking out their stalls.

Each lunch time I rewarded the most responsible young equestrians by choosing "eight stars" to help me feed the weary horses who had just finished going around and around the riding ring for three hours.

While Steve required each camper to wear appropriate riding attire – jodhpurs, boots, and riding helmets – I somehow managed to teach each day clad only in riding boots, navy blue swim trunks and a "Rama" helmet right out of an exotic African movie. For some unknown reason, when it came to my breach of riding attire, Steve looked the other way. So, I happily got my coveted tan as I taught each day looking like a half-naked jockey on Safari.

At each midday feeding time, I would line up my eight "star riders of the day" and assign each two horses.

Once a "feeder" was designated for each of our 16 horses, I would lift the steel lid off the large metal barrel containing the horses' oats. After I shook the feeding bag free of stale oats, I then dipped the oats scooper deep into the barrel and dumped the loaded scooper of oats into one of the feedbags.

As this process began, the horses typically got very excited, snorting and stomping their hoofs in anticipation of the feast they would enjoy as soon as their feedbags were hung over their necks by one of my eight "star riders."

On the particular day in July 1961, I followed my normal routine and placed the first feedbag on the tack room floor. I then dumped the oats into it. To my horror – a vile little gray mouse – surely full of lice – suddenly jumped out of the feedbag. For country people, mice are not a big thing; but for this city slicker, any mouse, including this little bugger, was a huge problem.

Determined as I was to always be Mr. Cool Camp Counselor – role model to my pupils – I said, with feigned calmness, "Oh, look at that, a mouse must have somehow gotten into the oats barrel." I obviously was not thinking clearly since in reality, that mouse would have had to be a rodent version of Arnold Schwarzenegger to lift the heavy steel lid that covered the oats barrel.

"Ok, Mr. Cool," I thought, "stay calm and feed the horses – or they'll start kicking their stalls down."

Streetwise as I was, I now very carefully moved the oats scooper around the barrel. To my relief, there were no other mice in the barrel. "Thank God," I thought, "can you imagine the stampede that would have occurred if our fractious horses started eating their oats, and suddenly discovered that a live rodent had been added to their entrée?"

Confident that the mice crisis was behind me, I pulled the second feedbag off the hook, shook it free of any stale oats from yesterday's lunch, and put it on the tack room floor. I filled it – waited – and as expected, no mouse jumped out.

By now, the horses were showing increased annoyance at the mealtime delay with their snorting and stomping reaching a fever pitch. Hastily, I reached up, got the third feedbag off the hook, and vigorously shook it.

And then it happened.

Without the slightest warning, three full-grown mice flew out of that feedbag and ran right down my bare chest as they fell to the tack room floor. Not one – not two – but three full grown brown and gray field mice pursued their exit strategy across my freckled, shirtless chest.

And I lost it!

"Holy shit – Jeesus Christ", I screamed, as Camp Olympics' panicked senior riding instructor bolted out of the tack room at a full gallop.

Only when I was safely 30 yards away in the dusty paddock did I realize what I had just done. As I looked back at my totally startled – and first time ever-speechless eight "star riders" – I realized that I had permanently obliterated my "Mr. Cool Guy" camp counselor image.

My reputation lay shattered on that tack room floor. And not only that, I actually had said, "Shit" and had taken the Lord's name in vain all in one sentence.

Humiliated at my total breech of good counselor conduct, and increasingly aware of the cacophony of snorts and frantic hoof stomping now emanating from the still unfed horses, I returned to the tack room. There, the eight brave "star riders" stood with total disbelief on their innocent young faces.

"Mike, are you afraid of mice?" came the first incredulous question. And then a tidal wave of laughter as they shouted, "Mike's afraid of mice, Mike's afraid of mice."

When the horses were finally fed, we all walked up to the camp's lunch grounds. Almost instantly, the story of "the three mice running down Mike's bare chest" and my "cursing and running away" spread like a forest fire. To my chagrin, following lunch that day – and for every day until the summer ended, the entire camp serenaded me with, "Mike's afraid of mice, Mike's afraid of mice!"

Years later, when I was living as an image conscious bachelor in Georgetown, I occasionally ran into several of my "star riders" at Georgetown's Safeway. Invariably, these unforgiving teenagers would once again loudly greet me with "Mike's afraid of mice, Mike's afraid of mice."

Timberlawn: Another Home Away From Home

In the fall of 1961, President John F. Kennedy and his photogenic siblings dominated the media and life inside the Beltway. And I was totally caught up with the magic and drama of the Kennedys – their administration, their family and their friends. So, to my great delight early in October of my sophomore year at Georgetown, my Irish luck brought me a terrific "professional" opportunity: training fractious horses for President Kennedy's favorite sister, Eunice Kennedy Shriver.

One day when my father was playing a round of golf at Georgetown Prep with Father Dixie Duggan, S.J., my normally modest Father proudly proclaimed to Father Duggan that, "Mickey has become quite an equestrian – in fact, I think he can make any horse do what he wants." At 19, I had become an accomplished horseman, thanks to Stephen Benedek.

According to my Dad, the mere mention of horses caused Father Duggan to explode about the horse and pony hoof marks found all over the fairways and greens of the Prep's nine hole golf course. While Dixie Duggan did not actually see the stampeding trespassers, other Prep faculty members had seen Peace Corps Director Sargent Shriver riding wildly with several of his young children across the Prep's pampered golf course. On one occasion, Father Duggan – a horseman himself – apparently saw Sargent Shriver bite the dust when thrown by his 18½-hands Irish Hunter.

Terrified that the Shriver clan and their out-of-control horses and ponies would return to the Prep's golf course, and fortified with my Father's boast that I could train any horse, Father Duggan decided to pursue a preventative strategy. He called President Kennedy's brother-in-law and told Sargent Shriver "you need help with that big horse of yours! And I know just the kid who can teach that animal not to buck."

Happily, the kid was me.

Following Father Duggan's instructions, I promptly wrote "Mr. Shriver" at the address he provided and boldly affirmed that I could make his huge 18½-hands Irish hunter behave.

Four days later, I received a call from a secretary who stated – coldly and firmly: "Eunice Kennedy Shriver wants to see you at Timberlawn, 4:00 p.m. sharp tomorrow afternoon. And be in riding attire." Bang went the phone. I was being summoned for a "riding audition" with the President's sister.

King of Sprinkler Lane

For an Irish Catholic kid from Chevy Chase, D.C. who was addicted to presidential politics, this was a big deal. Even if the 18½-hands monster horse threw me off, I would still get to meet the President's sister. Accordingly to press reports, Mrs. Shriver was so close to the President that they had shared a house in Georgetown when the President was a lowly Congressman.

At 3:45 p.m. the next day, I drove through the gates of Timberlawn and parked in front of a sprawling white mansion that looked like a southern plantation.

With Tessie's admonition echoing in my ears to be my confident self, I knocked firmly on the front door. After what seemed an interminable delay, a disheveled middle-aged man opened the door and said with a very foreign accent: "oh – you're the horse kid. Well, go down there – to the riding ring, the Madame's waiting for you." He paused and then grinned from ear-to-ear, "Gude luck kid – you'll need it."

At the riding ring, they were waiting: Eunice Kennedy Shriver; her precocious little daughter, Maria on her pony Miss Buck; and Maria's riding instructor – an elderly Shriver cousin from Baltimore. Tied to the nearby fence was the huge, magnificent horse that had been unseating her husband.

After very brief and chilly introductions, I was asked to ride "Mickey," the fearsome, enormous Irish Hunter. "No problem," I said. However, there was a slight problem; at five foot six, I needed a ladder to mount the huge four-legged creature. Since no mounting block was in sight, I simply approached Mickey – who was not snorting – looked him square in the eyes, patted him and literally did a high jump, miraculously getting my left boot in his left stirrup. I was in the saddle.

For the next 20 minutes, "Mickey" and I worked out – first in the ring, and then galloping in the adjacent field. Bottom line: Mickey was a piece of cake – steady, responsive, smooth. He unquestionably was the finest and biggest horse I had ever ridden. We bonded after the first two canters around the ring.

The no nonsense Mrs. Shriver came up to me after my brief workout with Mickey and said: "I'll pay you $5.00 an hour. When can you start?"

"How's tomorrow?" I replied. Mrs. Shriver surprised me: "I'd like you here at least three times a week, and you also need to ride Miss Buck as well as Mickey on each visit."

Trying to be cool, I replied: "No problem – I'll see you tomorrow."

As I drove out of Timberlawn's driveway that day, I was thrilled. First, I had just met President John F. Kennedy's sister, and I was going to see more of this family, close up. Second, I was going to haul in substantially more tax-free money, augmenting my earnings each week from working two days at the GU Shop and teaching riding each weekend at Camp Olympic. Third, I would be riding that exquisite Irish hunter Mickey three times a week. I couldn't believe it: I would be getting paid $5 an hour for riding the most beautiful, stately, Irish hunter in the entire Washington, D.C. area!

The Timberlawn Family

Since I would ride at Timberlawn three afternoons each week during much of the 1960s, I quickly got to know the staff. Happily for me, the eccentric Timberlawn staff embraced me with open arms and occasionally even shared gossip.

The best source of tidbits was the Shrivers' rumpled master chef, Leonardo. While I never knew Leonardo's last name, I learned quickly that this Belgian had a fierce temper and a big heart. Every time I finished riding the glorious Mickey, Leonardo had hot tea waiting for me. And when Mrs. Shriver was traveling, Leonardo also had a plate of Madame's "tres cher" French cookies next to my tea.

Another staffer who added to the mischief and merriment of Timberlawn was the witty Irish nanny, Winnie Butler. A recent arrival from the Olde Sod, Winnie's Irish accent was as thick as a big slice of paddy's pig. A devout Catholic, Winnie was great fun.

Another of the Shriver's most memorable staffers was their gregarious chauffeur and jack-of-all trades, Richard "Rags" Ragsdale. A big barrel chested man who was ready to help in any pinch, "Rags" was the 24/7 guy who never lost his sense of humor. Given the frantic and often demanding nature of life at Timberlawn, Rags was an indispensable part of the Shriver household.

Because of Mrs. Shriver's deep private and public commitment to advancing the cause of the mentally retarded – now known as the mentally challenged – the "Madam," as Leonardo called her, insisted on hiring mentally retarded women to help Leonardo serve meals. Given Leonard's impatient and perfectionist ways, this sometimes lead to fireworks in the kitchen.

On one unforgettable afternoon when I was scheduled to ride Mickey, I got a call from Mr. Shriver's assistant telling me to go "immediately to Timberlawn" where Leonardo apparently had threatened "the help and Mrs. Shriver." With obvious stress in her usually ice-cold voice, the confidential assistant added that, "Leonardo has quit and said he would only talk to "Mike the horseman."

"No problem." I said, "I'm on my way to Timberlawn right now." Intrigued, I sped out Rockville Pike. When I drove through the gates of Timberlawn, it was unnaturally still. No screaming kids, no bikes, no dogs roaming around, no Mrs. Shriver – it was unreal.

As I screeched to a halt in the driveway, a totally frazzled Leonardo bounded out of the kitchen. "Mike, Mike – do you know what the Madam did? Not only does she hire that idiot woman to work with me, the Madam comes into my kitchen after lunch today and tells me the hamburgers are too thick. Too thick! And then she yells that I'm wasting her dollars. I am the Master Chef; and I'm cooking hamburgers for Bobby's birthday lunch – for his friends, those brat kids: and the Madame tells me the hamburgers are too thick!"

I quietly agreed: "Leonardo – you are the best; everybody knows that. That's why you worked for the President's Father: that's why everybody knows the Shrivers' dinner parties are better than Ethel's or Joan's. You're the best. So don't get so upset with Mrs. Shriver's suggestions; she's only trying to save money."

Instantly, Leonardo's bloodshot eyes widened. "Saving money, saving money – are you crazy Mike?" he shouted.

I decided to change my approach.

While Leonardo didn't know the details, he knew from the staffs' schedule that the Joseph P. Kennedy Foundation that Mrs. Shriver had talked her Father into funding, would be awarding a million dollar grant for mental retardation research to a Chicago hospital on the following day.

"Okay Leonardo, so you yelled at Mrs. Shriver." I asked, "What got everyone so upset?"

"Well I picked up the carving knife and chased the Madam out of my kitchen."

Oh my God – no wonder Timberlawn was so quiet; the whole household – dogs, kids and adults – were "locked down" behind Mrs. Shriver's bedroom door.

After letting Leonardo vent for nearly an hour, I suggested action.

"Leonardo, don't you think you should have left the knife out of this – even if you wanted to make your point with the Madam? After all Leonardo, you love these kids – most of the time – and their Mother means well, even if she's annoying about money. Don't you think you owe her an apology? You know you like your job – and everyone here at Timberlawn and throughout the whole Kennedy family, they all know that you're the master chef!"

Leonardo was easily flattered so I had hit a responsive cord. In reality, Leonardo was the best. Moreover, he liked his job.

As he noticeably mellowed, I went for the kill: "Leonardo, life is good for you here at Timberlawn. It's time to make up with the Madam and get back to work." By now, it was also time for me to get to work. The sunlight was starting to fade, limiting my ride on Mickey.

Finally, Leonardo sighed and capitulated: "Ok, call the Misters' office and tell them I don't resign anymore. I'll stay – but damn it Mike, tell them that I – Leonardo – decide how thick the hamburgers will be!"

And that was that. Leonardo went back into the kitchen and put on his tall white chef's hat; I called Mr. Shriver's secretary and announced the truce – and by the time I had saddled Mickey and was trotting on Timberlawn's front lawn, Mrs. Shriver, the kids and dogs were all playing outside.

And on the next day, Mrs. Shriver gave a million dollars of her Father's fortune to a medical research center in Chicago that would do pioneering work on behalf of the mentally challenged.

THE BLACK CAR CHASE

Another Timberlawn incident of note happened on that dreadful day when President Kennedy was assassinated.

Right before my two o'clock history class was to begin on November 22, 1963, I parked on P Street near the Georgetown campus planning to spend the afternoon in a series of back-to-back classes. As I gathered up my books, a radio bulletin announced a shooting in Dallas involving President Kennedy's motorcade.

And then the shaken voice of Walter Cronkite, "The President died today at..."

Like most Americans, I was more than stunned. Emotionally shocked, I needed my anchor: I needed to go riding. So without a thought, I drove to Timberlawn.

Saddled and out into the glorious fall day, Mickey and I galloped and galloped and galloped around one of Timberlawn's huge back fields adjacent to Old Georgetown Road.

Oblivious to anything around me except the graceful horse under me, I exhausted myself and Mickey. Even with the crisp fall air, we were soaked.

Suddenly a blaring sound startled us.

At first, I thought a car horn had gotten stuck on Old Georgetown Road; but the intrusive honking grew louder. And it kept getting closer.

When I finally looked over my shoulder, I couldn't believe my eyes. A big black car was bearing down on Mickey and me. And the damn fool driver had his hand firmly on the horn. As the sedan sped closer to us, Mickey started to rear up.

"What the hell are you doing?" I screamed.

Now, just 15 yards behind us, the horn stopped blaring as the big black sedan skidded to a stop on the thick green turf.

In a rage, I trotted Mickey to the driver's side of the black car.

"Who do you think you are? You could have gotten me thrown," I shouted.

Then both front doors opened, and two humorless muscular looking guys in dark suits stepped out. Before I could say another word, the unsmiling driver said, "Get off that horse, kid. This place is locked down." He held up his badge: "United States Secret Service."

"Buddy, you could have gotten your head shot off if some nut thought you were a Kennedy. This is a bad day, and we're making sure no other Kennedy family members get killed."

I suggested that they were overreacting: "You can't be serious. No one is going to think I'm a relative of the President."

The other agent stepped forward and pointed his finger in my face: "Listen, smart ass, you're riding right next to this road, and everybody knows that the President's sister lives here. So get your ass off that horse and get the hell out of this field."

End of conversation.

For me, and most Americans, that day and the ensuing days of Oswald's murder and the President's funeral were traumatic – and even today, they remain somewhat blurred.

But one visual image is still crystal clear in my mind: a black sedan chasing Mickey and me at high speed through the fields of Timberlawn.

The Shriver Horse Show for the Mentally Retarded

In the mid-1960s, Mrs. Shriver's opened a pioneering summer Camp for the mentally challenged at Timberlawn. I say, "pioneering" because Mrs. Shriver's efforts in the 1960s were truly revolutionary, pushing the envelope for the mentally handicapped in ways never dreamed possible in those days.

Long before she launched the Special Olympics in 1968, Eunice Kennedy Shriver determined that the American public must realize that mentally challenged people could live productive lives in society. And what better place to showcase this controversial concept than at your own home – in this case, the lush green fields, riding ring and huge swimming pool at Timberlawn.

So for several summers in the 1960s, dozens of mentally challenged youngsters who otherwise were confined to home or some drab institution, would come to Timberlawn for what often became a life altering experience – succeeding at a sport. For many of these challenged youngsters, riding a horse or "swimming" in Timberlawn's pool was much more than their first athletic outing; their brief visits to Timberlawn were huge self-esteem building experiences.

Since I had never had any contact with a mentally challenged person before Timberlawn, I marveled at Mrs. Shriver's resolve to create a new world order possible for this special, but largely invisible portion of our population. So when Mrs. Shriver asked me in the spring of 1965 to help her on a project involving horses to showcase the abilities of these children, I agreed at once.

In this case, Mrs. Shriver had decided on a media generating event that was unprecedented in the horse world; we would organize a full blown Maryland-registered Horse Show at Timberlawn to financially benefit the mentally retarded. And here was the hook; we would use teenage boys from the Joseph P. Kennedy Institute for the Mentally Retarded in Northeast Washington who, together with the Shriver kids, their Kennedy cousins and friends, would set the jumps, collect the parking fees, cook the hot dogs, even announce the classes!

I, nonetheless, was immediately skeptical.

"Mrs. Shriver – are you sure this is a good idea?" I asked. "After all, registered Maryland Horse Shows are not casual county fairs; everything will have to be done right. Do you really think it will work?"

"Of course it will, Mike," she impatiently replied. "The only thing those boys at the Kennedy Institute need is some help and they'll be terrific. You wait and see. This show will be a great eye opener because we'll get all the press out here, and they'll see what's possible if you just give retarded teenagers a chance."

As it turned out, Mrs. Shriver was right. For three consecutive years – she and I organized the first, second and third annual Shriver Horse Show for the Mentally Retarded. And with each May show, we got even better press and television coverage than the year before. Together with the Shriver kids and scores of Kennedy cousins, the fearless young men from the Kennedy Institute outdid themselves. Since one of Washington's top horse show experts, Gigi Winslatt volunteered to handle the course layout, the Shriver Horse Show for the Mentally Retarded even passed muster with the most competitive equestrians.

To make the one-day annual show a "must" for the media, Mrs. Shriver would suggest names of notable cup donors for me to contact. It was great fun to call President Theodore Roosevelt's daughter, Alice Roosevelt Longworth or Senator William J. Fulbright or Jimmy Hoffa's fearsome attorney, Edward Bennet Williams. And because I was calling on behalf of Eunice Kennedy Shriver, most Washington celebrities happily agreed to contribute the $25 needed to buy the Sterling Silver cups for our blue ribbon equestrians.

But I also had to find funding for some of those 24 sterling silver cups on my own, so I asked my parents, their dear friends, Helen and Steve Barabas, and Patrick Lennon's sister, Theresa.

By 1965 – and the First Annual Shriver Horse Show, I had known Theresa Lennon for eight years – but always as Patrick's sometimes stern older sister. Theresa often blamed me for fun loving Patrick's ample indiscretions.

Theresa had a long memory, but she also had a big heart – especially when it involved children. So, when the First Annual Shriver Horse Show was taking shape, I determined to "hit Theresa up" for a cup. At 23, Theresa was already the founder and Headmistress of the respected Georgetown Montessori School. "What better PR," I argued "than having some of your students present the Georgetown Montessori School cup at the Shriver Horse Show. Come on Theresa, every media person in Washington will be there."

Fortunately, Theresa was a good sport. So on the third Sunday in May 1965, she and three of her most precious pre-schoolers arrived at Timberlawn to present the Georgetown Montessori School cup to the winners of the junior jumping class.

Since it was raining, the media-wise Theresa had her three little students decked out in eye catching, bright yellow rain slickers. And sure enough, while the reporters were dazzled by all the Kennedys and Washington celebrities presenting cups, photographers were all eager to capture the three little pre-schoolers in their matching yellow slickers presenting the Georgetown Montessori School Cup.

The Washington Post's huge article on the Shriver Horse Show appeared the next morning, there on the front page of the style section was a half page, photo above the fold, of the three Georgetown Montessori students in their yellow slickers. The trouble was, they were only identified by name without one single reference to the Georgetown Montessori School. Nowhere in the six-column story of "yesterday's highly successful Shriver Horse Show for the Mentally Retarded" was there one mention of Theresa Lennon's Georgetown Montessori School.

Sometimes I'm amazed – giving our checkered history – that our marriage has worked out so well.

While Theresa Lennon and a host of Washingtonians continued to support the next two Annual Shriver Horse Shows, Mrs. Shriver was already moving on to the national arena as she envisioned something bigger for the mentally challenged. And I stood nearby as Mrs. Shriver officially opened the first Special Olympics in Soldiers Field in Chicago on a sunny July Day in 1968.

MICKEY AND THE BLIZZARD OF 1965

Another memorable event at Timberlawn took place on a snowy morning in February 1965.

Following graduation from Georgetown, my six months of active duty in the Coast Guard, and then a rigorous six-week stint as a "messenger-all purpose grunt" on the Johnson-Humphrey Inaugural Committee, I needed a permanent full time job. Somewhat reluctantly, I entered the Sears Roebuck "executive training program" and was assigned to a Sears Store all the way across town in Southeast Washington. Having grown up in the all white Northwest Washington, my 22-month tour of duty at the Sears-Alabama Avenue store turned out to be an invaluable learning experience.

Even though I knew after a few months that the financially rewarding life of a Sears Roebuck General Manager was not for me, I had made a commitment to the two-year program. After numerous discussions with my Dad, I decided that I was honor bound to complete this program. As my Father said, "You must stick it out Miguel – and you'll learn in the process what the next professional challenge should be."

One of the good things about the training program was my flexible work schedule. As a Sears "junior executive," I could set my own 40-hour week schedule. As long as I was on duty on Saturday – a "must work day" in retailing – I could take a whole day off in the middle of the week to ride Mickey. For me, having ample horse time each week made life at Sears tolerable.

As I dressed for my ride with Mickey on this particular mid-week day off, I bundled up since it was snowing. The drive was trickier than I expected, and it quickly became clear that the snowstorm was turning into a blizzard.

Despite the heavy snowfall, by noontime Mickey and I were cantering with ease through 6 inches of snow. The only problem was very bad visibility, so I decided to use the four feet high rail fence as my guidepost while Mickey and I circled the huge field in front of Timberlawn.

Galloping along close to the fence, Mickey suddenly reared up.

Scrambling to stay in the saddle, I tried to calm the agitated Mickey, And then I saw why Mickey had reared up.

Not five feet in front of us was a little old lady wearing a huge hat secured by a dark scarf around her head and chin, and she was walking right towards us.

Shocked, I asked: "Madam, can I help you? Are you lost?"

Before I could say another word, she bellowed back, (in a scratchy, but impatient voice), "Of course I'm not lost. I'm taking my walk. And please be more careful young man; I have another eight laps around this field."

I knew that voice. It was Rose Fitzgerald Kennedy, the late President's Mother. I had just come within two seconds and five feet of trampling her.

I couldn't get to the barn quickly enough. After hastily stabling Mickey, I plowed my way up to the main house to alert Mrs. Shriver that her mother was, in fact, walking outside.

I bolted into the house and asked Leonardo where Mrs. Shriver was. "In the dining room Mike; they're waiting for the old lady to come in for lunch." As an after thought, Leonardo added, "Can you imagine that silly old lady is out there walking in this storm?"

When I excitedly reported to Mrs. Shriver that Mickey and I had nearly trampled her Mother, Mrs. Shriver laughed. "Mike, my Mother walks two miles everyday regardless of the weather and no matter where she is. Don't worry, Mike. But I'm glad you didn't ride over her."

On a much sadder, stifling night in early June 1968, I accompanied the Shriver family in their car in Senator Robert Kennedy's funeral motorcade from Washington's Union Station to Arlington Cemetery; there, Rose Kennedy's third son Bobby Kennedy was buried a stone's throw away from her other assassinated son, President John F. Kennedy.

As I walked with Mrs. Shriver down the path from the graveside where Robert Kennedy's last rites had just been held, I was struck by Rose Kennedy's incredible stoic reserve as she sat tearless – all alone – in the back of her limousine. When her daughter Eunice leaned in and asked her mother if she was all right, she said with some impatience: "Of course, I'm alright Eunice. Bobby's with God."

The Caroline

In 1967, Eunice Shriver offered me a ride to Palm Beach on the Caroline – JFK's presidential campaign plane in the 1960 election.

Corporate planes were a rarity then, so a ride on a private plane was a significant event for me. But a ride on the Caroline, this was truly special.

In my GU Shop blazer and white linen slacks, I waited at Washington's Page Terminal for the Shriver's entourage to arrive for the flight to Palm Beach. First to arrive were Joan Kennedy and her three young children along with a shell-shocked nanny. Then the Shrivers showed up en masse with bikes, tennis rackets and their faithful nanny Winnie Butler.

Within minutes, the Caroline was airborne for what was the wildest plane ride I could ever have imagined. While bikes were tearing up and down the aisle, tennis balls flew overhead! Somewhere over the Carolinas, the beleaguered steward passed out luncheon menus: lobster tails or filet mignon – or both. I couldn't believe my good fortune.

Mindful of Tessie's guidance to always be cool, I tried to mask my euphoria. So, when Mrs. Shriver asked, "Mike, how do you like the Caroline?" as I was chowing down on my huge lobster tail, I replied, "It's a nice little plane, Mrs. Shriver."

Mrs. Shriver merely smiled; she knew full well that were it not for my free ride on the Caroline, I would not be flying to Palm Beach or anywhere else for Easter.

Since the Shrivers were traveling on to a private estate in Eleuthera where I would join them on Easter Monday, Joan Kennedy, her family with their now totally disheveled nanny and I were the only passengers deplaning the Caroline in Palm Beach.

When the Caroline touched down at the Palm Beach airport, there was a problem: Ambassador Kennedy's driver was new and had gone to the commercial terminal – not the adjacent private terminal where the Caroline landed. To get to the private terminal, he would need at least 20 minutes to circle the airport – an eternity since the Kennedy cousins were now out of control and in desperate need of their naps.

My host in Palm Beach, Mrs. Hugh Woodward, had sent her stately but ancient driver James to pick me up. As we taxied to a stop, I could see James standing beside his big black Cadillac.

Confronted with Joan Kennedy's obvious distress about the tardy driver, I did what any Palm Beach gentleman would do. I said, "Joan, would you like my driver to take you and the children to Ambassador Kennedy's house."

Before she could answer, Mrs. Shriver, standing next to me at the Carolina's open door, burst out laughing as she exclaimed: "My driver! My driver! Mike Gardner, you are sooo very thoughtful!"

I started to laugh at my own pomposity. Somewhat bewildered by a joke that only Mrs. Shriver and I were sharing, Joan Kennedy graciously declined my offer for a ride: "Thank you, but with their bikes and all of our luggage, we better wait for the Ambassador's station wagon."

As I walked down the stairs from the Caroline to James and my waiting car, I looked back to a still laughing Eunice Kennedy Shriver.

My second trip on the Caroline took place ten days later when the vacation weary Shriver clan, flew back to Washington. On this flight, the chaos and excitement of the pre-Easter flight to Palm Beach was gone. School was starting the next day for the Shriver kids – and very little homework had been done in Eleuthera.

While the "youngsters" frantically tried to play catch-up with their spring break assignments, I went to the private bedroom cabin at the back of the Caroline and took a nap in President Kennedy's bed.

Bobby's Big Sister

One morning in July of 1967, I was drafting a press release at my public affairs job at the Office of Economic Opportunity, the Johnson Administrations' War on Poverty. Although I was working officially as an appointee of OEO Director Shriver, I was a junior staffer. Fortunately, I was working under the tutelage of the renowned newspaper journalist Marshall Peck, a former top editor for the International Herald Tribune; Marshall was a nurturing but exacting mentor who taught me how to write something other than Sears Roebuck action memos.

On this July morning, I received a rather peculiar call from Director Shriver's office manager: "Mike, can you be at Timberlawn tonight by seven?" "Sure," I replied – "I'm planning to ride Mickey before it gets dark, so no problem. What's up?"

It turned out that Mrs. Shriver had decided unexpectedly to return to Washington to attend a meeting the next day of the President's Committee on Mental Retardation. Since Sarge was on the West Coast, and the Shriver kids and staff were already at Hyannis Port, Mrs. Shriver wanted me to spend the night "for safekeeping" at Timberlawn.

After a dinner of stale crackers, tea and some old cheese that I scavenged from Leonardo's virtually defunct kitchen, Mrs. Shriver insisted that we watch a special news show featuring her brother Bobby, then the junior Senator from New York. The show, using a quasi debate format, pitted her brother against several prominent conservatives. As a dedicated liberal at that point, I naturally sided with Bobby's anti-Vietnam, anti-establishment views.

After the show, Mrs. Shriver asked, "Mike, who do you think won this debate?"

I almost laughed. "Of course your brother Bobby did; he destroyed the conservative lunatics," I exclaimed – somewhat incredulous at the question.

"No Mike" Mrs. Shriver shot back, "you're wrong. Bobby didn't have an adequate grasp of the facts on some issues. He didn't do his homework."

Before I could reply, Mrs. Shriver bounded to the phone in the nearby den and promptly got her younger brother Bobby on the phone. Bluntly, Mrs. Shriver then detailed how he could have done better. Reading point after point from the yellow legal pad on which she jotted notes during the show, the Senator from New York's older sister made it clear – in no uncertain terms – that her brother's performance was not up to her standards – or his.

"Big sisters are big sisters," I thought as I climbed the stairs to go to sleep.

When Eunice Kennedy Shriver died at 88 in 2009, I wrote the following article that appeared in the Huffington Post. I don't think it overstates the living legacy of this special, God-centered woman.

EUNICE KENNEDY SHRIVER'S LEGACY

"Eunice Kennedy Shriver died this week at the age of 88. This younger sibling and special friend of the late President John F. Kennedy left five children, 19 grandchildren, and a devoted husband, this country's first Peace Corps Director, Sargent Shriver. Most importantly, Eunice Shriver left a vibrant global legacy: a world where developmentally disabled children and adults now live with dignity and the real promise of productive lives.

Eunice Shriver's legacy is profound -- and more important in its long-term humanitarian impact than all the accomplishments of a Kennedy family that has been such a vital part of this country's political landscape.

In the early 1960's, as a Georgetown University undergraduate, I watched first hand as the tireless sister of the 35th President pioneered the use of sports -- including horseback riding -- to demonstrate how mentally challenged children could succeed.

In those days, mentally challenged children were largely out-of-sight, hidden away because of the pervasive stigma associated with their limitations. The prospect of these youngsters succeeding at anything -- especially sports -- was viewed as preposterous.

But it wasn't preposterous to Eunice Shriver. Through her summer camp for challenged youngsters at Timberlawn, the Shriver's Rockville, Maryland estate, and through an annual accredited Maryland horseshow at Timberlawn staffed by those youngsters, the press began to appreciate the validity of Eunice Shriver's vision about the mentally challenged: if given a chance, this scorned segment of our national population had enormous untapped potential.

On Capitol Hill and in State Houses across the country, Eunice Shriver seized every opportunity to use her Kennedy family status to persuade policy makers to recognize the long neglected legal rights of the developmentally disabled. Because of her relentless advocacy, laws were enacted at the federal and state level, and courts began to recognize that the Constitution did, in fact, apply to this country's mentally challenged.

I was there on a hot July day in 1968, just weeks after her younger brother Bobby died of an assassin's bullet, Eunice Shriver walked through Chicago's Soldiers Field, enthusiastically cheering on hundreds of mentally challenged youngsters participating in the first Special Olympics. Despite her grief, Eunice Shriver was determined to create an exciting national media event that would showcase the unlimited potential of mentally challenged youngsters. And despite initial cynicism about an "Olympics for the retarded?" the first Special Olympics proved to be an exhilarating event for the hundreds of exhausted young athletes and the thousands of volunteers energized by Eunice Shriver.

In December 1968, as the wife of the U.S. Ambassador to France, Eunice Shriver persuaded the very private Madame Charles de Gaulle, wife of France's President, to attend a televised Christmas party for mentally challenged youngsters at the U.S. Ambassador's residence in Paris. As newlywed house guests of the rambunctious Shriver family, my wife and I marveled at Mrs. Shriver's media savvy in recruiting the French President's wife to help open the minds and hearts of French citizens who hid their developmentally disabled children from public view. Ironically, the public had no knowledge of the De Gaulle's deceased mentally challenged daughter, Anne. When French television aired footage of the animated children interacting with the puppeteers and Madame de Gaulle, Eunice Shriver shattered another taboo: she showed viewers throughout France that these children could laugh and play, just like "normal" kids.

Throughout the past five decades, as the pivotal force behind the Joseph P. Kennedy, Jr. Foundation, Eunice Shriver aggressively used her senior sibling status in the Kennedy clan to direct millions of dollars into medical research to benefit the developmentally disabled. And as officials know at countless medical institutions across this nation, no one could get more bang from her family's foundation dollars than Eunice Shriver.

Today, the Special Olympics have become a global success -- annually attracting tens of thousands of spirited mentally challenged competitors to games in 165 countries. Importantly, regardless of who wins a gold medal, every Special Olympics from Capetown to Chicago has been a self esteem enhancing adventure for these young athletes.

Beyond the obvious success of the Special Olympics, these international games also have been the catalyst for a global cultural change in attitude: today's mentally challenged children and adults in this country - and throughout the globe, enjoy lives full of dignity, acceptability and hope. For countless future generations of developmentally disabled women and men, they too will live in a world where their lives can be productive and joyful, thanks to Eunice Kennedy Shriver."

Domino Rebels

Another humiliating Camp Olympic event occurred several years after the mice caper when I took Theresa Lennon on an autumn trail ride.

On these multi-hour Gardner-Lennon cross-country excursions, I always rode Domino, my favorite horse in the barn even though he was definitely the ugliest of Camp Olympic's mounts. Only 15 and a half hands tall, Domino was jet black except for a white star on his forehead and a white sock on his lower left leg. Unfortunately, Domino looked like a mule – with huge ears that suggested a very eclectic gene pool. When Domino first arrived at the Camp Olympic, most people – including me – snickered at his looks. But Steve, the Hungarian horse whisper man, knew better. "Michael" Steve prophesied, "don't laugh at him – Domino has a big heart and one day he will be a champion."

Besides bad looks, Domino also had a bad temper. I learned about that painful side of his personality one day during feeding time when an impatient Domino used his left rear leg to send me airborne into the paddock. But over time, with a lot of "tough love," this mule-like horse was transformed.

Incredibly, Domino loved to jump any kind of jump, man made or natural. Despite his small stature, Domino was fantastic – and sailed with ease over jumps taller than me at 5'6".

So when Theresa and I went for a ride on a crisp fall day in 1966, I expected nothing but smooth sailing from my loyal mount. At this point, it is important to note that riding was the first and only sport at which I had succeeded. Winning ribbons with Domino had greatly increased my self-esteem, and quite frankly, I used riding on the perfectly trained Domino, to impress dates.

When it came to sports, Theresa had grown up at the Homestead, trained for the Olympics in swimming, was captain of her college tennis team, and had ridden every day of her life at the Homestead on horses that made most of the Camp Olympic stable look like milk wagon nags. So, when it came to trail rides with Theresa Lennon, I looked for any device that would help me maintain the upper hand.

And that's where a stunning but very spirited 17-hand tall horse named Second Chance came into play. After only a week in our barn, I knew that Second Chance was a handful – even for experienced riders.

When I suggested to Theresa that, "you might want to try our new horse, she's a real beauty," she agreed without hesitation.

So, off we went, me leading the way on Domino with Theresa right behind on Second Chance. As we trotted into a large open field, I was surprised – and a bit disappointed – to see that Second Chance and Theresa were getting along. There was no snorting and no rearing up like I had experienced when riding Second Chance just two days earlier – just a smooth fast trot with Theresa in control.

Ten minutes into our ride, we came to a creek that Domino and I had crossed a thousand times. Since we just had several days of hard rain, the stream was running rather high. "Not to worry," I confidently told Theresa, "Domino will plow right through."

But for the first time in our half-decade relationship of total equine obedience Domino balked.

I ordered him forward, "Domino, let's go. I'm serious."

Once again, nothing happened. Domino would not budge.

"Okay" I thought, "I'll have to use my crop," not used in years on my push-button, horse Domino.

The crop stung across Domino's flanks.

Still nothing.

Domino was firmly planted before this rushing stream.

"Damn," I thought, "this can't be happening to me – right here in front of Theresa Marie Lennon."

Another "wham" on Domino's rear-end, another firm "Domino – let's go!"

And again, nothing!

Suddenly from behind me, Theresa piped up: "Mickey, why don't you let me and Second Chance lead the way."

Before I could respond, Theresa steered her horse in front of Domino, and with one firm kick, she and Second Chance plowed forward into the stream – with Domino following.

Busted at the French Embassy

Crashing key social events in Washington had become a routine, cash-free way for several of my bachelor friends to enjoy a fine evening – free food and drinks, attractive women and interesting people from all walks of life in official Washington.

Whether it was Washington's Christmas Debutante Ball at the Mayflower Hotel or the black tie dinner dance officially opening the annual D.C. International Horse Show, my friends and I were always ready in our tuxedos for a crash. Sometimes several ex-debutantes came with us wearing old ball gowns.

After a few years, we had become so adept at crashing that we maintained a collection of glasses from the various hotels where we'd crashed. So if we were crashing a Mayflower Hotel event, we would have cocktails in Mayflower Hotel glasses at one of our houses before the event; we would then take our half-consumed drinks with us as we drove to the hotel. Leaving our topcoats in the car, we'd enter the hotel's lobby and move with authority to the ballroom carrying Mayflower glasses. If stopped by a security guard, we would say with feigned annoyance, "Hey pal, we went out to get some air. See the glass – we're guests here. Now bug off!"

Our rebuke to the security guards always worked. Policemen routinely replied: "Sorry gentlemen. Go right back in."

So in the spring of 1965, several of my friends and I put on our tuxedos to crash a reception at the home of the French Ambassador on Kalorama Road in the swish in Embassy Row section of Northwest Washington, D.C.

Before the party my new roommate, Peter, asked if he could join us. Certain that this shy guy from Toledo didn't own a tuxedo, I replied, "Sorry Peter, it's black-tie."

"Oh, no problem" he replied, "I had to buy a tuxedo for my brother's wedding last Christmas, so I'm all set."

What could we do? Reluctantly, we agreed that Peter could join us on his first ever crash. While I liked Peter, he was somewhat socially awkward. So, while Peter quickly changed into his tux, we wisely passed the time practicing the little French we had learned at Georgetown.

On our arrival, it was clear that this reception was an important affair. Limos everywhere, D.C. cops galore, and dazzling bejeweled women entering on the arms of gray haired diplomats.

As we approached the massive open doors of the Ambassador's residence, I turned to Peter and reminded him "Be cool, Peter. Just smile, and remember – say "enchante," and as soon as you shake the last hand in the receiving line, get lost in the crowd."

As I gazed around, Peter nodded in agreement, but he looked very pale. In fact, Peter was ashen; he had totally lost his color.

By now, it was too late to abort our plan. We were already in the French Ambassador's grand foyer, and just ten yards ahead was the seven-person receiving line.

I was almost through the line when this elegant French woman with piercing eyes held onto my hand a bit too firmly and said, "Je suis, Madame Alphand, le ferme de l'Ambassador de France. Jeune homme, comment t'appelles tu?"

While my French was miserable, it was good enough for me to realize that this woman, who now had a death grip on my right hand, was none other than the French Ambassador's wife. More troubling was that she wanted to know who I was, far more information than I wanted to share.

Fumbling, but continuing to smile with forced confidence, I spoke, "Je m'appelle Michael Gardner et je suis invit— du maison de Monsieur Dean Rusk, le Secretaire de l'etat."

Smiling, but with a steely glare, Madame Alphand reluctantly let go of my hand. From her cold stare, it was obvious that the French Ambassador's wife did not believe me when I explained that I was a "houseguest" of the Secretary of State, Dean Rusk.

With my heart pounding, I then quickly shook the outstretched hand of the guest of honor, the French Minister of Culture. Fortunately, he was the last person in the receiving line.

Sensing vulnerability, I determined to immediately blend into the crowd.

Gliding toward a champagne bar, I glanced back at the receiving line. To my horror, I saw Madam Alphand still gripping Peter's hand with her right hand while holding her left hand high over her head. She was pointing at me, directing her security guards to catch the other crasher, the alleged houseguest of the U.S. Secretary of State.

At this point, it was survival of the fittest. As for me, five feet away at the crowded buffet table stood Texans Dale and Scooter Miller. From daily press stories, I knew that the Millers were best friends of the recently inaugurated Lyndon Johnson, and his wife Lady Bird Johnson. While the Millers didn't know me, I had seen them frequently during my recent six-week stint of grunt work as a "messenger" on the Johnson Inaugural Committee, a Committee chaired by Dale and Scooter Miller.

Just then, two security men in dark suits and with wires in their ears approached me.

Desperate, I butted right into the Miller's conversation with Senator J. William Fulbright: "Oh, Mrs. Miller, how are you – and wasn't it a terrific inaugural that we all worked so hard to put on for our great President and the country?"

Somewhat stunned by my sudden intrusion, Mrs. Miller, nonetheless, replied pleasantly: "Lyndon and Lady Bird – I mean the President and Mrs. Johnson – were so pleased with that Inaugural. Now remind me, young man, what inaugural office did you work for?"

That was all I needed; I was on a roll as I shamelessly dropped names for the next 12 minutes. And throughout my monologue, the Millers listened, smiled and acted – at least to the hovering security men – like we were all old friends.

After the Millers had convincingly created the false impression that I belonged, the puzzled security guards huddled nearby with Madam Alphand who was clearly perplexed.

When Mrs. Miller subsequently introduced me "as their dear young friend from the Inaugural Committee" to the French Minister of Culture, the French Ambassador's wife wisely called off the cops. She obviously decided that it would be risky to arrest a young American crasher who somehow was well acquainted with the President's friends – the Millers. Years later when I read the obits on those nice Texans – the Millers – I realized what good sports they were.

While I brazenly partied with vigor once the security guards were called off, the events of that night proved too stressful. I decided to end my crasher career while I still had a clean record. As for Peter, he escaped even a misdemeanor for trespassing. The DC cops were so impressed with his remorse that they let him off scott-free outside the Embassy grounds.

Dino – the Canine Matchmaker

Christmas 1967 was a special one for me. On that Christmas Eve, before they left for Palm Beach, the Shriver family surprised me with a beautiful three-month-old yellow Labrador retriever named Dino of Timberlawn.

I was a bachelor living alone in a shabby second floor apartment at 3921 W Street in the then low rent Glover Park section of Northwest Washington, so I was blown away by Dino, my new roommate.

While Dino's arrival at my flat brought welcome companionship, my lease said "absolutely no pets." And the tenants who lived below me on W Street, were obnoxious.

No matter how quiet I was when taking Dino in and out, the downstairs neighbors were always standing at their open door, yelling, "Get that fucking dog out of this building." While the building's cockroaches apparently were of little concern to them, three-month old Dino was viewed as a serious health risk!

So, my top priority that Christmas was finding a suitable place for Dino to spend the workday.

I knew that Patrick Lennon's sister loved dogs. So I called Theresa at the Homestead to say "Merry Christmas" – and to share the news of my Christmas gift and – our housing dilemma.

Since Theresa already had a beautiful German Shepard named Sweetie living in her Georgetown townhouse with a real backyard, I suggested that Sweetie should have a little yellow playmate named Dino.

When I broached the Sweetie-Dino workday co-habitation proposal, it took Theresa about a minute to respond. "Sure, Mickey – I'd be glad to help out, but is Dino house trained?"

Well, Dino wasn't exactly foolproof, but I assured Theresa that he was a quick learner. So the canine co-habitation arrangement at Theresa's house began on January 2, 1968 when she returned to D.C.

Three months later, due to my daily early morning and late night Dino "drop offs" and "pick ups" at her house on T Street, I realized that I had fallen completely in love with Theresa Lennon.

From DC Kid to Washington Man

I finally grew up in 1968.

In late February of that year, my Father Joe suddenly passed away. He was 59 – and we had become best friends just five years earlier. I was devastated.

Fortunately, my Father – who was my mentor, my interest-free banker and my most constructive critic – had left me with a treasure trove of wisdom, and a clear sense of what a good man should be. In a 25th birthday letter to me – just three months before he died – he wrote me:

Michael R. Gardner

J.T. Gardner
5311 Nevada Ave., N.W.
Washington, D.C.
November 19, 1967.

Dear "Miguel",

    Just a brief note on your 25th Birthday, happy to have had such a pretty good son, for this quarter of century.

    As a matter of fact, and your mother, I am sure joins me, that you haven't been just a pretty good son, but a truly fine one, which will be substantiated even more so by your actions, these next 25 years. It matters little indeed to us, whether you become President of the United States, a successful business man, or what (although all such things are fine), as long as you continue to be a fine American man. There is hardly anything better than the fine American man, for he's personable, competitive, kind, God-fearing, fair, and with all this, perhaps on account of it, a content and happy guy.

    Reviewing on this memorable occasion, a few pleasantries of these 25 years of yours; I'll not forget one night back in 1945, when I went in your room on Military Road, having just left my ship, for a couple days leave, just to take a peep at you, as you were presumably sleeping in your crib, and as I looked in, you gave with, "Hello, Daddy" (I hardly knew you could talk); then, shortly after we moved to Nevada Avenue, seeing pudgy you trekking in one Christmas Eve, dirty, with a dead-end kid's cap on your head, but with a handsome bunch of flowers for your mother, which cost you most of your long day's pay, as Florist helper; perhaps some of our fondest remembrances will be those wonderful years, when you were Mr. Camp Olympic, friend and instructor to your charges, as they embarked on their riding careers.

    So with all these happy years behind, and happier ones even, lying ahead I wish you a very Happy 25th Birthday, Miguel.

Your dad, Joe

    And just two weeks before his unexpected death, my father and I had a profound conversation even though I didn't fully appreciate its significance on my life. Our conversation took place on the first Sunday night of February 1968; I rarely missed Sunday night dinners at the Nevada Avenue house; Sunday night was the best opportunity to get together with my parents. This Sunday night I was particularly worn out as I had ridden Dominio cross-country for several cold hours. With my mother visiting my sister Sheila and her new baby in Missouri, my father Joby enjoyed his favorite bourdon, Old Fitzgerald, while I downed my regular dry Beefeater Martini.

While my father generally and studiously stayed out of my love life, he nevertheless inquired about my relationship with my good friend Patrick's sister, Theresa Lennon. Joby knew that Theresa was the only woman who could rival me on challenging horse outings – and he obviously noticed the special rapport we enjoyed when Theresa and Patrick visited the hospitable Nevada Avenue house.

"Miguel" he asked, "How is that Lennon girl. She's very attractive and has a lot of character. And character is essential for a long term successful partnership."

"Dad" I gasped. "You've got to be kidding. Theresa Lennon is too strong." Resorting to equestrian lingo, I added, "Dad, she'd need a double bit – and life would be a challenge. Anyway I still may accept Ambassador Shriver's invitation to work for him in Paris."

Joby paused for a long minute or two. And then he looked me square in the eyes and softly opined.

"Miguel, don't you think you've already gained a great deal from working with both Ambassador Shriver and his wife? Sometimes people stay too long at one job – and even though Paris would be fine, it may be time to go your own way professionally."

He paused, and added: "As far as that Lennon woman, if you're challenged by her already – and you obviously are – you can be sure that you won't be bored when you're 50 if she's by your side."

End of pep-talk – a prophetic talk indeed.

In June 1968, Dino of Tiberlawn died in an accident at my buddy Bob's farm. It was a tough year.

But, at least, I still had my special friend, riding companion, tennis coach – Theresa Lennon. While she helped me see the good things in life during those difficult times, her mercy was limited. On a 10-day trip to Bermuda that spring, Theresa humiliated me daily on the Castle Harbour Tennis Courts. After 10 days of early morning and late afternoon matches – with the Portuguese grounds keepers cheering her on wildly – the blonde bombshell won 40 consecutive sets – 39 of which were 6-0 victories.

November 30, 1968, Theresa Lennon and I were married by three wonderful Jesuits at a candlelight Mass at the Homestead; and as my father predicted on that Sunday night in February 1968, I wasn't bored at 50, 60 or 70.

After being crowned King of Sprinkler Lane, I pose with the newly crowned Queen of Sprinkler Lane, Jeanne McManus.

Sheila (left) and I (right) share a laugh on the front yard of our row house on Military Road in Northwest Washington, D.C.

Eva (Nana) Bennett Johnson (left) and her older sister Tessie Bennett Bradley (right) sit at the kitchen table of the Nevada Avenue house ready for the poker game to start. Close at hand are the requisite cans of beer and Nana's ever present cigarettes.

The Gardners, minus older brother Tim, pose with our beloved Irish Setter Finnegan on Christmas Eve in the Nevada Avenue house.

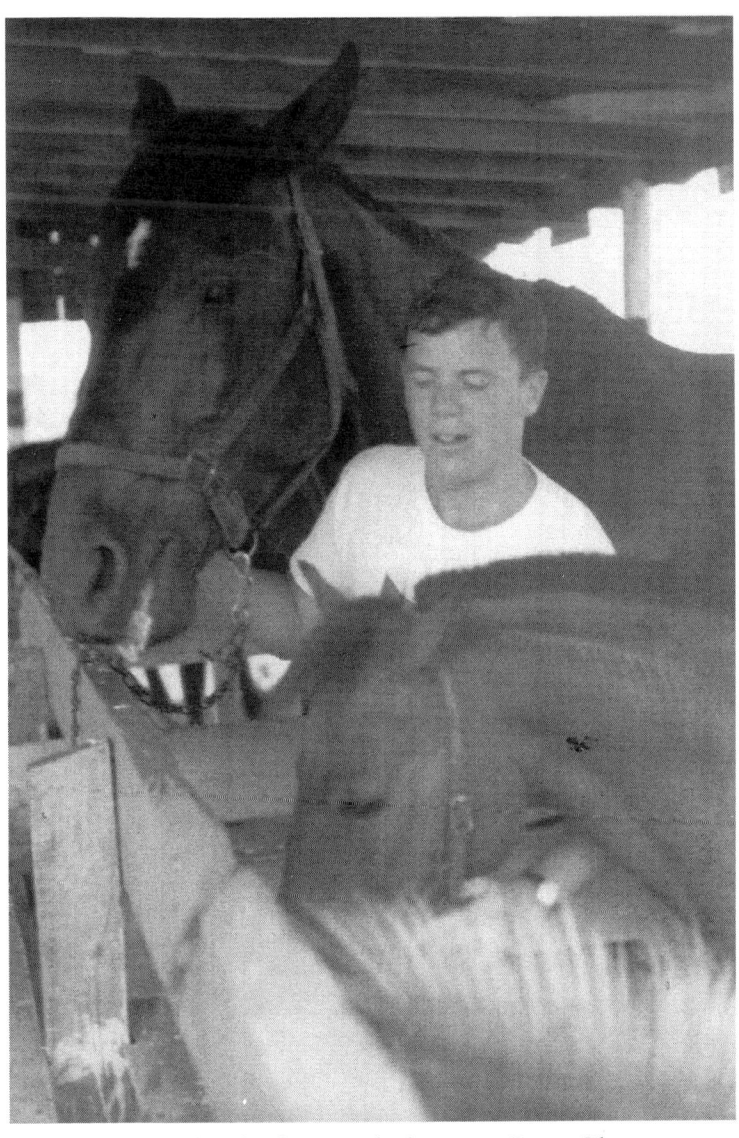

Feeding a well earned lunch of oats to the horses at Camp Olympia was one of my favorite duties as the Head Riding Instructor for the Hungarian Olympian gold medalist Stephen Benedek.

Yours truly and my fellow seaman apprentice mess cooks at sea in Guantanamo Bay, Cuba doing what we did every day – peeling potatoes!

Me with young Timmy Shriver on Sargent Shriver's huge Irish Hunter appropriately named Mickey. Timmy would later carry on his Mother's work as Chairman of the International Special Olympics.

Eunice Kennedy Shriver (President Kennedy's sister) asking me how I liked travelling on the Caroline, the plane used by JFK in the 1960 Presidential campaign.

Peace Corps Director and head of LBJ's War on Poverty, Sargent Shriver and I discuss arrangements at the Shriver's Horseshow to Benefit the Mentally Challenged.

Noël à Paris 1968

The newlyweds Theresa (3rd from right) and me (4th from right) with the Shriver family for a fun filled honeymoon stay at the U.S. Ambassador's residence in Paris. Bobby (far left), Maria (far right), Timmy (2nd from left) and Mark (3rd from left) standing in front of his mother, Eunice Kennedy Shriver and Ambassador Sargent Shriver (2nd from right).

Theresa (center) and 1 (right) pose for a photo in Bermuda with her brother and my best-man Patrick Lennon (left). A great fun friend, Patrick overcame a challenging physical hurdle to become a scratch golfer and a world class dancer.

PRESIDENTIAL POLITICS

Democrats for Nixon (DFN)

After our first year as newlyweds, a sometimes challenging year in which two Alphas learned to compromise, Theresa and I moved in 1970 to a small house at the very top of Washington's Foxhall Road. I would later distinguish our modest block of Foxhall Road as the only stretch of Foxhall Road where residents cut their own grass.

Three doors away, a bright young attorney named David Young lived with his charming wife Suzy. David had left New York's prestigious law firm of Milbank Tweed to work at the Nixon White House. A 24/7 guy, David was thrilled to be working closely with National Security Advisor Kissinger and his deputy, General Alexander Haig. While always discreet, David was clearly deep in the mix of things at the Nixon White House. In fact, we later learned that David apparently had earned the high regard of President Nixon himself for uncovering a serious breach of security apparently being conducted by a Navy Yeoman assigned to a clerical job on the NSC staff. David's reward would be a subsequent transfer from the high maintenance Kissinger to one of the Nixon White House's two top officials, John Ehrlichman. Ironically, David's promotion from Kissinger to Ehrlichman's team would end ultimately making this well-intended young attorney from New York one of the infamous "Plumbers," an important part of the Watergate scandal that forced the 37th President to resign.

From mid-1970s to early 1972, Theresa and I got to know David and Suzy Young reasonably well. At neighborhood dinners or just over cocktails, David provoked animated political discussions that often went on until late at night. A true Nixon devotee, David seemed impressed with the fact that I had worked for Sarge and Eunice Shriver, voted for Hubert

Humphrey in 1968, but by 1971, was determined to vote for Nixon in his 1972 re-election bid.

David was aware of my political evolution from a young, roaring liberal to a moderate Democrat. Because of my Democrat credentials, David immediately thought of me in early spring of 1972 when the White House's political hatchet man, Chuck Colson, was looking for a person with Democratic credentials to staff the Secretary of the Treasury, John B Connally. Connally was expected to resign his post and lead a Democrats for Nixon re-election committee.

"Hey Mickey," David excitedly said, "the White House is looking for someone with your kind of Democrat background to staff Secretary Connally if he agrees to head up Democrats for Nixon. Do you want me to put your hat in the ring with Chuck Colson?"

I was immediately intrigued at the prospect of working for the larger-than-life former Democratic Governor of Texas, John B. Connally. Ironically, Governor Connally was the second man shot in the Lincoln convertible on that fateful November 22, 1963 when Lee Harvey Oswald murdered President Kennedy.

So I said yes.

David promptly went to work and got my bio to Chuck Colson the following morning. Within 24 hours, I was sitting across from Colson in his Old EOB office overlooking the West Wing of the White House. A tough ex-Marine who was devoted to Richard Nixon and obsessed with his re-election, Chuck Colson minced no words.

"I hear you're going to vote for Nixon even though you voted for Humphrey and hang around with the Kennedy crowd. Damn, you even worked for Shriver and his wife. Why would you want to work for a conservative like John Connally?"

I was in one of those no-lose situations: if I got the job, it would be great fun, and if I didn't, no big deal! In either case, I still had my little PR-public policy shop to pay the mortgage. So I said, "yes, I'd like to work for Secretary Connally; he looks like a very interesting guy."

No apologies offered.

Colson and I talked for another twenty chaotic minutes – with frequent phone interruptions. Even though I only heard one-half of these tense discussions, they confirmed that hatchet man Chuck was juggling dozens of political balls. I would later learn firsthand why Chuck was called the hatchet man when it came to all kinds of balls.

Leaving Colson's office, I figured I'd "struck out," but at least I had visited the old Executive Office Building for the first time.

Next morning a very officious Colson secretary summoned me to a "5:30 ish" afternoon meeting with Mr. Colson and added that he didn't like it if people were late.

"Well, maybe this thing has life," I thought.

I arrived promptly at the Pennsylvania Avenue entrance to the Old EOB at 5:25 pm – and waited in the lobby until 7:20 pm!

Then a secretary came to escort me back to the same cluttered high ceiling office that overlooked the West Wing. "He's really pissed-off but don't take it personally," was all the secretary said on our short walk to Colson's office.

"Sit down," Colson barked, "this is the deal. Connally is resigning Treasury after he takes a 17-nation farewell blitz that the Old Man wanted to use as a thank you for a job well done. If the Democrats run that liberal mad-dog McGovern, Connally might – I repeat might – run a separate re-election Committee called Democrats for Nixon. It's a big "if"; Connally's very coy. But in the meantime, we need someone with Democratic credentials to recruit important conservative Democrats to this yet-to-be formed Democrats for Nixon committee."

Pausing briefly to sip his coffee, Colson went on: "You'll get $2,000 a month, an office at the Nixon re-elect committee; secretarial help if needed and you'll report to me in person every night with the results of your outreach to prominent Democrats who we've identified. Sometime in the next month, we'll know if Connally agrees to head this effort. If he does, it's up to him whether he keeps you around until Election Day in November."

"Yes or No?"

"Okay," I replied, "as long as I can still service my clients."

"Sure if you want to work 24 hours a day, that's your choice. But I want daily results." Colson wasn't smiling.

The Slush Fund

On my first visit the next day to the lively Nixon Re-election Committee, I was hosted by an altar-boy looking young official named Jeb Stuart

Magruder. He was exceedingly gracious, introducing me to key officials as "Connally's man"- clearly a premature characterization since I'd never met Secretary Connally nor had he hired me to be on his staff. While everyone I met was gung-ho, I felt a bit out of place: a solo Democrat hired by the much feared Chuck Colson to work for the President's favorite Democrat, John B. Connally. So I decided to work out of my own office in North Georgetown just 15 minutes away from Chuck Colson's old EOB office.

The daily drill was the same: I would receive names and phone numbers of leading Democrats from around the country who had told the President or one of his aides that they would be publicly supportive of the President when appropriate. My job was to call each of these Democrats to explain that "The White House was hopeful of launching a national Democrats for Nixon Committee as soon as George McGovern was formally nominated in mid-July by Democrats meeting in Miami Beach. So hold on; there will be a lot for you to do; we're even going to have separate Democrats for Nixon state committees in key battle states!" My message was a simple place holder: keep key Democrats like Virginia's conservative Governor Mills Godwin and Philadelphia's Mayor Frank Rizzo on ready alert. Also on the list of targets provided by Colson's office were various celebrities including Frank Sinatra, Mickey Mantle, comedian Milton Berle and a varied list of celebs who needed to know that they weren't being ignored or forgotten by the President.

One reality I quickly learned: everyone took my call after I explained that "I was calling at the specific request of President Nixon's Senior Advisor, Chuck Colson." And what a trip to be talking directly to potential DFN committee members - Democrats who disdained the liberal capture of their party by McGovern forces.

The nightly visits to Chuck Colson's office were fascinating. Usually sandwiched in between 5:30 and 7:30 pm, I gave Chuck my updates while Colson would take calls, summon staff members, and openly discuss controversial campaign issues.

On numerous occasions, Colson would get a call from the President and wildly wave me out of his office. Often, these calls would be just a few minutes long, but on some occasions, the Nixon-Colson calls would last 20, 30 even 40 minutes. While these Presidential conversations apparently originated from venues where the phone calls were not taped, their frequency and duration confirmed for me early on Colson was not a solo player; he was a very close and strategic advisor to Nixon.

For about six weeks, I worked closely with Colson's staff out of my PR firm's office. And then one day, the Nixon re-election official with whom I had first met, Jeb Magruder, asked to see me. Greeting me warmly, Jeb said he had heard that I was "doing a great job for Chuck and Secretary Connally." He said however, "we're concerned that you've haven't been paid yet – and you're nearly seven weeks on the job." Whether at Colson's direction or in an effort to get close to "Big John Connally's man," Jeb offered to pay me $3,000 in cash for my six weeks on the job. He further opined that the creation of the national Democrats for Nixon could still be weeks away – and I shouldn't have to wait that long. He then turned his chair around and started to turn the key into a locked credenza behind his desk.

Without hesitation, I blurted out: "Thanks Jeb, I'll wait until Democrats for Nixon is officially in business!"

Why I did this is inexplicable. I was owed the $3,000 – a huge sum to Theresa and me in the spring of 1972 when our funds were stretched thin. At that time, Theresa ran her successful Georgetown Montessori School, but I was just building my PR-public policy shop. So $3,000 was important to a young couple.

As it would later come out in the Watergate scandal, Jeb Magruder's slush fund from which I would have been paid my $3,000 became a notorious, radioactive war chest for nefarious campaign activities; that fund would be the reason that the likable Magruder was among numerous Nixon Administration officials who served time in federal penitentiaries.

BIG JOHN CONNALLY IN PERSON

Shortly after Secretary Connally's return from his global farewell trip as President Nixon's Treasury Secretary, the Democrats met in Miami Beach, Florida and enthusiastically nominated Senator George McGovern as their presidential candidate on July 14, 1972.

Once that occurred, the former Democratic Governor of Texas formally announced, with great fanfare from the White House, that he would chair a committee of concerned Democrats – "Democrats who had been deserted by liberal extremists who had wrestled control of the party

King of Sprinkler Lane

from moderate and conservative Democrats." Chairman Connally went on to explain to the press that his Democrats for Nixon Committee would solely support the re-election of President Nixon; it would assiduously avoid any involvement in Congressional, gubernatorial or state elections.

Soon after Secretary Connally's press announcement, I met with him in his huge two bedroom suite at Washington D.C.'s then lavish Madison Hotel. In my first meeting with Connally, I briefed him on my conversations with leading Democrats who were identified by Chuck Colson. He glanced over his half glasses, nodded a few times and said very little. As far as the ongoing recruitment effort for Democrats for Nixon, Connally instructed me to continue to work on Democrats who were suggested by the White House, but "make no commitments, I'll pick the final list of members for the national Democrats for Nixon committee, not Colson or anyone else from 1600 Pennsylvania Avenue!"

Once Connally was on board, my new office became the empty bedroom in the Connally's expansive Madison Hotel suite. Several trusted Connally colleagues came to Washington and were non-stop visitors to the Connally suite.

After a few weeks of working closely with Secretary Connally he opened up a bit.

"You're doing a good job," Connally muttered early one morning. The fact was that I was putting in 12-14 hour days, even on weekends when the Connally entourage returned, often by private planes, to Texas.

"But I want you to keep Colson and the re-election Committee people at arms' length. No more late afternoon meetings at the White House; I'll report directly to the President on our progress."

"No problem," I replied.

And it was a great job, but for one irritant - the always present creep Jake Jacobsen, the former LBJ aide who acted like an adoring butler to "the Governor" in Connally's Madison Hotel suite.

"Why is that slimy guy always around?" I asked my bride late one night when I returned home after 11:00 pm.

But I listened to my wife who counseled to not let one weirdo spoil it.

And progress we made. In less than a month, Connally would hold a mobbed press conference in the Madison Hotel, announcing a stellar list of 40 leading Democrats for Nixon from state governors, Hollywood celebs and heroes from the world of sports. Reporters gasped as they quickly read the committee's membership list, and not surprisingly, the President promptly called Big John after the press conference to thank him for his "superb efforts."

And then, just as we were about to celebrate our launch, my pride really took a hit. It happened immediately after the very successful press conference in the standing-room-only Madison Hotel ballroom. Connally, George Christian, Jake and a few other members of Big John's Texan-only inner circle returned euphoric to the Connally suite for club sandwiches.

At Connally's instruction, I phoned the order into room service and then went into my makeshift office-bedroom to make some follow-up calls. Absorbed with my calls, I didn't realize that room service delivered the club sandwiches for the luncheon celebration until Jake walked into my multipurpose office with a club sandwich. "Enjoy your lunch," was all Jake whispered as he slipped out and firmly closed the door connecting the suite's living room to my "office."

That was it – the door had always stayed open, and now Jake was telling me to be a good little staffer, eat my lunch in silence, as laughter and good cheer permeated the living room full of Texans.

Then and there I decided to resign.

All that was left to do was to give Connally my resignation in a professional fashion. So, as Connally and I were driven from NBC's WRC-television studio the following Sunday, where JBC was on Meet the Press, I turned to him: "Sir, I wanted to tell you that now that Democrats for Nixon is launched, I've decided to go back to my PR firm fulltime." I was surprised how calm I was – no edge, no rancor, just matter of fact.

Looking up from the New York Times as we drove around Ward Circle, Connally looked at me quizzically.

"What...what are you talking about Mr. Gardner?"

"Sir, it's time for me to move on. The committee is in good shape – and that's what Chuck Colson hired me for." My response was calm and devoid of any edge.

"Now just a minute young man, no one quits on John Connally, and that includes you," the former Treasury Secretary declared. Turning in his seat and looking quite perturbed, he asked: "What's really going on here? Is Colson giving you a hard time? Is it the crowded suite? You know we'll be into our new offices in 10 days? What is it?" Connally demanded.

I was surprised by his concern, so I decided to be candid.

"Mr. Secretary, I'm either a full member of the team, or I'm not going to be on the team, and when Jake Jacobsen closed the connecting door at lunch after the press conference, it was clear to me that I wasn't a full member of your team." I managed to keep my voice steady.

Connally stared at me, paused, and for the first time, smiled warmly.

"Mickey, you've done a great job and I value you – professionally and personally. At first, I wasn't sure about you because Colson and the White House gang recommended you so strongly, but you acted with integrity and you are a trusted and important part of my team. And don't concern yourself about Jake; there will be no more closed doors."

And there were not any – not in the remaining Democrats for Nixon effort, not during Connally's year long preparation sessions for his trial with his attorney Edward Bennett Williams; nor were there any closed doors or whispered conversations when Presidential candidate John Connally honored me in 1978 (only one year after my graduation from Georgetown's night law school) by making me the general counsel of his campaign. From that conversation in 1972 where I tried to resign, Connally and I never exchanged a harsh word.

SARGE – MCGOVERN AND CONNALLY

Following our weeklong honeymoon stay in December 1968 with the Shriver family at the official U.S. Ambassador's residence in Paris, I got busy with a new job, marriage and by 1971, a beautiful infant daughter, Courtney.

Then in June 1972, something happened: Democratic Presidential nominee George McGovern's running mate, Senator Tom Eagleton of Missouri, confirmed that he had once undergone shock treatments for depression, and it became a major negative news story. So in July, news bulletins declared that Sarge Shriver would replace Eagleton on the new McGovern-Shriver ticket.

"What a bummer," I said to Theresa. "What if they ask me to help out?"

Theresa chuckled: "Get real, you were never anywhere close to being a top, vital assistant to Sarge Shriver – they won't be calling you, so don't worry."

Early on Monday morning, a woman who identified herself as "confidential assistant to Eunice Kennedy Shriver" called and asked if I could meet Mrs. Shriver later that day.

Surprised, and starting to feel queasy, I asked what the meeting was about.

"Oh, Mrs. Shriver wants you to coordinate her activities in support of the McGovern-Shriver ticket," she said.

I'd do anything for Mrs. Shriver, but I'd been working for John Connally and Democrats for Nixon for almost two months.

"Listen, Miss…" I uttered. "I've got a problem. I've already committed to Governor Connally. I'm helping him with a campaign committee called Democrats for Nixon. I just…I just couldn't go back on my commitment. Please tell Mrs. Shriver that I am really sorry, but I'm ready to help her anytime with the Special Olympics or anything else. Will you please tell her that?"

Silence. Then more silence. Then her voice turned ice cold.

"I will tell Mrs. Shriver you're unavailable."

The Kennedys don't forgive breaches of loyalty, and while I would have played a relatively minor role, I knew that I would now be viewed as a traitor – especially since I was helping to organize <u>Democrats for Nixon!</u>

As the campaign moved forward, I had one late evening, spontaneous encounter with the Shriver kids as their father's campaign plane landed at Washington's Page Terminal just after wheels down for Connally's leased private jet.

Greeting me with smiles, 18-year-old Bobby chanted "Mike's a traitor. Mike's a traitor." Maria, age 16, was smiling as she said, "Dad's going to win Mike! You're on the wrong team." Already like her mother, Maria believed that anything was possible.

For the next year, I neither saw nor heard from any of the Shrivers. Then one Saturday morning, Sarge's beloved, can-do-anything man, Richard "Rags" Ragsdale appeared unexpectedly at the front door of our house on Foxhall Road.

"Rags," I shouted. "What are you doing here? Man, it's great to see you."

A smiling Rags held out his hand and gave me a keychain with one key on it.

"Mike, the Misses said Mickey is getting fat and you're probably also getting fat. So she told me to give you the key to the new tack room so you can start riding him again."

THE MANILA ENVELOP EPISODE

Once the membership of the national DFN committee was released to the press, the pressure was less intense. And that's when John Connally gave me a brief but very memorable tutorial. When he was in Washington, my routine was to start the day by briefing the teetotaler ex-Governor of Texas on the status of various DFN priorities. On this particular morning I stood up to leave when I finished my overview.

"Sit down, Mr. Gardner," JBC said firmly.

I immediately thought something was wrong.

To my surprise, the reserved and often taciturn Connally smiled and started to talk in an unusually relaxed tone:

"You've done well Mickey by keeping Colson and the re-elect committee at arms' length. That's good and especially important now that we're officially open for business. Colson and others may try to use us to do something that has nothing to do with our limited mission - to get Democrats voting for the President. And you may be put in situations that are harmful to the integrity of Democrats for Nixon. So watch out; this can be a tough game. When you have any doubts at all, call me and if I'm at the ranch or in Jamaica and you can't reach me, talk to George (Christian). And under no circumstances let anyone give you an envelope because if will probably contain cash. If it ever happens, just get up and leave."

End of Presidential campaign lecture 101.

I was temporarily speechless. The thought that I could be a bag man was foreign to me. "Yes, Sir, thank you Mr. Secretary," was all I said as I returned to my office.

But two weeks later, on a rainy Monday morning when Big John was still in Texas, his lecture took on a new meaning. On occasion, Colson's office would steer some important Democrats to our headquarters on 15th Street across from the Washington Post for a show and tell and mini-briefing on the DFN. Connally would do the honors if he was in Washington and if the visiting Democrats for Nixon were of sufficient stature. On this particular Monday, I acted as a surrogate host for Connally.

The two Democrats who were expecting to meet Big John were noticeably disappointed when they got me. After I showed the two portly, middle aged men in raincoats around the headquarters, including Chairman Connally's spacious digs, I took them into my office and offered them a coffee.

"No, no…no thank you," the shorter man exclaimed. "We're just here to see Governor Connally, but since he's not in Washington, we'll leave this with you. But be sure he gets my card."

And with that the short fat man pulled a large, bulging manila envelope from out of his rain coat!

Speechless, I bolted out of my desk chair and literally ran into the hallway outside my small office. The nearby secretaries looked puzzled as I finally blurted out, "Gentlemen, there's some mistake. We don't take cash here." I realized that my voice was shrill – and the two startled men in my office were now on their feet with incredulous expressions on their faces.

The taller man's face was blood red.

"What the hell's going on here? We were told to see Connally. Are you sure you're his assistant? This is really screwed up," he demanded.

Not another word was said by me or the two men in raincoats as they stormed out of the DFN headquarters.

Big John was spot on – and his sage admonition saved me from a possible felony charge in the subsequent far flung Watergate investigation that would begin early in 1973, just months after Richard Nixon's landslide reelection.

CONNALLY AND ROCKY

One of the nation's most admired Republicans in 1972 was moderate Nelson Rockefeller, the hard charging three-term Governor of New York. While 1972 was clearly a promising election year for the GOP, Rocky nonetheless wanted to make sure that Connally's popular Democrats for Nixon committee didn't prove damaging to New York's Republican nominees. So even though Connally repeatedly and publicly stressed that the DFN was a Presidential only effort, Rocky needed personal assurance from Connally.

So off we went to New York City one hot summer morning for Connally's meeting at Rocky's 5th Avenue duplex. Arriving early for the

1:00 P.M. meeting, Big John and I walked around mid-town, stopping only once at the Waldorf for Connally to get a shoe shine. On the walk we passed a raggedly dressed beggar standing on 50th Street near the side entrance to St. Patrick's Cathedral. Despite the heat, the bum wore an overcoat. As we passed this man, he implored us to help him get some food. Awkwardly, I gave him a dollar bill. Connally ignored him.

As we turned right onto 5th Avenue for the final short hike to Rocky's apartment, Connally asked: "Did you see that guy's shoes?"

What a weird question, I thought.

"No, Sir," I replied. "I saw and smelled his overcoat – that was enough."

Connally shook his head. "Their shoes tell you if they're really hurting, and that guy you just gave a dollar to had on a reasonably new pair of Johnson and Murphy shoes that retail for $200." That's all he said – but my street philanthropy has been guided ever since by that little pearl of wisdom. When confronted by a panhandler, look at his shoes.

At exactly 1:00 PM, a smiling doorman with an Irish brogue said: "Governor Connally. Good day to you, Sir," as he opened the heavy ornate doors, to the impeccably dressed Connally and me.

"Sure enough, the Governor is expecting your Sir, it's the 11th floor button," his thick brogue suggested he was a Galway lad. Two men in dark blue suits stood discreetly at the far side of the lobby, obviously part of Governor Rockefeller's security detail.

When the elevator reached the 11th floor, the doors opened directly into the most lavish, art-filled living room I had ever seen, even in the movies. A stern lady with a slight Scandinavian accent dressed in a black uniform with white collar and cuffs, greeted us with a curt: "Governor Connally, this way please; the Governor is waiting." Not missing a beat, she added: "Should this young man wait out here?" "No," Connally replied. "He'll join me."

We were immediately ushered into a very small, wood paneled den with a spectacular view of Central Park. Rocky greeted Connally vigorously but with some reserve. It was like two old bull elephants meeting once again at the watering hole. Governor Rockefeller then introduced his aide, at least 60 years old, who after saying a bland "hello" never spoke again. With virtually no small talk, Rocky immediately probed John Connally about Democrats for Nixon with a barrage of questions.

Connally was totally matter of fact. Without any warmth or feigned friendship, he, nonetheless, tried to assure that New York Governor that Democrats for Nixon was exclusively a nationwide organization intended to help committed Democrats to cast their first-ever vote for the GOP's presidential nominee in 1972.

During this frank exchange, we were served several cups of coffee; soon Connally excused himself to use the rest room. Suddenly it was Rocky, me and the assistant alone in the tiny den.

"So kid," Rocky asked. "Are you a Texan too?"

"No Sir."

"Where you from, kid?"

"Washington D.C., Sir."

"Where in Washington?" Rocky asked. "My brothers and I have an old house on Foxhall Road in Northwest Washington. Where do you live?"

Suddenly, I was uncomfortable. I couldn't tell the Governor of New York that I knew his Foxhall Road estate rather well, that I had skinny dipped in his pool on numerous late evenings and that I had often shared a six-pack of beer on his dark driveway with some of the coeds from Mount Vernon Junior College, just 200 yards away on Foxhall Road.

Struggling, I managed to say: "Governor, I know where your house is: it's a great spot."

Persisting, Governor Rockefeller asked again "Kid, where exactly do you live?"

Connally had now re-entered the den. That's when I decided on candor.

"Governor Rockefeller, I also live on Foxhall Road, but I live on the part of Foxhall Road where you cut your own grass!"

Silence – then a roar of laughter from the Governor of New York.

"John, where'd you get this Kid? That's terrific - the part of Foxhall Road where you cut your own grass!" And another roar from Rocky.

And that was it. The two bull elephants met, as Attorney General John Mitchell and President Nixon had requested, and we never heard again from Nelson Rockefeller about Democrats for Nixon. Rockefeller would serve out his third term as Governor and later he would be named Vice President by Richard Nixon's successor President Gerald Ford.

And as I would later find out, Rockefeller never forgot the answer from the little Irish kid from Foxhall Road. At a black-tie, stag dinner hosted by President Nixon early in 1973, I was grabbed by my shoulders and forcibly spun around. Shocked, I realized that my attacker was New York's Governor Nelson Rockefeller. Smiling broadly Rocky roared once again, "Still cutting your own grass kid?"

THE HATCHET MAN AT LARGE

On a Friday afternoon in late summer of 1972, a few weeks after the manila envelope episode, I got a call from Chuck Colson saying that "Secretary Connally had approved a press release to go out on DFN stationery." He added that a White House messenger would bring it over so that it could be retyped on DFN stationery and be given exclusively to the New York Times by 5:00 PM.

At first, I thought this was a little odd, but Connally and George Christian did have lunch at the White House earlier that day – JBC with the President and George with Colson and some other senior White House types.

Within fifteen minutes, the White House messenger arrived with a two-page draft press release that for some inexplicable reason savaged the sole surviving Kennedy male, Senator Ted Kennedy.

Feeling uncomfortable and after sharing my anxiety with a seasoned press aide to George Christian, I tried to call Connally on the private jet that was taking him for a long weekend at Tryall in Jamaica. No luck – even the signal corps operators at the White House couldn't make contact and the ETA was three hours away. I then tried to reach George Christian who had left Washington on a commercial flight to spend the weekend with his family in Austin. Again, no luck – George's plane had been delayed and had only just left Washington's National Airport.

It was now 10 minutes after four – and Colson's office had already called "urgently" three times.

Knowing that I was flying solo since Connally and George were airborne at least until 6:30 pm or even 7, I decided to take Chuck Colson's fourth call.

"Did you get the draft to the Times?" Chuck bellowed.

"No, Chuck, I want to clear it with Secretary Connally when his plane lands in Jamaica. He'll be there by seven at the latest," I replied with a great effort to appear calm.

"What do you mean you've got to clear it with Connally? For Christ's sake, he was here today having lunch with the Old Man. And Christian also signed off on it. Now get the fucking thing over to the National Editor at the Times – he's waiting for it." Slam went Colson's phone.

19 minutes later, Colson was back on the line.

"The guy at the Times has seen nothing. What's going on, you little asshole? I told you that both Connally and Christian signed off on it – what the fuck are you waiting for?" Colson screamed.

Trying to appear calm – a major challenge, I amplified my prior message: "Chuck, we've got your draft retyped on Democrats for Nixon letterhead, and as soon as I get clearance from Secretary Connally or George, we'll get it to the New York Times. I should be 6:30 or 7:00 at the latest."

Silence – and then a loud guttural noise. Colson screamed: "Look you little shit. I want that release to go to the Times now – before 5. Do you hear me? You fucking wimp."

Even if he was one of the President's most senior and most trusted advisors, my temper was now taking hold.

"Chuck, you can scream all you want; it's not going out until Connally or Christian tell me it's ok!" I no longer was trying to mollify him – it wasn't going out.

Colson wasn't finished.

"Let me tell you something Gardner. If that press release isn't out in ten minutes, you'll never work in Washington again. You'll be finished – and believe me, I'll cut your balls off!" Slam went Colson's phone.

For a long moment, I reflected on what had just happened. Then I did what I always did in difficult times: I called my wife Theresa.

"Well," she calmly stated, "you don't need them for a job; you've still got your PR firm. But I hope he's not serious about your private parts!"

Connally would arrive in Jamaica exactly at 7:00 pm, hear the press release that I read to him over a signal corps line, and confirm that the release should <u>not</u> go out, that he had never approved it.

Relieved, I left the deserted DFN headquarters and headed home.

It wasn't until the following Tuesday that Connally returned to Washington. When he came to the office at about 10:00 am, he called me in:

King of Sprinkler Lane

"You did well, and you won't have to deal with Colson again," Connally assured me. I never knew who Big John complained to – the President, Haldeman or even Colson himself – but his prediction was correct; Chuck never called me again until the day before the November 2 election.

Ironically, Colson's call then was most cordial. He was calling to make certain that I had all the tickets we needed for the various election night parties. And in subsequent conversations, Chuck was a prince – surely in large part because of the Nixon landslide, but also possibly because he respected people who could push back.

NIXON AND THE 30 RABBIS

Once the Democrats for Nixon committee was officially launched, John Connally became Nixon's most publicized re-election advocate. Photogenic and gifted with an imposing command presence, Connally was everywhere on talk shows, at special fundraisers, and even the sole moderator of a 30-minute, paid for primetime network tutorial – a tutorial where Big John dramatically portrayed the fatal harm to the United States if George McGovern was elected the 38th President.

As Connally's star rose, I benefitted in numerous fun ways: several Oval Office meetings where Nixon and his #1 Democratic cheerleader talked strategy; frequent lunches in the White House's Situation Room and Mess, and even substituting for Connally at DFN events where I was asked to introduce supportive Democrats to the President.

In one meeting in New York's Waldorf Towers, 30 of the nation's most influential Rabbis gathered in the hallway outside a small suite to meet the President. Without warning, a Nixon re-election advance man cornered me: "Mickey, you're going to introduce these Rabbis to the Old Man!"

"Why me?" I replied. "I only know one Rabbi who is on the committee."

"Well, wing it then. This is a Democrats for Nixon event, Connally's not here, so you're it," the harried advance man retorted.

Suddenly the 37th President and several secret service agents entered the suite through a side door. The President came right up to me, shook my hand (he never could remember my name), and asked "How is the Governor. He's down on his ranch, right?"

"Yes, Sir."

"Well, let's get going. They're 30 of them right?" And with that a long line of bearded men dressed in black and wearing Yarmulkas were ushered into the suite to be introduced by me to the President of the United States. Some names were easy, but I mangled most. But no one seemed to mind, least of all the President.

One oddity I noticed that evening and at subsequent meetings with Richard Nixon: he rarely made eye contact with anyone he was greeting; instead he seemed to look at your lapel. I mentioned it one day to Secretary Connally after a meeting with the President in the Oval Office. Connally's reply was instructive: "The President is basically a shy man." That seemed particularly strange given that Nixon, the politician, was one of the most, if not the most, resilient President in the country's history. For Nixon to lose the California Gubernatorial race so pathetically in 1962 and then to win the huge re-election landside for President ten years later gives new meaning to the word "resilient."

THE DEMOCRATS FOR NIXON – TEXAS HOE-DOWN

John and Nellie Connally's Picosa Ranch in Floresville, Texas was their pride and joy, so when the President suggested an early fall hoe-down for leading Democrats for Nixon at Picosa Ranch, Connally was thrilled.

For me and the small DFN staff, the DFN dinner at the ranch became an overwhelming priority. And once the White House leaked word of the dinner, invitations to the Connally's "Hoe-down" became the hottest ticket in town.

The day of the actual dinner, Theresa and I flew to San Antonio, a long hot trip made more uncomfortable by the unknown fact that the reason for Theresa's upset stomach was her pregnancy with our second daughter, Christine. Air conditioned buses were on hand at the hotel to ferry those excited Democrats for Nixon who didn't arrive by private jets landing on Picosa Ranch's runway; however, with Theresa's queasy stomach, we decided to rent a car and take our time driving to the ranch.

So we left almost an hour after the shuttle buses. When we turned into the Picosa Ranch's long driveway, I was stunned to see the lineup of large and small private planes that had already landed.

While I was impressed with the collective wealth reflected on the runway, Theresa was dumbfounded by the dusty, burnt-out brown landscape surrounding a golf-course green stretch of grass that encircled Picosa Ranch's large elegant main house. "Mickey, this place is ugly – everything is brown except for their front yard."

When we parked the rental car, we immediately bumped into George Christian who was talking with Virginia Governor Mills Godwin. Governor Godwin greeted Theresa warmly, having known her and her family well from frequent visits to the Homestead Hotel in Bath County, VA.

Greeting George and the Godwins, Theresa declared: "Good God, this place is brown!"

George Christian laughed and with a big smile on his face, sternly warned my wife: "Theresa, you better not let Governor Connally hear you say that; he spent a small fortune keeping every square foot of this lawn green." Before George could finish, Nixon's confidential aide, a great guy named Steve Bull, suddenly appeared.

"Mickey, where the hell have you been? They're waiting to start the receiving line and you're supposed to introduce each of the Democrats to the Old Man. They've already lined up."

Entering the huge living room, I was greeted by an obviously annoyed Secretary Connally, who murmured. "We've been waiting for you," and then re-introduced me to the President and Mrs. Nixon.

"Now Mickey," Connally barked, "You get the names of each guest and introduce them to the President," who was now immediately on my right. "Then each couple will stand between the President and First Lady, and Nellie and me for their photo to be made. Now they're a lot of folks (420) so keep it moving. We don't want to be here all night," Connally was smiling, but he was clearly still annoyed that I had delayed the long receiving line for a good 30 minutes.

To my surprise, things went pretty well – people were especially thrilled to have their photos snapped with their favorite Governor and the 37th President. After the first hour, I was so relaxed that I even innovated, not only telling the President the next couple's names but adding the city they were from. For some reason – probably Texan pride – many guests gave me their names as well as their hometowns.

Then it happened.

A crusty old guy with his much younger bride in a very low cut dress was next. He gave me his name, and added he was from Pasadena. Since

I knew Pasadena was in California, I decided to tell California native Richard Nixon that this crusty fellow was also a Californian.

"Mr. President, this is Mr. and Mrs. Smith who came all the way from Pasadena, California to honor your tonight."

The President extended his hand but before they connected, the crusty old guy abruptly turned back to me and bellowed in an angry voice:

"Hell, boy. I'm not from California. I'm from Pasadena, Texas, and damn proud of it!"

Everyone was startled, including the two secret service agents across the room.

After an awkward pause, Governor Connally jumped in and re-introduced the well-known Texan oil man to the Nixons, and they quickly had their group photo.

Before I could introduce the next somewhat unnerved couple, Big John leaned over behind President Nixon and firmly, but quietly admonished me: "Forget the geography lessons."

And so I did, for another 50 minutes until every couple met the Nixons and had "their pictures made" as Connally would say. But before the Presidential party moved to the huge, tented buffet, a thoughtful John Connally asked, "Where's Theresa? We need a group photo."

The photo of the Gardners with the Nixons and the Connallys was taken and I've never given a geography lesson again.

Election Night – 1972

Election night 1972 should have been one of Richard Nixon's happiest moments ever. He realized his dream, winning 49 states (Massachusetts was the solo loss) and winning a huge mandate of 520 of the 537 Electoral College votes. Instead of celebrating, the President holed up with a few key aides and instead of praising his Cabinet, he requested a resignation letter from every one of them to be on his Oval Office desk the next morning.

As for John Connally, he had accomplished his mission. Millions of Democrats across the United States cast their first vote for the Republican Presidential nominee.

A week or so after the Election while the small DFN staff and I were in the process of closing Democrats for Nixon, Connally called me in "to talk about the future." I was quietly thrilled that my first six-month tour of duty with Presidential politics might not be ending.

Connally was, as usual, very matter of fact. "Mickey, the President wants to solidify the switch over of so many Democrats so that they become permanent Republicans in the new, broader-based GOP that he will build in the next four years. They want me to stay involved; I've been promised that I'll be consulted on every important Democrat appointee made by Nixon in the second term. They also want me to select someone to serve as Special Assistant to the President for the new majority. Obviously, you're the one I would select for the White House Liaison job. But I've got to warn you; Haldeman doesn't like you…he thinks you have too high an opinion of yourself." Then Connally added with a smile: "Oh, he also thinks your hair is too long."

Before I could speak, Connally moved on. "I plan to help the President and would like you to help, either in the White House job or at you're PR firm when you're back fulltime. No rush. Just think about it and we'll talk in a few weeks." Connally added.

For the next six weeks, I was inundated with calls, requests and even invitations from the White House. Chuck Colson and others wanted to make sure that every important Democrat for Nixon got Inaugural tickets, possible appointee consideration, and even invitations to special White House Christmas receptions. Theresa and I were on every list, "Not because your important," my wife would repeatedly state, "but because the President wants Connally to help him herd a lot of Democrats into Richard Nixon's new majority party."

And party we did, from a Sunday White House prayer session conducted by Billy Graham to festive Christmas receptions.

After talking it over with Theresa, I decided not to be a Special Assistant at the Nixon White House – a White House that would soon be embroiled in a growing Watergate scandal. Instead I would be "Connally's man" in Washington, where his Houston law firm had not yet opened an office. And the White House never named a special assistant for the new majority during the next traumatic 18 months prior to Nixon's resignation on August 9, 1974.

During much of those 18 months, White House staffers would routinely check with me to get Connally's input and approval when it came to Democratic appointees to regulatory bodies, etc. And as a thank you gesture from the President in early 1973, I would be named a member of the President's Committee on Mental Retardation where I would help continue the work started by Eunice Kennedy Shriver – the force behind the launching of the first President's Committee for the mentally challenged.

The Connally Trial

A secondary plotline in the all encompassing Watergate scandal that drove President Richard Nixon from the White House on August 9, 1974 was the criminal indictment and trial of Nixon's Secretary of Treasury, former Texas Governor John B. Connally.

Dubbed the Milk Fund Scandal by the national media, John Connally's accuser was Texas lobbyist Jake Jacobsen who represented the milk industry. Jacobsen, a long time LBJ aide and friend of Connally, alleged that millionaire Connally accepted a $10,000 cash bribe from Jacobsen in the Secretary of Treasury's office. Importantly, at the time he made his claims against Connally, Jacobsen was negotiating a plea bargain for his alleged role in clandestinely funneling two million dollars of milk industry funds to Nixon's re-election effort in 1972.

With decades of possible jail time facing him, Jacobsen was a desperate man, in part due to his 24/7 devotion to his ill wife Floreen. In 1973 and 1974, Jake was a welcome ally for federal Watergate prosecutors who did not know then that the U.S. Supreme Court would rule on July 24, 1974 that President Nixon must release the politically fatal smoking gun tape – a court ruling that ended Nixon's chances of retaining the White House.

But a year before the high court's ruling on Nixon's secret tapes, Watergate prosecutors were looking for any means to bring Nixon down – and John B. Connally might be the winning lottery ticket for the unleashed prosecutors.

Their theory was simple: if Connally, the former Texas Governor and Treasury Secretary from central casting, was indicted for any reason, he would plea bargain to avoid jail time – and his only way to get full immunity would be to finger Richard Nixon. The prosecutors were convinced that Connally was a key player in the alleged two million dollar illicit milk industry contribution to Nixon - a payoff allegedly facilitated by Jake Jacobsen.

In the midst of the Watergate investigation, John Connally was in the crosshairs of the Watergate prosecutors who jumped at negotiating a plea deal with Jake Jacobsen if he would finger Connally. A complicated theory? Really not. All it required was Jacobsen to provide enough evidence before a District of Columbia federal grand Jury to conclude that there was a mere preponderance of evidence that Nixon's crony Connally was the bag man for the powerful milk industry. Remember, residents of Washington, D.C. were drowning in Watergate garbage, and John Connally was just another Nixon appointed actor in a bad national play.

Jake Jacobsen would work tenaciously to get full immunity: All the frail, soft spoken Jake had to do was to convince a majority of grand jurors from the Nation's Capital that the former Treasury Secretary, John B Connally took $10,000 from him in the very office once occupied by Alexander Hamilton.

When events surrounding the milk fund scandal started to move quickly and the media were daily publishing devastating alleged testimony by Jacobsen before the federal grand jury, Governor Connally finally realized that attorneys from his Houston Law Firm were not up to the task at hand: preventing Connally's indictment.

But this was early spring in 1974 and most qualified-Republican leaning criminal attorneys had already been retained by the dozens of Nixon aides and fundraisers who were snagged in the Watergate Kabal. So who should Connally hire to prevent his indictment?

Driving Connally in from National Airport on a clear springtime night in 1974 – I had a bold, if not radical idea:

"Mr. Secretary, why not try to get Edward Bennett Williams to handle your case? Yes, he's a fierce Democrat who has represented everyone from Jimmy Hoffa to LBJ's Bobby Baker; and yes, he is Katharine Graham's trusted counsel for the Washington Post. But that's all plusses now. Williams is a brilliant pit bull in the court room, and the Washington press loves him. So it's a twofer if he takes you on: a great defense lawyer and a credible Democratic friend of the press jackals who might tone down the damaging press coverage you face each day if Ed Williams is leading your defense!"

Connally look quizzical. "Kay Graham (CEO of the Washington Post and the number one Nixon hater) would never let Williams represent me. But it's an intriguing idea." Connally fell silent.

"Mr. Secretary. What can you lose? Just give it a try. Williams is a fierce advocate. Look how he took on Bobby Kennedy when Bobby was AG." I was lobbying pretty hard, and John Connally didn't like being pushed.

Silence prevailed until we reached the private side entrance to the Mayflower Hotel. As he left my light blue cutlass convertible, Connally looked over his shoulder and merely said, "I'll think about it."

An hour later when I was home telling Theresa about my Ed Williams proposal, the phone rang. "Mickey, this is John Connally. Ed Williams' phone is unlisted. Can you get it?"

Five minutes later, I gave Connally Ed Williams' unlisted home phone number. Twenty minutes later, our phone rang again. "Mickey, this is John Connally. Ed Williams is coming down to the Mayflower tomorrow morning to have breakfast with me. He didn't even call Katherine Graham. Sounded very interested. I'll let you know what happens."

The next day's breakfast evolved into an all day debriefing. Two huge lawyers with equally large egos hit it off from the get go and the imperious John Connally finally turned himself into a cooperative defendant. Within a matter of weeks, the Watergate prosecutors had finalized the comprehensive immunity package that Jacobsen insisted on before Jake would fully tell his Connally bribery tale to the federal grand jury.

Once Jacobsen testified, the prosecutors easily secured their indictment of President Nixon's former Treasury Secretary, the formidable John Connally.

The prosecutors did show a degree of mercy for Connally after they got the grand jury vote on a Friday – the night before young Mark Connally's wedding; they decided to wait until the following Monday morning to issue the indictment. I got word of the pending indictment from the tenacious *Dallas Times Herald* reporter and Connally friend, Margaret Mayer who asked me to give the painful heads-up to the Governor. So from a pay booth on Friday night at Georgetown Law School, I reluctantly conveyed the bad news to Connally that he would in fact be indicted and the indictment would be released on the Monday following his son's wedding festivities.

Ironically, Connally would be arraigned, including being fingerprinted and a mug shot taken, in the D.C. federal Courthouse on August 9, 1974 at the very same time that Richard Nixon delivered his resignation speech.

It was also ironic that Connally's indictment, possible only after Attorney General Saxbe okayed Jacobsen's extraordinary immunity package, would be issued at the time when Watergate prosecutors no longer needed John Connally to finger President Nixon. Nixon, as it turned out, was done in by the U.S. Supreme Court when they ruled that the smoking gun tape confirming Nixon's criminal complicity in the Watergate cover up had to be released to the public. That development however, was not on the Watergate prosecutors' radar screen when they decided six months earlier to use the discredited Jake Jacobsen to provide the meat for Connally's very own indictment.

Once Connally's indictment was handed down, the brilliant legal strategist Ed Williams went into high gear. Together with the shrewd young attorneys Mike Tigar and Richard Keaton, Williams determined to slow things down, trial-wise. With the stench of Watergate and Nixon's resignation hanging over Washington, D.C., Williams wanted sometime to pass before 12 residents of Washington, D.C. would have to decide on the fate of a very visible and well-know member of the shamed Nixon Administration, the President's flamboyant Secretary of Treasury, John Connally. So thanks to Williams' maneuvering, it would be a springtime 1975 trial for Connally, not a fall 1974 trial sought by the Watergate prosecutors.

For Georgetown night law student Mickey Gardner, sitting in on some of Ed Williams prep sessions with Connally were live theater. What an eye opening experience for any law student, and when the Watergate prosecutors subpoenaed me, the real live, hands on experience was even greater. And the timing couldn't have been better since I was taking my criminal law course at that very time.

When I was subpoenaed, Theresa and I wondered if I needed my own lawyer to prepare me for my Grand Jury appearance. We were particularly concerned since more than a year earlier, the now notorious Watergate Plumber, David Young, had warned me about the relentless efforts of prosecutors to "trip you up" on the simplest issues so that they could pressure you with a frivolous perjury charge. To make sure that I was adequately prepared, I called the beleaguered Secretary Connally at his Houston law office.

"Mr. Secretary," I said with some concern. "I've been subpoenaed by the Watergate Grand Jury, and I wanted to know if I needed to retain counsel, and if so, who would you recommend?"

Connally immediately responded.

"No, you don't need a lawyer. Just tell the truth and you'll be fine."

And so, I waited with some excitement combined with trepidation for my grand jury appearance.

On the day of my appearance, I was seated on a hard wooden chair in a hallway of the Federal Courthouse in Washington, D.C. And then a short, disheveled man came up to me and said he and his colleague wanted to privately visit with me before my testimony. As it turned out, these two men were Connally's lead prosecutors. Leading me into a small empty office the short prosecutor started to talk in a very chummy way about the legal problems I could have due to my work for John Connally in 1972 at Democrats for Nixon Committee.

"You know, Mr. Gardner, the Nixon re-election committee had a huge cash war-chest that took care of lots of people like you. And I don't have to tell you what IRS problems you might have for taking cash and not paying taxes on it." Pause. "We can help take care of your legal problems..."

"Wait a minute." I snapped. "I didn't take any cash from anybody, and I don't have any IRS problems!"

Bemused at my rebuff, both prosecutors just shrugged their shoulders. "Have it your way, Mr. Gardner."

Good God, I thought. These guys think I handled dirty money and will need immunity – obviously immunity that depended on my damaging grand jury testimony. Now I was mad; screw these smarmy guys. I couldn't wait until I was actually before the Grand Jury.

After another 40 minutes in the hall sitting on my hard wooden chair, a security guard led me into the spacious grand jury room. Sitting on bleacher type seats along one wall were a disparate group of grand jurors – all ages, all races. Then I was led to a small table and chair, and sworn in. The same two disheveled prosecutors seated themselves directly in front of me, and a Court stenographer was at my right. David Young's sage words of caution echoed in my ears as the rapid fire questions came from both prosecutors.

"How many times did you see Jake Jacobsen at the Democrats for Nixon office?" "Rarely."

"Did Governor Connally meet with milk industry representatives?" "Not during my six months at Democrats for Nixon."

"When did you last talk to Secretary Connally?" one of the prosecutors asked.

"Three weeks ago, when I got your subpoena," I calmly answered.

"Who called whom, Mr. Gardner?"

"I called Secretary Connally."

"Why?" the sleazy prosecutor asked.

Looking squarely at the pathetic duo of prosecutors, I replied. "I asked Secretary Connally if I needed a lawyer to help me prepare for today?"

Smiling, the shorter prosecutor sneered: "And what did President Nixon's Secretary of Treasury say?"

"He told me I didn't need a lawyer. That the only thing I needed to do was to tell the truth."

That clearly wasn't the prosecutors' desired answer; in fact, it seemed to catch them off guard. The 90 minutes witch hunt ended after a few more lame questions.

Sharing a bottle of red wine with Theresa that evening, I had a new first hand appreciation for the treachery that was swirling around.

As Ed Williams prepared for the delayed Connally trial (that ironically started on April Fools' day, April 1, 1975), an important element of Williams preparations involved identifying credible and compelling character witnesses who could personally attest to Governor Connally's integrity and honesty. When the possible list of witnesses was dwindled down, it included a wide cross-section of illustrious Americans from former First Lady, Lady Bird Johnson to outspoken Watergate critic, African American Congresswoman Barbara Jordan to former Defense Secretary Robert McNamara, and even worldwide evangelist Billy Graham.

While character witnesses are strictly limited in their testimony to giving their opinion about the defendant's reputation for integrity and honesty in the community, skillful Edward Bennett Williams succeeded in generating goodwill for Republican Connally with the

12-member D.C. jury made up overwhelmingly of African Americans and Democrats.

For example, President Lyndon Johnson's widow, Lady Bird Johnson went far beyond the normal scope of character witness testimony as she responded to Ed Williams' questions:

> Q. "Mrs. Johnson, would you state your full name, please, for the record.
> A. Claudia Taylor Johnson, Mrs. Lyndon Johnson, also known by the nickname of Lady Bird.
> Q. Mrs. Johnson do you know the defendant in this case, Mr. John Connally?
> A. I do.
> Q. How long have you known him and under what circumstances?
> A. Since 1938 or '39. I am not sure which. When he came to work for Lyndon.
> Lyndon was in the House of Representatives and John worked for him. And so I have known him - - that is over 35 years, both working with him and spending time with him and knowing his family.
> Q. Have you had, from the time when you first met him, Mrs. Johnson, regular contact with him through those years or was there any hiatus?
> A. Yes, sir; we have.
> Of course, there was a period when he was off in the war and it was - - one's opportunities to be together were limited.
> And then he went to Ft. Worth to practice law after, I think it was - - in 1950.
> But we still saw them frequently, so it is all of the 35 or more years.
> Q. Did you see him in the 1960's frequently?
> A. Yes, Sir.
> Q. Have you maintained a close relationship with Mr. Connally and his family?
> A. Yes, sir.
> Q. Mrs. Johnson, I want to ask you if you know and will tell His Honor and the jury what John Connally's reputation for

> *integrity and honesty is, both in your home state and here, if you knew him during that time?*
> A. *Well, John is a man of integrity and a man of honor and he is so known in our state - -"*[1]

At this point in her expansive, "chatty" testimony, Lady Bird Johnson, had gone too far for the cranky federal Judge George L. Hart, Jr., Chief Judge of the United States District Court:

> *"Wait just a minute,"* Judge Hart bellowed.

> *"Mrs. Johnson, you may not give your personal opinion as to his* (John Connally) *reputation for honor and integrity, but only the opinion in the community concerning same."*[2]

Judge Hart was clearly annoyed when he tried to discipline the soft-spoken former First Lady of the United States. But Mrs. Johnson never missed a beat.

In a very strong voice, Lady Bird Johnson politely rebuffed the agitated Judge Hart.

> *"Your Honor, it is the opinion of the community in the state and the people that we have known together in Washington that he is a man of integrity. Some folks don't like him, but I don't think any of them doubt his integrity."*[3]

Shortly after Lady Bird Johnson was excused and left the witness box, a hush fell over the courtroom as a tall man with sparkling eyes took the stand to answer questions from Attorney Williams.

> Q. *"Would you state your full name, sir?*
> A. *William Franklin Graham, Jr.*

---

[1] RG 21. US v John Connally - CR 74-7440. Transcript of April 14, 1975; page 899-900 – U.S. National Archives & Record Administration

[2] RG 21. US v John Connally - CR 74-7440. Transcript of April 14, 1975; page 900 – U.S. National Archives & Record Administration

[3] RG 21. US v John Connally - CR 74-7440. Transcript of April 14, 1975; page 900 – U.S. National Archives & Record Administration

> Q. *What is your occupation, Doctor Graham?*
> A. *I am a clergyman.*
> Q. *How long have you been so occupied?*
> A. *About 33 years.*
> Q. *Where do you presently reside?*
> A. *Montreat, North Carolina.*
> Q. *What is your work at the present time, sir?*
> A. *I am an evangelist preaching the gospel of Jesus Christ all over the World."*[4]

As Dr. Graham proudly affirmed his work as "an evangelist preaching the word of Jesus Christ all over the world," a female juror sitting in the back row of the jury box, uttered "Amen!"

While the official court transcript omits any reference to this juror's spontaneous "Amen", it was clear to every lawyer in Judge Hart's courtroom that at least one juror was in the Connally camp. And as Edward Bennett Williams knew so well, the federal prosecutors needed all 12 jurors to agree that millionaire John Connally took a $10,000 bribe from a discredited, multi-indicted milk lobbyist.

The coup de grâce in Ed Williams' effective and strategic use of character witnesses came later in the day when one of the "heroes" of the Nixon Impeachment effort, Democrat Congresswoman Barbara Jordan took the stand. A large woman with a booming deep voice that gave no hint of her Houston inner city background, Barbara Jordan had been one of the most visible – and surely the most memorable, Member of the House Judiciary Committee's public hearings just a year earlier calling for President Richard Nixon's impeachment. As a result of her forceful and articulate leadership on the House's impeachment committee, Barbara Jordan enjoyed enormous credibility.

After Ed Williams established the fact that Ms. Jordan was the elected Member of Congress from "the heart of Houston, Texas," Williams had some critical additional questions for Barbara Jordan:

> Q. *"Prior to coming to Congress, Rep. Jordan, did you serve in the Texas*

---

[4] RG 21. US v John Connally - CR 74-7440. Transcript of April 14, 1975; page 906 – U.S. National Archives & Record Administration

> *Legislature?*
>
> A. *I served in the Texas State Senate for six years, prior to my coming to Congress.*
>
> Q. *And beginning in what year did you begin your service in the Texas Senate?*
>
> A. *Beginning January 1967.*
>
> Q. *And did you know the defendant, John Connally, at that time?*
>
> A. *I did.*
>
> Q. *What was his occupation at that time?*
>
> A. *At the time I began service as a member of the Texas State Senate, John Connally was Governor of Texas.*
>
> Q. *For how long did your periods of service overlap?*
>
> A. *For two years.*
>
> Q. *Now, I am going to ask you, Rep. Jordan, do you know what the reputation of Mr. Connally was and is for honesty and integrity?*
>
> A. *Yes.*
>
> Q. *What is it, Ma'am?*
>
> A. *As far as I know from my association with him he has a very good reputation for honesty.*"[5]

As Congresswoman Jordan concluded her unequivocal testimony in support of defendant Connally, there was a noticeable flurry in the courtroom. Not only was Ms. Jordan's elocution compelling, she had been the national poster child just a year earlier for the impeachment of President Nixon. And today, this Democrat from Houston had just testified that Republican John Connally – a former Treasury Secretary for the disgraced Nixon, "has a very good reputation for honesty."

Who better to assure this jury of citizens from Washington, D.C., that the defendant John Connally was an honest man?

When the jury reached their verdict on April 17, 1975, three days after the testimony of numerous character witnesses, John Connally was found not guilty.

---

[5] RG 21. US v John Connally - CR 74-7440. Transcript of April 14, 1975; page 941 – U.S. National Archives & Record Administration

For a town still recovering from the trauma of Watergate, it was a verdict that few cynics expected. And to this day, Edward Bennett Williams' strategic selection and use of character witnesses in the Connally trial is legendary.

INTERESTING TIMES

Theresa and Cary Grant – at the White House

When the Watergate boil finally burst with President Nixon's resignation on August 9, 1974, Washingtonians of all political persuasions were exhausted, relieved, angry in some cases, but most of all, in need of some carefree times. And the new President, Gerald Ford and his fun loving wife, decided that one of the best ways to bring some laughs and smiles to the beleaguered White House in the new year was to have a full blown State Dinner on January 30, 1975.

The news of a pending White House's celebrity-packed dinner was the talk of the town. Not only would British Prime Minister Harold Wilson be the honored guest, the gifted opera star Beverly Sills would perform her magic at a post-dinner entertainment program in the East Room. The 120-person guest list for the State Dinner would include Ford Administration officials, a large group of Brits traveling with the Prime Minister and a group of celebrities, including British born actor, the elegant Cary Grant.

Fortunately, President and Mrs. Ford decided to augment the number of guests for this memorable evening by inviting another 120 "after dinner" guests – a diverse group of notables who would arrive at the White House as the State Dinner ended, go through a receiving line that included the President and Mrs. Ford and the Prime Minister, then mingle briefly with the State Dinner guests before going into the East Room to hear the indomitable Beverly Sills.

Three weeks before this special White House evening, we received an invitation to the entertainment part of the State Dinner for Prime Minister Wilson.

I was flabbergasted. But Theresa was very cool. "Mistake or not, we'll go and have fun."

Ironically, as we waited with other guests to go through the receiving line in the marble entrance hall of the White House, we had the pleasure of talking to Texas Congresswoman Barbara Jordan, the most articulate and compelling Member of the House of Representatives' Judiciary Committee where she advocated for Richard Nixon's impeachment. Theresa, always the Montessori teacher, asked the formidable Congresswoman: "How did you ever learn to speak so forcefully and effectively?" After all, Barbara Jordan was a product of inner-city public schools in Houston.

"Madame," Ms. Jordan proudly answered, "I taught myself and I wouldn't stop working on my elocution until I had totally lost my Texas accent!"

After we went through the receiving line – where the Fords were particularly relaxed and gracious, a wonderful protocol chief named Bill Codus grabbed my arm.

"Mickey," Bill said with a big grin, "we have a bit of a problem. Cary Grant is here solo, and we need someone fun to be his date for the entertainment program. Do you think your wife would agree to be escorted into the East Room and sit with Mister Grant?"

"Are you kidding Bill? Theresa's been a Cary Grant fan all her life – she's seen *To Catch a Thief* six times."

And so it was. Thanks to the mischievous Bill Codus, my bride walked into the East Room on the arm of the tanned, debonair Cary Grant. Seated to his right, Theresa, who never got tongue tied, clammed up despite Grant's rapid fire questions: "Are you from Washington?" "How do you know the Fords?" "Have you seen Beverly perform before?"

When I realized that my wife, for the first time since I'd met her at age 13, was speechless, I leaned over my mute but stunning wife and started to answer the questions from "her date" Cary Grant; while engaged, Mr. Grant was clearly more interested in hearing from the blonde sitting next to him, than her husband.

Then Theresa suddenly spoke: "Mr. Grant, my daughter Courtney (who was only three) is a big fan of yours, would you autograph my program for her?"

Relieved that Theresa could finally talk, Cary Grant said, "Of course Theresa, I'd love to write your daughter Courtney a little note. How do you spell Courtney – you know there're several spellings?"

Theresa gave Cary Grant her White House embossed program (light blue with a red tassel) and started to spell, "C..o..u…"

Then an unfortunate thing happened; Cary Grant's ballpoint pen literally exploded, sending the spring and back end of the chrome pen past Theresa and me, and right into the left breast of the famous Babe Paley, who was seated between me and her renowned husband, CBS founder and CEO Bill Paley.

Cary was instantly on his feet – "Please excuse me," he said to the unsmiling Mrs. Paley.

"I do apologize." Cary added. But neither of the Paleys spoke, nor did they smile. In her defense, Mrs. Paley had probably had so much "face work" done that smiling was a physical impossibility.

At any rate, the smiling Cary Grant returned to his seat, screwed the ballpoint pen back together, and with his trademark British accent, said "Now Theresa, let's try again: Court – what is it – ney or ny?"

Now back in full voice, Theresa said: "ney – and thank you for being such a good sport."

"Glad to do it Theresa," the Hollywood superstar responded with a smile – just as Beverly Sills started to sing.

The Reagan Years

When the Connally for President Committee ran out of gas in early spring of 1980, I was finally able to go back fulltime to practice energy law as a partner at the Washington office of Houston's Bracewell & Patterson.

The Bracewell brothers, two jovial, shrewd gentlemen from old Houston, had been very generous to me after my completion of Georgetown Law School in December 1976, making me a full partner two months later when I passed the D.C. Bar exam. The firm also enthusiastically supported my decision to serve as Governor Connally's General Counsel in his Presidential bid. But wearing two hats had a price: I had to spend half of my 12-14 hour work days at the sparse

Connally for President headquarters in nearby Arlington, VA and the rest of the day at Bracewell's elegant Washington, D.C. law office.

After the Connally campaign fizzled in the South Carolina GOP primary, I was totally finished with the Presidential sweepstakes; it was time to see more of my family.

As we closed the Connally committee, there was one positive thing I could say about my job as General Counsel: we never were cited by the Federal Election Commission (FEC) for any campaign law violations – a real accomplishment when dealing with a lot of devoted, rich Texans who wanted to donate far more than legally allowed to Connally's Presidential committee. And the only thing I would miss from the Connally committee's closing was the incredible wit and humor of my fellow non-Texans on the Committee, Connally's irreverent press Secretary Jim Brady and Connally's brilliant and funny southern Regional Director Haley Barbour – both of whom remain valued friends.

Ironically, after spending $14 million on his campaign, Governor Connally had won only one(1) delegate – a rather compelling reason to close shop!

So it was a relief to be back at the law firm, free of the crazy, frantic problems facing any Presidential campaign, Democrat or Republican.

And then a call came in that changed my life.

"Mickey Gardner, is this Mickey Gardner?" the seemingly confused male caller asked.

"Yes, I'm, Mickey Gardner. Who are you?"

"I'm Loren Smith, General Counsel of the Reagan for President Committee and I'd like to meet with you."

"Loren, nice to meet you by phone but there's no reason to meet. I'm back at my law firm full-time and I'm exhausted," I protested.

But this Mr. Smith wouldn't give up.

"Just a quick coffee, please. And by the way, those 17 one pagers you put out on various FEC do's and don'ts are really helpful," Loren casually added.

Good God, I thought. The Reagan Committee is using our simple white papers written in non-lawyer, layman terms for Connally committee officials and volunteers. What the hell, I quickly concluded. If they helped us stay out of trouble, all the better if these one-pagers were helping the Reagan forces.

Blown away by Loren Smith's candor and good cheer, I agreed to have breakfast with him the following week. The meal would become the first of hundreds of fun encounters I would enjoy with Loren – a brilliant, loving and witty man who would become one of my closest friends.

At our first breakfast, Loren was all business. Realizing that I was really tired of the back-to-back 12 hour days of Presidential campaigns, Loren had a very simple request: he wanted me to serve on a small, informal committee that would be a sounding board and independent advisor to him, and through him, to the Reagan for President Committee. All that would be required was one early morning breakfast a week – no briefs to prepare, no issue papers to develop, nothing but my participation with four or five so called "wise-men" in a frank, off the record discussion of troublesome issues and/or opportunities facing Governor Reagan's trusted legal counsel.

So, why not, I thought. I had been impressed with Ronald Reagan since his 1964 speech at the Republican Convention that nominated Barry Goldwater; now that Connally's election hopes had bitten the dust, I was planning to vote for Reagan anyway.

"Okay, Loren, we've got a deal, but remember, I'm not drafting anything, right?" I asked.

And how interesting those early morning breakfasts turned out to be. Besides a core group of four or five attorneys, Loren would arrange for Ed Meese, Bill Casey and other notable Reaganites to discuss thorny issues with us. Very interesting indeed, and Loren kept his word, there was no heavy lifting, just brainstorming.

By Election Day 1980, it was a foregone conclusion that Governor Reagan would win the White House; the only question was by what margin?

Several nights following Election Day, the phone rang in our bedroom. It was almost 11:00 pm – far too late for a civilized caller.

When I picked up the phone, I was greeted by the same, somewhat confused voice that I had heard on my first call from Loren Smith eight months earlier.

"Hello, hello – is Mickey Gardner there?" Loren was barely audible with all the noise in the background.

"Loren, it's Mickey. Yes it's me. Are you in a bar celebrating?" I asked.

"No, no – I'm, at the Reagan committee office, and I forget to mention something to you." Loren was still barely audible.

"Mickey, we want you to head up President-elect Reagan's FCC Transition Team; is that ok with you?"

Still trying to hear him clearly, I said, "Loren you mean the FEC (Federal Election Committee) don't you?"

"No" he shot back, "The FCC – the Federal Communications Commission! We need someone who is politically seasoned and doesn't have any client matters before this independent regulatory commission. You'll enjoy it."

"Loren, thanks but my practice has been energy – and of course the FEC when I was working with the Connally campaign. If you need me, I'd be glad to help with either of them," I replied.

"No, no Mickey. The FCC is politically sensitive – and that's where we need you." Loren was insistent but I was very wary about this out-of-the blue assignment.

"Loren, I know absolutely nothing about communications policy and law. I can barely change a light bulb…"

Before I could continue, Loren interrupted. "No problem. There're several former FCC Commissioners and engineers lined up to be on your team and you have a good seven weeks before your Transition Report will be due. Ok?"

"Listen, Loren, I'm flattered you thought of me, but I think I'm the wrong guy. Let me talk to Theresa and call you back first thing tomorrow?"

Always agreeable, Loren said, "Sure. Talk to you tomorrow."

Relieved, little did I know until I read the front page of the Washington Post the next morning that I was already listed as FCC Transition Team Chairman in the Reagan Committee's press release – a press release that had been distributed to the media hours well before Loren's 11:00 pm call the night before.

And so it was – for the next seven weeks, I would immerse myself in the FCC. Under the Transition Act's authority, I would interview all the incumbent FCC Commissioners, Bureau Chiefs and even mid-level staffers. Helped by a 30-plus person transition team of communications lawyers and engineers, I would learn all about the key issues; I also learned to filter out some recommendations that were client driven by some on "my team." Importantly, I would have the fun task of helping President-elect Reagan re-shape the then seven-member FCC with four appointees – two of whom, the late beloved Jim Quello and decorated Vietnam Veteran Henry Rivera, would become cherished lifetime friends.

Only after my extended Transition duties ended in April 1981 with the Senate confirmation of the final Reagan FCC appointee, did I agree to represent a communications industry client. And what a field to enter in the early 80's – communications technology was exploding as cell phones first appeared, new satellite technologies were introduced and the contentious era of Reagan-inspired deregulation took off.

And I would be a part of it for the next 30 plus years, thanks to Loren Smith.

Jim Brady - My Hero

I first met Jim Brady when he was recruited to be Press Secretary to Gov. John B. Connally in Connally's ill-fated bid for the White House in 1980. During the early campaign committee's senior meetings, I was initially struck by Jim's irreverence – a rare quality for the key campaign aides to the much revered former three-term Governor of Texas. While most aides were easily intimidated by the silver-haired presidential candidate from central casting, the Illinois born Brady was often the only Connally campaign official who had the temerity to say "Governor, that's a bad idea." While Jim frequently admonished his boss that some hair-brain idea was "just plain stupid," he was usually out voted. Nonetheless, Jim Brady did his professional best for candidate Connally through the South Carolina GOP Presidential primary in March 1980 where Connally lost miserably and wisely withdrew from the Campaign.

Sometime later in 1980, Jim Brady was named Press Secretary for Presidential candidate and former California Governor Ronald Reagan. It was a brilliant selection because Jim Brady's reputation for integrity and wit would prove to be welcome contributions to the Reagan campaign. Only once was there a bump in the road for Jim when he put his wit to questionable use during a controversial environmental policy period towards the end of the campaign; as the Reagan for President press plane landed near a forest in Louisiana, Jim loudly pointed to "the killer trees."

Apparently candidate Reagan's wife Nancy and some of the ranking Reagan campaign committee officials were not amused so Jim was in hot water for a brief spell. But wisely, after his overwhelming victory, President-elect Reagan named Jim his official press spokesman. For Jim Brady, it was the highest professional honor, and one he would carry out with distinction until March 30, 1981 when he and "his Boss" were nearly assassinated in front of the Washington Hilton Hotel.

When the media stories started to fill the airwaves that grim afternoon, I called Governor Connally to commiserate; and while we were talking, one of the networks incorrectly announced that Jim had been mortally wounded. Soon the press correctly reported that the President and Jim were both in surgery; and that's when the brilliant neurosurgeon Dr. Art Kobrine performed his miraculous work on Jim's shattered brain. Once he survived the skillful surgery that Art Kobrine performed, it would take years of hard work on Jim and Sarah Brady's part to restore his damaged brain; but with Dr. Kobrine's guidance and Sarah's determined coaching, Jim would make remarkable progress with daily painful therapy sessions.

And then there came a point in his protracted therapy that "the Bear" (as Sarah fondly called her husband), revolted! No more sessions with those women-in-white; he was through with these therapists who were so vital to Jim's continued progress.

And that's when I had an idea. I asked Sarah: "why don't I get my trainer Gary Figler from the Metropolitan Club's Athletic Department to come up to my office when Gary's workday ends at 3:30 pm to workout with Jim in my large conference room?" Sarah answered. "why not," and for the next decade, twice a week, Jim and Gary met. No white dressed therapists – just the often protesting but macho Bear Brady working-out with Gary, the no-nonsense muscle-bound Met Club trainer.

It was a match made in heaven: Jim instantly responded to Gary's stubborn urgings, and before long, Jim was able, with Gary's help and encouragement, to stand up, then take a few steps and before long, walk the length of the long conference room. The only problem occurred early in the Brady-Figlar workouts; Gary gave Jim the ok to verbally express his frustration anytime he was in pain – thus there were frequent Brady issued F Bombs! Sometimes, when Jim was particularly pained, his resulting Brady F bomb would reverberate throughout my law firm and the adjacent

USTTI offices. But not to worry – Jim Brady was doing the impossible – walking with minimal assistance.

As our families' friendship grew close over almost two decades, I got to know Jim well – so well in fact that I rightfully concluded that Jim Brady was and is the bravest person I know.

Being born a Mensa, Jim knew early in life that he was smart, really smart. And he was good at what he did, being named President Reagan's Press Secretary was proof of Jim's professional prowess. But then to be at the top of your game, and have some nut shoot a bullet through your brain, and literally to have to start all over to say and do the simplest things – that would be an impossible hurdle for most of us. But not Jim Brady; a man who knew he was diminished but still determined, as was Sarah, to live a full life. No self-pity, not vengeance, no bitterness, just pushing forward in every new day.

One night at our favorite Italian restaurant in Adams Morgan, I was feeling sorry for myself about some injustice, and Jim looked across at me and said: "Miguel, shit happens and it's not about what happens that counts, it's how you react that matters." I went home that night embarrassed that my friend Jim Brady would have to give me a pep talk after all this brave and forgiving man dealt with everyday of his life.

On a more positive occasion, the Gardner and Brady families were celebrating Thanksgiving together in Bermuda. On the Friday night after our Thanksgiving feast at our rented beachfront house, we decided to have dinner at the Mid Ocean Club in Tuckerstown. Once seated in the Club's dining room overlooking the Atlantic Ocean, we ordered drinks with Jim getting his all-time favorite Bermuda drink, a Dark and Stormy. One round led to two and since our food service was slow, we even got to three rounds of these popular but powerful drinks.

No sooner had the third round been consumed when the Bear firmly exclaimed: "Mickey, get me out of here, I need some air!" I immediately stood up and steered Jim's wheelchair to the double doors that led to the Mid Ocean Club's tiny elevator. I pushed the ample Bear Brady front ways into the tiny elevator; to my surprise I could only get Jim two-thirds in. "No problem" I thought, "I'll back in, pulling Jim's wheelchair side-ways so that the elevator door could close."

I was wrong.

When I backed him in and turned the wheelchair side-ways, Jim's legs blocked the elevator door from closing. When I tried to exit the elevator, I realized that the wheelchair's rubber handles had effectively locked me in; I couldn't move forward or sideways.

Panicked, I told Jim "we're stuck." That's when the Bear roared out with an F bomb that echoed through all three floors of the staid Club. And every time the elevator door tried to close, Jim delivered another F bomb.

Finally, the maitre d' arrived; perplexed, he tried frantically to pull Jim's wheelchair back out into the third floor lobby. But he was not up to the job; it needed someone who had real strength. And that's when Jim Brady's devoted care provider, Mary Dickerson, came to the rescue. Admonishing Jim for using the F word, Mary reached into the cramped elevator and literally lifted the wheelchair with Jim in it, up and out.

Thank God for Mary Dickerson! We returned to the dining room as if nothing had happened and when we finished our dinner, the great Mary Dickerson steered the brave Jim Brady safely to the waiting van.

Nairobi and Hollywood

By late spring of 1982, my law practice had shifted completely to the fast growing, exciting world of communications policy. By that time, the Reagan-appointed Chairman of the FCC, a former broadcast attorney named Mark Fowler, was aggressively pushing for sweeping deregulation of the U.S. broadcasting industry. While I supported deregulation, I favored adherence to a basic recommendation of my FCC Transition Report – namely prudent deregulation. And prudent deregulation is what the Hollywood community wanted – thoughtful, incremental deregulation that would still prevent the three networks from abusing their collective, gatekeeper control over every program aired in primetime. This was an era before cables' and satellites' pay programming and digital services offered consumers nearly unlimited choices. So, Hollywood moguls, confronting a particularly determined deregulator with the Reagan Administration's FCC Chairman Fowler, knew they were especially vulnerable if the FCC eliminated three sister rules – the Prime Time Access Rule (PTAR), the Financial Interest Rule and the Syndication Rules (Fin-Syn).

Adopted almost a decade earlier by the Nixon FCC and codified into consent decrees between the then three networks and the Justice Department, the PTAR and Fin-Syn rules had opened up prime time programming to creative independent producers who thrived because they produced and distributed diverse entertainment (and sometimes socially provocative) programming like The Cosby Show, All in the Family, Dallas, the Golden Girls, etc. The then three national television networks tenaciously sought the repeal of the PTAR and the Fin-Syn rules – rules that deflected a $5 billion annual revenue stream to Hollywood by restricting the three networks from producing or syndicating prime time television programming.

As it turned out, my first communications client after my FCC transition duties ended was a group of competitive Hollywood television programmers who were born under the shield of the PTAR. Fortunately, for me and my growing communications law practice, in spite of FCC Chairman Fowler's efforts to repeal the PTAR, my Coalition blocked this potentially precedent setting deregulation by one vote.

The three networks were stunned – and the new FCC Chairman was furious. After all, this was supposed to be the era of total deregulation – not prudent deregulation!

As my luck would have it, my successful defense of the Prime Time Access Rule made me the go-to guy for the Hollywood Studios when CBS, ABC and NBC turned their attention in 1982 to repealing the Fin-Syn Rules. From the networks perspective, the repeal of Fin-Syn was understandably a multi-billion dollar priority; in the networks view, it was time to let the networks once again produce and syndicate their own prime time schedule, not Hollywood's studios and independent producers. Billions in annual revenues were at stake, and with the Reagan Administration's and Chairman Fowler's deregulatory agenda, CBS, ABC and NBC had the stage set for victory.

But that's before the legendary Lew Wasserman, Chairman of MCA and its Universal Studio, determined that the Fin-Syn Rules should remain unchanged.

I got lucky; Lew Wasserman hired me to run a new Hollywood Coalition appropriately called "The Coalition for Prudent Deregulation." Wasserman told me years later that he decided to hire me because of my past success in 1981. If I could beat the networks' over repeal of the weakest of the three rules, I had the stuff to protect the Fin-Syn Rules. So I became the lead Counsel of a Coalition consisting of all the major Hollywood studios, and importantly, the 250 plus independent producers who created the television shows that aired Monday through Friday nights on the three networks.

As it turned out, I became Lew Wasserman's communications attorney for the next two decades. For twenty plus years, one of the most respected men in Hollywood mentored me, shared his incredible insights about all the Presidents he had been close to from JFK to Bill Clinton, named me to the Board of Directors of MCA's spinoff broadcast company when he sold MCA to the Japanese, and even gave me and Theresa the use of his Belgravia townhouse when we were in London. He would become a great force in my life – but first we had to derail Chairman Fowler's number one priority: total repeal of the Fun-Syn rules.

And that's when Lew assembled the initial team: me as lead counsel, the pioneering female lobbyist and former aide to Governor Ronald Reagan, Nancy Reynolds; the legislative troops from Akin Gump; and MPAA's energetic CEO, Jack Valenti. While our ranks would grow to include dozens of other lawyers and lobbyists during the 10-year plus long Fin-Syn fight, Lew Wasserman's handpicked original team would keep the networks (that grew to include Fox) regulated until the Fin-Syn rules were finally repealed in the early 1990s.

While Hollywood's Coalition for Prudent Deregulation was starting in the spring of 1982 to engage Chairman Fowler and the three resourceful networks in battle at the FCC and on Capitol Hill, a totally unrelated thing happened. The Reagan White House, with the urging of some key GOP friends, asked me in June 1982 to head the U.S. delegation to a United Nation's Telecommunications Treaty Conference in Nairobi, Kenya. Scheduled to take place at Nairobi's huge Kenyatta Center from September through mid-November 1982, the U.N.'s International Telecommunications Union's (ITU) Plenipotentiary Conference would require extensive bilateral meetings around the world for the U.S. Ambassador if I accepted the job. Moreover, the job would require building a long-overdue consensus between warring officials from the U.S. Department of State and U.S. Commerce Department. Friction was so bad between the federal telecom policy experts that each Department put out separate, often differing, white papers on the key 76 issues to be addressed at the conference – 152 different white papers in all.

But, as bad as things were between the federal members of the U.S. delegation, and as busy as I was organizing the Coalition for Prudent Deregulation, I was really intrigued: a six-month Ambassadorship with pre-conference travel around the world – followed by 10 weeks in exotic Kenya.

And happily, Theresa, who had sometimes shown a strong antipathy toward ambassadors, was on board.

"Okay Mick, I'll do it – as long as Courtney and Christine and I can share as much as possible in this experience – and that means travel to Africa and phone calls from you every morning and every night." Theresa, a Montessorian, knew the great educational value of travel and exposure to varied cultures; in fact, when Courtney was just seven and Christine was five years old, Theresa chose a three-week family Christmas trip through Western and Central Europe, rather than buy drapes for our new house. So taking the girls now 10 and 8 to Kenya for a pre-conference bi-lateral was a priority.

However, there were two big hurdles yet to be scaled before I could accept:

(1) I needed a free watts line to call home twice a day, as well as to stay in touch with clients as we built up the Coalition for Prudent Deregulation, and
(2) I needed the FCC Chairman to delay, for at least six months while I was doing the Nairobi gig, the just commenced FCC rulemaking to repeal of the Fin-Syn rules.

How could I go off on this tempting assignment and leave Lew Wasserman and wonderful independent producers like Marian Rees and Marcy Carsey to the vagaries of the networks' legions of lawyers and lobbyists?

Miraculously, both of my needs were promptly met: I'd have the only secure watts phone line in Kenya and the Fin-Syn rulemaking would be put on the backburner, at least until I was permanently home from Nairobi.

So, I immediately started reading the 152 policy papers and began scheduling the "must do bilaterals" – meetings intended to build consensus around major U.S. positions. And when consensus wasn't possible, I had to at least flush out the opposition so there were no big surprises when the U.S. delegation arrived in Nairobi.

One issue "you definitely don't have to worry about Ambassador Gardner", a senior State Department official confidently confirmed, was the expulsion of Israel from the United Nations due to Israel's devastating assault on Beirut, Lebanon. Earlier in 1982, Israel's massive invasion of Lebanon (the Beirut Massacre, as it was commonly called), resulted in harsh global anti-Israel criticism with the promise of expelling Israel from the United Nations when the U.N.'s General Assembly took place in New York in late September. Even though the United States was privately angry at Israel for overreaching in Beirut, I was assured that issues related to Israel would not be addressed in Nairobi.

Confident that there would be no anti-Israel mischief in Nairobi, it was time for me to conduct pre-conference meetings with Ministers of Communications from all over the world. After the first few meetings with leaders in Europe, Scandinavia and the Caribbean Basin, I was told that it was "a priority" for me to meet the key Kenyans who were hosting the ITU Plenipotentiary Conference in Nairobi. So with Courtney and Christine out of school, the Gardner Family headed to Kenya with the exciting prospect of seeing lions, elephants, rhinos, monkeys and other wild animals in the bush.

On our arrival in Nairobi in late July, we were met by U.S. Embassy officials who quickly cleared us through customs and dropped us off at the Nairobi Hilton. Since Theresa's father was the respected President of the five-star Homestead Hotel in Hot Springs, Virginia, the head of the Hilton had arranged for us to have the huge Presidential suite for the cost of a single room. Luxurious as the hotel was, we all were struck by overwhelming poverty evident everywhere in Nairobi. When I told the Embassy driver that I would get myself to my meeting later that day with the U.S. Ambassador to Kenya, he protested, "Not safe, Sir, not safe! Too many beggars; not safe!"

And an hour later after we enjoyed chicken sandwiches in the Presidential suite, I would find out how correct that driver was. As I tried

King of Sprinkler Lane

to get into a cab in front of the Hilton, I was literally encircled by a mob of Kenyans – children dressed in rags, disabled or handicapped beggars on makeshift roller boards, even elderly people frantically holding out their cups for a few coins. While I had seen firsthand some really poor Americans when working for Sarge Shriver at the Office of Economic Opportunity (AKA the War on Poverty), I had never seen such raw and pervasive poverty as I saw on my first outing in Nairobi.

When I mentioned my shock to the U.S. Ambassador at the U.S. Marine guarded U.S. Embassy, the Ambassador looked bemused. "What did you expect?" he said, "This is Africa."

Annoyed, I told this beleaguered Foreign Service Officer that I had seen a lot of poverty in the U.S., but nothing like this.

"It's explosive here," I said. "And when I return in September with my 28-person White House approved delegation I want Marine Corps protection for them, at the Hotel and at the Kenyatta Center," I declared. We clearly were off to a bad start.

"Mr. Gardner (not Ambassador), you're overreacting. Marine protection will not be necessary; moreover it would insult the Kenyan leadership."

Ending our brief meeting so I could meet with Kenyan officials, the U.S. Ambassador to Kenya offered an Embassy car and driver for our excursion the next day to the Salt Lick Game Reserve, followed by a two-night stay at Diani Reef on the Indian Ocean. "Thanks, but no thank you. I've made arrangements for a rental car."

That night, the four Gardners and a senior ICT official from the Commerce Department named Frank Urbany had dinner at a lobster restaurant highly recommended by Hilton Hotel's concierge. Once again, we were swarmed by beggars as we entered our cab at the Hilton. But after copious wine with dinner, world traveler Frank Urbany suggested we walk the two short blocks back to the Hilton. Theresa insisted we wait for a cab, but after a fruitless 15-minute wait and still no cab, we reluctantly took off on foot to the Hilton.

It was a foolish thing to do.

No sooner had we moved 50 yards from the restaurant, when a group of teenage boys appeared asking for "donations" as they encircled us. Fortunately, the doorman at the restaurant saw the menacing situation and ran towards us barking some harsh Swahili to the scattering teenagers. As he got to us, I finally realized that the big wooden staff that the doorman held while opening the restaurant's front door for patrons was not decorative; it was real and surely had scared away others in this crowded, impoverished city.

After profusely thanking the fearless doorman, we negotiated a deal: he would walk us the remaining 300 yards to the Hilton in exchange for $10 U.S.

Safely back in the Hilton, we said a hasty good night to Frank and took the elevator to the Presidential suite.

Riding with us to the hotel's top floor were two smiling Japanese businessmen who promptly presented their cards. Since they didn't speak English and our Japanese was limited only to a rough version of "Happy New Year," we shook hands, and repeatedly said, "Good night, good night."

Once inside our suite, I opened a beer.

"Theresa, we're going to the bush tomorrow and not coming back to Nairobi. We can fly from Mombasa – and never have to come back into the city. And believe me, when I come back, if the city doesn't blowup before the conference, I'll be coming back with Marine protection," I declared.

"Let's go to bed." Theresa urged. "We've got a big day tomorrow. And promise, you'll call the Ambassador first thing tomorrow morning and take him up on an Embassy car and driver."

No sooner had she repeated her wise plea for a driver, the phone rang. It was now midnight in Kenya.

To my total surprise, it was FCC Chairman Mark Fowler. "Hey, we just got through a Commission meeting and we wanted to see how you're doing in Kenya. Is it a fun place?"

Fatigued and stressed out, I made no attempt at civil conversation: "Mark, this place is the armpit of the world. Beggars everywhere, homeless people living in the streets – it's ten times worst than anything I've seen in the United States."

Pausing, Mark interrupted: "Oh, come on, Mickey, you're just jetlagged. It can't be that bad. The ITU would not have selected Nairobi if it was unsafe."

I was now sitting on the side of my bed with Theresa urging me to calm down.

"Listen, Mark, this place is going to blow up. I can feel it. And if and when I come back to Nairobi, tell Kenny (our mutual friend Ken Cribb at the White House) and Bill Schneider (Under Secretary at the State Department) that there better be Marines with the Delegation!"

Feeling my stress, Mark used his most soothing, broadcaster's voice to end the call.

"Sorry old pal that you had a bad day but get a good night's sleep Mickey, and I'm sure things will get better."

In retrospect, the Chairman's call was very thoughtful and he was very positive while I wasn't. But as time would prove, my intuition was spot on.

Promptly, the next morning, the Gardner girls dressed in their safari outfits for our 9:00 am departure from the Hilton to the Salt Lick Game Reserve – a mere four-hour drive according to travel brochures. The high anxiety of the prior night was replaced with our collective excitement of going on Safari in the Bush! And even though I had agreed to call the Ambassador to take him up on his offer for an Embassy car and driver, I stubbornly insisted on driving the rental car. Unfortunately, while we had booked a solid four-door Mercedes for our drive through southern Kenya, the rental agent could only come up with a tiny, stick-shift Toyota.

This was a bad omen especially since I had never owned a stick shift car.

But my bi-lateral meetings with Kenyan officials had gone well, and our focus was on our family adventure in the Bush.

Two hours out of Nairobi, I began to realize that I had really made a huge error of judgment when I declined the offer of an Embassy car and driver. The main highway south was a bad joke: mostly one lane each way, the dusty road was literally riddled with gapping potholes. Worst of all, Kenya truck drivers heading to Nairobi loaded with imports that had arrived at Mombasa's ports, rarely stayed on their side of the road! It was like "dodge-em cars" at the amusement park – but this was deadly real.

After another hour of dodging potholes and wild truck drivers, we suddenly hit a roadblock. And the heavily armed soldiers who examined our four diplomatic passports were not kidding around. When I politely asked "Why the roadblock?" I got no response, only hostile stares.

Trying to break the ice, I asked "How much farther to Salt Lick…you know the Salt Lick Game Reserve?"

Silence! Then one toothless soldier grudgingly replied: "Many hours… many hours," as he pointed south.

In the seventh hour of our drive from Nairobi to Salt Lick, we ran into another heavily armed roadblock. Same drill – same hostile attitude by the tense soldiers.

Theresa and I didn't want to upset the girls, but we were worried: what's going on with the roadblocks and the obvious ready alert of the Kenyan Army?

At 6:10 pm, four very weary Gardners entered the single lane, five mile long driveway to Salt Lick Lodge. Instantly the vagaries of our scary nine-hour drive were forgotten as we spotted zebra, a herd of elephants – even warthogs that scattered as we pulled in the lodge's dirt parking lot. Rushing up the ramp to the Salt Lick Lodge which was oddly built on tall stilts, we quickly checked in and passed tourists enjoying high tea on the deck as we took our luggage to our two adjoining rooms.

"Hey," I proposed, "Let's forget tea – and take a quick drive around the park!"

So down the ramp once again and into the tiny Toyota. While the Kenyan at the front desk gave us what he called a "map," it was just a piece of paper with four lines leaving the lodge like spokes on a bike wheel.

But no problem. We took the first single lane dirt road we came to as we circled the parking lot. About 50 yards later, we encountered a small stream bed with no more than a foot of water. Confident after my nine hours of experimenting with the stick shift, I glided the Toyota into the shallow crossing – and promptly got stuck in the mud. Theresa, frustrated all day by my insanity in turning down the Embassy car and driver, erupted.

"Put it in first and then reverse. Rock it – and if you can't do it, climb in the back and I'll drive." Theresa had had it.

Just then, a very awesome thing happened. The trees just 30 yards away started to move.

"My God, girls, they're not trees. It's a herd of giraffes," I exclaimed. And sure enough, there must have been 30 to 40 giraffes, some necking as they gently walked away from the noisy intruder, our Toyota.

And then something even stranger happened: the lights suddenly went out! And it was so dark we couldn't even see the giraffes. I then remembered that we were just south of the Equator and that's what happens. You go in a heartbeat from daylight to nighttime. We were now in total darkness in our rental Toyota.

Realizing that I had really misjudged things once again, I rocked the Toyota quickly out of the stream, put on the headlights, and started down that dirt path which represented one of the four lines on our bogus map. For the next 90 minutes we crisscrossed Salt Lick Game Reserve – a huge patch of God's bush that I would later learn was 28,000 acres in size. Needless to say, the tension in the car between the totally lost husband and the fuming wife (and concerned mother) had reached an all time high. And then our headlights shone on a small Kenyan farmer walking on the path in front of us. Responding to our collective pleas, the obviously amused young man who spoke excellent English said, "Go two more miles and you'll hit the main road leading to the lodge. Take a left – and it's just another mile."

Profusely thanking our guide, I sped off, parking in the same spot in the lodge's make shift auto park. Once again, we were greeted by several startled warthogs as we ran for the ramp. But to our horror, there was no ramp. As night arrived, and the wild animals, including predators, gathered around the lodge's watering hole, the ramp was always pulled up and the lodge became an animal-free fortress.

So we hollered. And after a few minutes, a totally shocked bellboy lowered the ramp for our climb to safety. Once safely inside, the equally bewildered lodge manager with a twinge of disgust explained that "No one - no one - ever goes out for unescorted night drives. You Yanks are very lucky indeed."

Once safely inside the Salt Lick Lodge, we quickly ate dinner in the lodge's now empty dining room – empty because everyone else had moved to the lodge's vast observation deck to watch the various wild animals' nocturnal visits to Salt Lick's huge watering hole.

Before long, the four Gardners joined the other tourists for hours of hushed game viewing. And the game viewing was spectacular – everything from a female lion with her three cubs to a large family of elephants who playfully used their long trunks to give each other shower baths. We spent the next 48 hours savoring the nearly spiritual experience of seeing God's creatures as they have lived for thousands of years undisturbed in the African bush.

But as remarkable as the sights were at Salt Lick, unbeknownst to us bad things were happening in Nairobi. Just before midnight on August 1st, the Kenya People's Democratic Movement (KEPDEMO) launched its bloody coup against Kenya's corrupt President, Daniel arap Moi. Led by mid-level Kenyan Air Force officers, the anti-capitalist revolutionaries quickly seized control of several key assets including Kenya's International Airport, the state owned broadcasting system, key roadways, etc. Importantly, the fighting that would go on sporadically for several days, would trigger violent rioting, looting and widespread rape of tourists who had packed Nairobi's hotels. And it wasn't just tourists and Kenya's Indian merchants who were targeted; we would later learn that foreign businessmen were also targeted by the anti-capitalist soldiers, including our two smiling Japanese friends from the Hilton, one of whom apparently was shot to death in the Hilton lobby when he didn't understand the order to empty his pockets.

When we reached the Diani Reef Resort on the Indian Ocean we learned of the violence that was raging in Nairobi. And even though we thought it odd that the state owned television channel was dark, it wasn't until I tried to reconfirm our flight from Nairobi to Zurich that I found out that all fights in and out of Kenya were cancelled "until further notice."

For two stressful days, I wasn't even able to reach the U.S. Ambassador. While Theresa and I were preoccupied with the uncertainty in Nairobi and our exit from Kenya's first and only attempted coup, Courtney and Christine were deliriously happy. The Indian Ocean was magnificent, the hotel had three pools, and there were festive African cookouts each night with Maasai warriors performing colorful native dances.

On the third day of our now extended stay at the Diani Reef Resort, I finally got through to the U.S. Ambassador's secretary. "Ambassador Gardner," she excitedly said, "where have you been? We've contacted all the hotels in Mombasa and we couldn't locate you. Even the White House is involved."

Relieved that we finally got through to our Embassy, I found it incredulous that Theresa, the Gardner girls and I would warrant White House involvement. As I would later learn, FCC Chairman Fowler who called during our last night in Nairobi was also an enthusiastic ham radio operator. And over the weekend, as our luck would have it, Mark picked up a live broadcast by none other than members of the Kenya People's Democratic Movement, declaring their short-lived victory over President Moi. Whether it was guilt driven or inspired by my sober prediction to Mark a few nights earlier that "this place is going to blow up," Mark apparently spread the word that "Mickey Gardner and his family are stuck in a coup in Kenya." The alarm then went out.

When I finally talked to the U.S. Ambassador later that day, he sternly asked, "Do the people at your hotel know you're a U.S. Ambassador? There're still some Air Forces officers causing trouble and the looters are everywhere."

For the first time, I sensed that this Foreign Service officer was really concerned. "Ambassador Gardner, it could be a serious problem if you and your family were located. But don't worry, we have four seats for your family on a chartered Swiss Airlines flight tomorrow afternoon that will be the first flight out since this nonsense started."

"How about getting us out of Mombasa?" I asked.

"No problem, we lined up a private piper cub to pick you and your family up at 10:00 am tomorrow. The hotel will know the airstrip's location – a little grass runway just south of Mombasa that's used by wealthy tourists." The Ambassador paused and then added. "And don't worry about paying the Indian pilot; he's one of our contractors."

And then another startling question from the top U.S. official in Kenya. "Oh, you never answered me when I asked if anyone there knows that you are a U.S. Ambassador? It's very important!"

"Mr. Ambassador, as you know, hotel guests in Kenya must surrender their passports when they check in. Of course the people at the front desk know – they greeted me as Ambassador Gardner every time I asked them to call the Embassy!"

Ignoring my frustration, the U.S. Ambassador to Kenya tensely concluded our call. "Remember 10:00 am tomorrow. And I'll have my key staffer with an Embassy driver and station wagon waiting for you at a private airport, Wilson Field."

I simply said. "Thank you" and hung up.

The next morning at 10:05 am, an open air single engine plane dropped out of the blue Kenyan sky and landed just feet away from us. A very slight Indian pilot jumped out.

"You're the Gardners, right? Okay, this trip will be rough, lots of going up and down cause they're still some crazy Air Force pilots flying around. Anybody get airsick?"

Silence. I managed to say, "Not normally."

The Indian shot back. "Well if you are going to be sick, just turn sideways and throw-up outside the plane, ok?"

"One more thing, I need $1,100 U.S. dollars before we take off. This is hazardous duty – so I hope you have $1,100 – cash or travelers' checks."

"Wait a minute. We were told by the U.S. Ambassador to Kenya that you were already paid. What's going on?" My temper was starting to act up and then Theresa gave me that look, and wisely said, "Just pay him."

Fortunately from my days as a Seaman's Apprentice in the United States Coast Guard Reserve, I had learned a valuable lesson after a fellow Seaman was robbed of every penny when on shore leave in grimy downtown Norfolk, Virginia: "Always keep your big bills in your socks, but leave some small bills in your pockets for the muggers who will at least feel good that they cleaned you out."

Without a word to our pilot, I pulled up my right leg pant, pulled down my long black sock, and took out a wad of 18 one hundred dollar bills. I peeled off 11 bills and handed $1,100 to the creep, who quickly pocketed the ransom.

"Okay," he then said looking at Theresa, "You lady, get in the back seat and put one girl on each side or you. You mister, sit up front with me. I'll put the luggage in the storage pocket."

And that was that. We flew for almost an hour, at various altitudes, without another word spoken. And to their parents' great pride and joy, Courtney and Christine never budged, never got airsick, never expressed any fear.

When we got to Wilson Field, a small private terminal with an asphalt runway, our pilot taxied close to a large white van-station wagon. No sooner had he landed when gunshots were audible as the single engine plane shut down. A pale young embassy official ran from the van and together with the Kenyan driver, quickly grabbed our luggage and hustled us to the van. More gunshots off somewhere but we were in the Embassy van – almost like reaching U.S. soil. Then the disturbing sights on our breakneck speed drive to Kenya's International Airport: shop windows broken everywhere;

burned out cars deserted in the streets, debris everywhere; but no people in sight. It was eerie.

As our white Embassy van entered the airport circular driveway, I saw dozens of Kenyan soldiers lining the long driveway; they were all holding rifles and most were with large rows of bullets crisscrossing their chests.

Ignorant of the sacred Kenyan tribal requirement to get permission <u>before</u> taking the photo of a male Kenyan warrior, I exclaimed, "Courtney, quick, give me your camera." I leaned out of the window and quickly snapped a few shots of the war torn scene with Courtney's nine dollar Kodak instamatic.

All hell broke out. Soldiers weary from 24/7 combat duty during the prior six days suddenly came alive. Shouting madly to stop, the Embassy's white van was immediately surrounded by angry soldiers. Short and tall, the soldiers had one thing in common – they all had red, blood shot eyes from their sleepless, non-stop military service, including regaining control of the bullet ridden, blood stained airport we were about to enter.

Not sensing the depth of the furor that my reckless photo taking had aroused, the soft-spoken U.S. Embassy staffer sitting in front of me said, "Please let us pass." Now surrounded by dozens of war weary Kenyan soldiers toting machine guns, the ashen Embassy staffer held up a white stenciled sign that read "Official USA Embassy Vehicle." Our Embassy guide pleaded once again, "Please let us pass. This is an official U.S. Embassy car and we're transporting Ambassador Michael Gardner and his family. Please let us pass."

That's when I felt the cold steel of a rifle's barrel pressed against my right temple.

"Get out…get out. You have insulted Kenya," were the angry first words from the short, muscular Kenya soldier. "Get out – and we won't hurt your family," he was very matter of fact – and very agitated.

Stunned, I knew I had no choice. The gun barrel that was pressed against my head could also injure or kill my wife and two daughters. I had a clarity that I never experienced before or since. I had to obey.

In a calm voice, I said, "I am getting out – just don't do anything rash."

It was like I was speaking Latin; the gun barrel stayed firmly against my right temple, and the angry Swahili chatter continued.

As I went to open the van door, Theresa coldly said: "Don't move Mickey; don't move." She simultaneously reached over Courtney who was immediately to my left, and dug her nails into the inner thigh of my left leg. When I tried to move, she dug deeper.

Then something beautiful happened. A tall Maasai soldier standing next to the van saw tears streaming down little Courtney's face. With authority, this six foot six Maasai warrior firmly addressed my captor: "Stop! Don't make the little girl cry!"

I remember the Maasai's command as if it was uttered yesterday.

Suddenly, the rifle was pulled away and the angry soldiers entered a serious debate about my suitable punishment. After what seemed like an hour, the short soldier walked back to my open window to deliver the verdict.

"Say you're sorry Kenya" he yelled.

"I'm sorry Kenya, "I immediately called out.

"Louder…much louder!" the frustrated soldier screamed.

So I responded in kind, and with all the energy I could muster, I screamed.

"I'M SORRY KENYA!!!'

Satisfied, the unsmiling soldier stepped back, and our supportive Maasai warrior stepped forward.

"Give me the camera."

Picking up the camera that had fallen to the car floor, I reached out and handed it to this kind man.

The Kodak was thrown on the roadway and immediately hit by dozen riffles butts that shattered it into little plastic pieces.

When we reached the main entrance to the terminal, guards and disheveled tourists were everywhere. So was dried bloodshed in the battle by soldiers loyal to President Moi who regained control of the Airport.

Knowing that our four tickets for the chartered Swiss Air flight were precious and coveted by the more than 5,000 tourists who fled Nairobi and were gathered for days at the Airport, we huddled closely together as we fought our way to the Immigration check point. Once there, we showed the stern Kenyan official our four tickets and also gave him our passports.

After a long minute, this ramrod straight Kenyan held up Courtney's passport and coldly said in perfect English: "This girl cannot leave. Her passport does not have a stamp showing her lawful entry into Kenya!"

I started to argue but after the events of just 20 minutes earlier, I became a gentle but persistent advocate:

"Sir, I'm a U.S. Ambassador and when all four of us were taken through customs last week, someone merely stamped three of our four diplomatic passports. I assure you that we all arrived together so obviously it's only a clerical error."

Unmoved, the unsmiling Immigration officer merely repeated his prior declaration: "The little girl's passport does not have an entry stamp. She cannot leave Kenya until this matter is worked out."

I knew it was either this flight – or many more dangerous days in war-torn Nairobi.

Then Theresa had an inspired idea: she turned to Christine and whispered: "Take out your packet of chewing gum and give it to the man – and smile."

And that's what eight-year-old Christine Lennon Gardner did. She gently pushed her half empty pack of Wrigley's spearmint chewing gum through the opening in the Immigration desk window and smiled broadly.

It was magic. The hard ass Kenyan melted, took the gum, smiled back at Christine and said: "Go-go; all four of you – go."

Within 10 minutes of our clearing the Immigration check point, we were seated side-by-side on a shabby Swiss Air already filled with many German and Swedish victims of the rampages that devastated Nairobi for the prior five days. While the body odors were horrible in the plane's cabin full of tourists – tourists who had spent three or four shower-less days at Kenya's International Airport, the worst part of the nine-hour flight to Zurich was hearing the horrendous stories from fellow passengers about the widespread rapes and unprovoked violence that was visited on "capitalist tourist." They also shared stories about assaults directed at industrious Indian merchants who had ably served the British colonialist who had abandoned Kenya in early 1960's when the corrupt dictator-President Jomo Kenyatta took control.

Passengers – some sobbing – needed desperately to compare their horrible stories – to expiate themselves from the traumas that had just altered their lives. And while we tried to shield Courtney and Christine from the anguished stories, they heard and saw more than we wanted. But isn't that one of the risks and benefits of traveling the globe – you see things that most American children were shielded from.

It would take eight months before Courtney's nightmares of the van incident were replaced by spectacular visual images of animals in the Bush; as far as Christine, she was quietly very proud of herself – and that smile (with the chewing gum) that saved her very best friend, her sister Courtney.

Israel, the Vatican, the Soviet Union and the USTTI in Nairobi

On the first full day after my arrival in Nairobi in September 1982 with a White House approved 28-person delegation of corporate executives and senior government officials – and a five-man contingent of young U.S. Marines, I received an urgent message from a Saudi Prince. The Prince, who was Head of the Saudi delegation, requested a meeting with me that afternoon either in my suite at the Intercontinental Hotel, or at the Saudi Arabian Embassy in Nairobi. "It was important," the note read with the green Saudi flag prominently embossed on the top.

Still jetlagged and juggling a lot of last minute issues before the formal opening of the ITU's Plenipotentiary Conference the next morning, I asked several of the State Department's members of the delegation what could be "so important." They too were puzzled since they had been assured, as I had, that the attempted expulsion of Israel from the United Nations would take place in New York when the General Assembly convened later in September. But regardless of what the "important matter" was on the mind of the Saudi Head of Delegation, I was strongly advised that I "had to meet with him" because of the Saudi's influence over all of the Arab delegations.

At a meeting later that afternoon, the Saudi Prince came to my Marine guarded-suite at the Intercontinental and handed me a two-page "demarche" officially notifying the Secretary of State, and me as his representative, of the Arab world's intent to expel the Zionist murderers - Israel - from the ITU, the specialized agency of the United Nations in charge of global communications. The Prince, a hugely obese man, was very quiet as I read the inflammable demarche, and then thanked me for my time and promptly left my suite.

As a novice diplomat, I was stunned at the radioactive tone and hate seeping through the demarche. And because there was so much hate during the heated debates of the next seven weeks, Kenyan officials would place machine gun toting police at the elevators on my floor. As the U.S. Ambassador to the ITU's Nairobi Plenipotentiary Conference, I was suddenly immersed in a diplomatic morass where the United States would daily be vilified as "Zionists loving pigs" by Iran, Algeria and other conference attendees. They were determined to punish Israel for the Beirut Massacre that took place earlier in the June 6, 1982 invasion of Lebanon by 60,000 PLO-seeking Israeli troops, and the September 16 "massacre" at PLO refugee camps of Sabra and Shatila in West Beirut.

Once the Israel Expulsion Resolution was formally introduced, the routine work of the ITU Plenipotentiary Conference became a very secondary concern. For the U.S. Delegation, our top priority was to preserve the fundamental principle of the "Universality of the United Nations" and that meant keeping Israel in the ITU at any cost. So my secure WATTS line in my hotel suite became a vital link to my friend and strategic advisor, the shrewd and seasoned Under Secretary of State Bill Schneider. In daily calls – several involving President Reagan's Ambassador to the U.N. Jeane Kirkpatrick and Vice President George H. W. Bush, Bill and I would compare notes.

One thing quickly became apparent: the U.S. intel network was horribly unreliable. While the State Department analysts, working with the CIA, would advise us initially that we were just a few votes away from preventing Israel's expulsion from the ITU, the Israeli Ambassador would privately tell me with certainty that we would lose by 25 plus votes if the vote was taken.

We didn't know who to believe so my mission was to delay a vote on the Arab-backed Israel Expulsion Resolution until we had the votes to prevail. So, for the next seven weeks, the U.S. delegation used every trick we could to delay the vote while simultaneously closing the huge 25 plus vote divide that Israeli intelligence confirmed.

One important target was the Soviet Union's Minister of Communications who effectively controlled 13 votes from Soviet-bloc countries. Nicknamed "Big Paw" because of his huge bulky hands, the Russian Minister was constantly on the conference's microphone, vigorously supporting the Expulsion Resolution while repeatedly blasting "the Zionists' strongest allies, the greedy capitalists from the United States."

After several efforts at neutralizing – or at least diminishing the Soviet tirades, I decided on a different approach: I would have my hand written note delivered to Big Paw inviting him for a one-on-one meeting in my suite. Delivered personally by the fearless Frank Urbany, Big Paw immediately responded with a note that said:

"Ambassador Gardner: Good idea. I bring the Vodka."

Well, if he brings the Vodka, I decided to share my huge supply of peanut M&M's that Theresa snuck into my luggage for the long trip to Nairobi. And so, in the midst of the ugly public fight over Israel's expulsion from the United Nations, we sat down with a liter bottle of lemon flavored Stolichnaya Vodka and two large yellow bags of M&M's.

So, it went: toe-to-toe shots of Vodka until the Minister's bottle was almost empty.

And then Big Paw got serious:

"Why does U.S. stand up for Israel? Everybody's mad at them for destroying Beirut, but you don't care"

Chewing on more M&M's, I shot back. "Israel is our trusted ally and we are not going to abandon them even if we are displeased with them about something. And, anyway, you certainly don't want the chaos in the global communication community that will happen if the U.S. withdraws from the ITU – and Minister, we will do that the minute Israel is thrown out of the ITU."

During a very long pause, Big Paw helped himself once again to my M&M's.

"Okay. We don't like it if ITU breaks up – and it will if USA no longer is member. But we still want to hurt Israel and embarrass USA for being only friend of Zionists. So here's my plan: USA gets Kenyans to do secret ballot on vote, and Soviet Union will split – you know, divide its vote. But don't play around with me: you get your own votes – and we will still attack USA for support of Israel."

At this point, I was still thinking straight – straight enough to know that the United States had just won an enormous concession.

"Minister," I said with a smile, "We have a deal. We'll get a secret ballot, and you do all the shouting against the United States you want. The key is that we both will still be members of the ITU."

And so it was, we worked the tedious U.N. processes and finally got agreement for a secret ballot. The only trouble was the fact that, according to the Israeli intelligence wizards including the young Benjamin Netanyahu, who came to Nairobi to help, we were still short 11 votes, even with the presumed split of votes cast by the 13 Soviet-Bloc countries.

And that's when U.S. Ambassadors around the world really went to work.

In our daily strategy conference calls, I would learn how effective the United States could be when it really wanted something. Whether it was friend or foe, the USA had something to trade when it came to securing a vote for Israel's continued membership in the U.N.'s International Telecommunication Union (ITU). And every vote mattered – even the vote of the Vatican, a full member of the ITU simply by virtue of the fact that the ITU was established many decades before the United Nations. So while the Vatican is not a voting member of the U.N., it is a voting member of the ITU.

So as votes were being gathered by U.S. Ambassadors all over the globe, I was assigned a special target – the Papal Nuncio in Nairobi.

When I arrived for my first visit with the Papal Nuncio at his palatial gated residence, I was struck by the Italian Archbishop's demeanor: not only was he a frail little man physically, the Archbishop seemed very shy – certainly not the typically outgoing Nuncios that were the Vatican's Ambassador to Washington, D.C.

After introducing my advisor Frank Urbany to the Archbishop and his assistant, a young Monsignor, we sat down for some delicious Kenyan tea. Then some small talk about the Catholic schools I attended. Then I asked: "Archbishop, we need your vote to keep Israel in the ITU. It's very important."

In halting but very carefully chosen English, the Archbishop smiled and said.

"Oh, Mr. Ambassador, we never vote. We're not political, and this issue regarding Israel is, as you know, very political."

I knew all about the political antics of the Vatican. A week earlier on September 15, Pope John Paul angered Jews everywhere by welcoming the PLO's leader, Yasser Arafat, to the Vatican.

So I tried again. Polite but firm, I reiterated my main point:

"Archbishop, keeping Israel in the ITU is very important to the United States. We must have your vote. The integrity of the United Nations is at risk."

The shy Archbishop finally made eye contact, and firmly stated: "It's impossible. It's too political."

"Archbishop, could I speak to you privately, without Colonel Urbany or the Monsignor present?"

Looking puzzled, the Archbishop paused. Then in a brief burst of Italian, the Archbishop dismissed his assistant. Without a word from me, Frank followed the Monsignor out of the Nuncio's large living room.

"Archbishop, I'm a Catholic and know very well how the Vatican uses its leverage to advance political goals around the globe. The United Sates may not be able to keep Israel in the United Nations without your vote. Now do you want me to tell my Secretary of State and the Israeli Ambassador that the Vatican would not help Israel? Remember the outcry from Jewish leaders around the globe when the Pope greeted Yasser Arafat last week. If the word gets out that you wouldn't help keep Israel in the United Nations, the uproar will be ten times louder. Do you really want me to have to tell the truth about your vote – that the Vatican wouldn't help Israel?"

The Archbishop was pissed.

"You, you Mr. Gardner should not threaten the Vatican. It's not a good thing. Anyway, I cannot decide alone. I must talk to Rome first."

"Okay Archbishop. How about tomorrow afternoon we meet again, right here?"

"Okay, tomorrow afternoon," the Archbishop answered.

Next day, I returned alone to the Apostolic Delegate's residence.

When I banged the heavy brass knocker on the Nuncio's front door, the Monsignor immediately opened it. The Monsignor was smiling: a good sign.

"Come in Ambassador Gardner; the Archbishop is waiting for you."

Back in the Nuncio's large drawing room, I was warmly greeted by a smiling Archbishop.

"Greetings Ambassador Gardner."

"I have talked to very senior officials in Rome who have also talked to your Ambassador in Rome. And we know how important this matter is to your government. So I can say "yes" to your request if you promise me two things." The Archbishop was very animated.

"First, you must secure a secret ballot…"

"Let me stop you there, Archbishop. We've already got an agreement for a secret ballot from the Kenyans." In fact, we had gotten word that very morning that the Kenyan Minister of Communications - the conference Chairman, had agreed. Now we would not only appease the Soviet Minister, we could also take care of the Vatican.

"Now, Archbishop, what is your second requirement?"

The little Italian Archbishop leaned close to me, like a co-conspirator and whispered: "Ambassador Gardner, you must promise me that no one will know about our vote for Israel – no one except your Secretary of State and the Israel's Ambassador here in Nairobi. No one else. Do you promise me?" His smile was gone; he was all business and deadly serious.

"Archbishop, no problem. I give you my solemn vow that no one will know except my Secretary of State and the Israeli Ambassador. I promise you that, and I thank you for your vote two nights from now."

Two nights later, 157 nations gathered in the cone shaped Kenyatta Center to vote on the Arab world's resolution to expel Israel from this important part of the United Nations. Because the vote had become a hugely symbolic issue covered by the international press, the galleries were loaded with journalists and camera crews from the BBC, the U.S. networks, the Arab Street, Tokyo, etc.

After hours of procedural delays, the secret ballot vote was ready to commence with each delegation casting its vote by checking, "yea, nay or abstain" on a letter sized piece of white paper.

If we lost the vote, my instructions were very precise. If Israel was expelled, I was to immediately take the microphone and announce that the United States was formally withdrawing from the ITU. Then I was to lead members of the U.S. Delegation down the stairs and walk the full length of the conference floor, passing before the rowdy Iranian and

Algerian delegations. I was then to issue a statement condemning the vote as an unacceptable assault on the U.N.'s cornerstone principle of universality.

Two or three minutes into the vote, there was some movement in the Vatican delegation's box, just nine rows below the large area set aside for the U.S. delegation. The young Monsignor was turning around, looking up at the U.S. Delegation. Then the Monsignor stood up and was handed the blank ballot by the Archbishop. They were both talking with some noticeable agitation, but were too far away for me or other U.S. delegates to understand.

And then an incredible thing happened: the young Monsignor turned and walked up the nine steps to where I was sitting. Sheepishly whispering as the global press corps watched, the cleric in his black cassock leaned over my shoulder, held the empty ballot in front me, and pleaded:

"Ambassador Gardner, the Archbishop and I are confused by the resolution; what box should we check off – yea or nay?"

By now the hush that had hovered over the Kenyatta Center was replaced with chuckles and laughs. The press obviously was amused by the Vatican's very visible support of the United States in this critical vote.

"Monsignor, the ballot is confusing. Tell Archbishop to check the "nay" box – but also tell him that the press here from around the world now knows that you – the Vatican – are supporting United States' position on Israel."

And so it was: Israel and the United States won the secret ballot by four votes, and while the press would speculate about how some nations actually voted, one thing was certain: the 110-acre Vatican in the heart of Rome cast one of those four crucial votes.

While the U.S.'s four-vote victory to keep Israel in the ITU was important, the Nairobi conference produced an added and long-term benefit as it provided me the venue and opportunity to respond to the pleas from developing country leaders who were being left behind as cellular technology and innovation in satellite usage were being deployed throughout the developed world. In the early 1980s the harsh reality was that unless a developing country could buy equipment from the global communications companies, the developing countries communications leaders simply couldn't get the training that was critical to their progress

King of Sprinkler Lane

in building a modern communications infrastructure. The problem was acute in the early 1980s where teledensity in most developing countries was a miserable ratio of less than one phone per every 100 citizen.

After countless bi-laterals where the U.S. Ambassador (me) was told that communications training for the poorest developing countries was their top priority, I complained – repeatedly to my bride Theresa – that the U.S. and the other G8 countries were going to be clobbered in Nairobi, at least budget wise. I felt strongly that the communications-rich countries had to come up with some credible response in Nairobi to this very legitimate request for free communications training.

Then one night after I had met earlier that day with several unhappy developing country Ministers of Communications, my wife Theresa blasted me.

"Mickey, do something! Don't just complain. These people should be able to understand their communications options, and the U.S. has always been a sharer. Focus on a way that you and your team can get some free communications training to these people."

And Theresa, as usual, was spot on. I would go to the leaders of AT&T, MCI, Comsat, etc. as well as my friends in government and ask them to finance and host tuition-free training for women and men from the developing world. But unlike the Peace Corps which sent its volunteers for year-long work around the world, we would use expert volunteer communications officials from industry and government who would conduct their intensive two or three weeks communications training in their offices and laboratories throughout the United States.

So as I and the 28 U.S. delegates to the Nairobi ITU Plenipotentiary prepared for the bellicose Nairobi conference, I together with a few daring friends including FCC Commissioner Henry Rivera and NTIA official Frank Urbany, legally established a non-profit joint venture between U.S. corporations and government officials called the United States Telecommunications Training Institute (USTTI).

And even though the Nairobi ITU conference would become a huge and nasty political battleground over Israel's right to remain a member of the ITU, the USTTI was launched to enthusiastic applause in Nairobi with the announcement of an initial 13 tuition-free course curriculum. I agreed to chair the USTTI for a year, but 30 plus years later, I still chair this non-profit that relies annually on hundreds of expert ICT volunteers from U.S. communications industry, academia, the federal government who each year conduct the USTTI's 80-plus annual curriculum. Importantly, since 1982, the USTTI has graduated 9,048 women and men working today in 171 developing countries to make modern communications a reality for their fellow countrymen and women.

Theresa was right: the United States has a long tradition of sharing – and the USTTI is a robust, living example of the Yankee spirit of volunteerism.

The Allure of Chauffeured Government Cars

In the winter of 1982, fresh back from Nairobi with a victory that kept Israel in the U.N's International Telecommunications Union, I was riding high.

After my successful three months in Kenya in a tense, victorious fight for the USA, a senior State Department official suggested the possibility of an appointment as U.S. Ambassador to Czechoslovakia or Yugoslavia. I was flattered and very intrigued.

Euphoric about the prospects of this new diplomatic adventure, I hurried home to tell my wife about the possible next chapter in our lives.

Running into our bedroom, I blurted out the good news: "Theresa, I've been offered an appointment as the U.S. Ambassador to either Czechoslovakia or Yugoslavia."

Without a pause, Theresa calmly responded. "If you want to do it, fine, do it, but do it with your second wife."

Stunned, I realized that this was not a debate.

Nonetheless, I pleaded: "Don't you think it would be great fun? And how about the girls living in a different country - learning a different language?" Before I ended my sentence, I knew I was losing.

Then with the same unemotional voice, my wife of 14 years continued: "I went along with the Ambassadorial thing in Nairobi because it was a great honor for you – and it was a good way for the girls to see Africa. But you've only been out of law school five years and you've been distracted and largely out of touch with us for the last six months. So it's time that we're a full time family once again, and if you're the U.S. Ambassador somewhere, you'll be totally absorbed in your work as you get driven around in your government car. Quite frankly, there's more to life than that. But go ahead and do it if it's that important to you – and the girls and I will go our separate way."

And that was that. I reluctantly told my White House, State Department and U.S.I.A friends the truth: it was time for me to get back to my family and to go back to the practice of law – fulltime.

The Vacation From Hell

Friends (now former friends) asked us one late night in the mid-1980s after lots of wine to join them at a beautiful villa located on 65 private acres on the Greek Island of Ios.

The invitation included our daughters Courtney (13) and Christine (11); to seal our acceptance, our would-be hosts showed us a photo album of the statuesque bright white villa just 50 yards from the Aegean Sea. Apparently owned by a group of Princeton graduates that included a then sitting U.S. Senator, our friend's Greek villa reportedly included six bedrooms with bathrooms en-suite, a fulltime cook, a butler/handyman – literally everything guaranteed to make our weeklong visit to Ios fun and carefree.

"Why not?" I asked my dutiful wife after our potential hosts pressed us for a firm late night acceptance.

"It's up to you Mickey. I've already been to Greece but if you think it would be a good experience for Courtney and Christine after the Kenya coup debacle (in 1982), I'll go with your call," Theresa agreed – but cautiously.

"Okay, that's it, we're on board," I blurted out to our generous friends.

The next morning when I was dealing with a horrendous wine-induced headache, Theresa reminded me of my pledge to join our lawyer friends – newlyweds with an infant – at their sparkling white villa next to the Aegean!

"I hope you know what we're getting into, Mickey," were the only prophetic words offered by my bride.

Flash forward to the third week in August. The Gardners have just arrived in Athens after a bumpy flight from Dulles to Frankfurt, followed by a long five-hour layover, then a brief flight to Athens for a quick visit to the Acropolis and a one night stay in Athens before our early morning boat ride to the gorgeous white villa on the beautiful Isle of Ios.

When we reached the Athens' dock to board the first class section of the "cruise boat" that would take us to Ios, we learned from a hostile middle aged Greek official that the "cruise boat" was in fact a dirty old ferry; moreover, first class consisted of a 30ft by 30ft fenced-in area at the front of the ferry that included a small cabin with 20-25 seats. When I say fenced-in, that is literally what the first class quarters consisted of with young, rugged tourist jammed in on the other side of the fence.

Originally scheduled to be a five-hour boat ride to beautiful Ios, we soon discovered that the captain of our crowded, grey ferry boat had decided to stop at every Greek isle on the way to Ios. This meant unscheduled stops at Syros, Paros, Sikinos, Santorini, Mykonos, Milos, etc. Suddenly our five-hour "cruise boat" ride to Ios turned into an 11-hour trip with stale cheese sandwich and thick Greek coffee being the only available sustenance. When I asked the deck hand "why the change in schedule?" he shrugged and replied, "Capitan do whatever he wants."

At this point, I began to remember our earlier family debacle into Kenya where I failed miserably in doing the minimal amount of due diligence. Privately, without sharing my new sense of dread with my Bride, I started to get nervous. After all, we had a puzzling phone call from our hostess a week earlier asking us to bring mosquito netting for their one-year-old daughter's crib; why would you need mosquito netting if the beautiful white villa was fully equipped with state-of-the-art equipment including screens as advertised in its marketing album?

When we finally arrived at Ios' small cluttered dock, we were four weary, sun-burnt, salt encrusted tourists. Nonetheless, we were excited. And then we spotted our smiling host who said the week earlier that he would line up his faithful boat captain to take us to the villa a good twenty minutes away.

"Is that the boat taxi?" I asked with incredulity as our host tried to help us load our copious luggage on to a small wooden motor boat docked 30 yards away from the ferry. "You've got to be kidding." I blurted out. The boat was full of dead fish heads – the waste from the fisherman's day long efforts in the Aegean. Weary, we tried to ignore the fish scales, rusty hooks and tangled lines on the dirty floor of our motorboat.

As soon as we maneuvered out of the chaotic harbor, Courtney and Christine started to giggle. My mood was not good, so I harshly asked, "What's so funny?" Instead of answering, my two Catholic school educated daughters smiled broadly and pointed to the crowded beach we were passing. And there they were – hundreds and hundreds of nude sun bathers waving at Courtney and Christine, who now were energetically waving back!

Turning to our host, I asked, "Is this a nude beach?"

"Hell yes, it's not just a nude beach; it's a nude island – even some of the cafes serve totally nude sun worshippers." Laughing, our one-time friend added, "Don't worry about the girls cause in a few more miles, we'll turn into the villa's harbor and private beach which are off limits to the tourists. We'll only see the nudists when we venture into town."

Quickly, things deteriorated.

As the fish smelling boat putt-putted towards the villa's private beach, I asked our host where the dock was.

"Oh, they haven't gotten to that yet, but it's ok because we use those rocks over there."

Still hopeful that things would improve once we climbed the long hill to the white villa, I followed our host onto the rocks and helped Theresa and the girls ashore. The fisherman, who spoke not a word of English, threw the suitcases onto the rocks, one of which fell back into the Aegean Sea. The 100 yards walk to the villa was literally "bloody" – as we had to walk through a blanket of tan sage brush that contained stubborn little thorns. As we approached the villa's staircase, a middle aged blonde lady approached Theresa whose ankles were now smeared with blood from the pricklies. We would later learn that this lady was a tenured professor from a major southern university; she and her professor husband had arrived via Tuscany a week earlier, loaded down with ten cases of Pinot Grigio. She walked to Theresa, hugged her, and whispered, "It only gets worse."

What prophetic words!

Since there was no sign of the promised butler-handyman, we dragged our luggage – including the wet suitcase, to the villa's large tiled deck overlooking the sapphire blue sea. Exhausted from the 11-hour ferry ride, we all were in need of water. When asked what we wanted, our hostess explained that "the villa was not quite completed," including digging a well which would one-day provide ample clean drinking water. "White wine or a little coke-a-cola," were the options our embarrassed hostess explained. "We have to go easy on the cokes because it's a three mile walk to the town – and six packs of soft drinks prove to be very heavy after the first fifteen minutes."

Now the reality of our world for the next eight days on Ios was starting to sink in. And then an extraordinary thing happened. As we are gathered on the deck watching the beginning of a spectacular sunset, Christine was sitting on the deck's white edge sipping her half a glass of rationed coke. From the ground level below the villa's main deck, something furry and all black popped onto the ledge not more than 12 inches away from Christine. At first, I thought it was a black cat. And then my memory from my days as a mess cook in the Coast Guard in Guantanamo kicked in. The black cat was, in fact, a huge wharf rat.

"Jesus Christ, Christine, move away!" I yelled.

Suddenly, our host clapped his hands several times – and viola, the huge black rat was gone.

"Oh Mickey, don't worry about the rats. They occasionally scavenger around for crumbs, but quickly retreat," our host opined.

Stunned at our host's cavalier attitude, I decided right then to clear out of Ios the next day.

But first we had to take our bags to our bedrooms and then have an authentic Greek dinner, prepared by the full-time cook who was married to the mystery butler-handyman. Climbing the wide stairwell to the second floor, our hostess casually mentioned that only one of the four bathrooms on the second floor worked. She also urged us to use ample amounts of bug repellant "when we're not enjoying a strong breeze from the sea," adding that, "a land breeze brings the mosquitoes." The fact that Theresa had explained on the phone to our hostess a week earlier that I was very allergic to mosquitoes had apparently mattered not at all as long as our hostess got the requested mosquito netting for her one-year-old.

Now, I was getting mad: at myself for not doing due diligence on Ios, and mad at our hosts who failed to candidly tell us that the beautiful, modern Greek villa portrayed in the marketing brochure was in reality, a half-finished, rat and mosquito infested dump.

Dinner was the next but certainly not the last straw. While our hostess set a beautiful table using copious candles and wild Greek flowers, the grilled lamb and rice were cold and barely eatable. And the so-called fulltime cook was a grouch who sprinkled hot peppers on everything. Clearly, people like me with an Irish stomach were out-of-luck. Fortunately, the professors' plentiful wine was the saving grace.

As the meal was winding down, my intake of white wine prompted the need for me to visit the villa's sole working bathroom on the second floor. As I approached the pitch black living room and stairwell, I asked, "Where's the light switch?"

Silence – and then our host called out, "Oh, they haven't connected the electricity yet. But we have a generator that keeps the ice box cool."

"You've got to be kidding," I uttered.

"Don't worry, Mickey, we've got tons of candles. Come back and take one off the dining table," our host glibly replied.

How could this be happening? We had known our hosts for three years, and they were fine. Yes, they were going through a rocky patch with the children from his first marriage, and yes, she was a new mother two decades younger that her husband, but they had always been perfect hosts. But no one would have let friends travel to their rented villa once they got there and saw what a mess it was.

Years later, we could only surmise that the friction between the young, newlywed mother and the weary would-be stud father was so bad that they wanted others there to keep things civil. Whatever their rationale, the Gardners were on the next ferry to Athens.

When the sun broke through the next morning, Courtney and I were dressed for the hour long trek into Hora, Ios' main city. While our host slept in, the good natured professors agreed the night before to guide us into town. While less than three miles away, the walk to Hora was very challenging; the pathway was at most a foot-wide, rocky and full of the nasty underbrush that had pricked our feet and ankles on our arrival just 12 hours earlier.

But getting off Ios, that day if possible, was our number one priority. So off we went.

After 40 minutes in the hot morning sun, we passed a partially full beach – and yes, everyone was nude. Courtney giggled – and it soon became nothing more than a humorous sight.

Ten minutes later, we arrived at the little town of Hora where most people were at least dressed in shorts. We immediately located the shabby little office for the ferry. A big red sign said "Closed – until 9:30." It was only 8:25 am, yet the bright Greek sun was beating down on us. To kill the hour, Courtney, the professors and I entered an open-air-café; we had wonderful lemon quiches – still warm, washed down with thick Greek coffee. After our treats, the kind professors decided to return to the villa in order to avoid the midday heat that was apparently unrivaled.

While waiting for the ferry boat office to open, we asked our waiter where we could buy coke-a-cola. "Only the bar up the hill sells coke. Right up there," he pointed. Sure enough, we bought the bar's entire inventory of cokes – 33 10oz cans. Dividing our important find into plastic bags – Courtney carried 10 cans and I took the remaining 23 cans.

It was now 9:25 a.m., so we walked down to the ferry boat office, next to the dock. The smell of dead fish was everywhere; a dozen young college kids had already lined up at the ferry boat door where the "closed" sign still hung. At 9:45 a.m., the front door finally opened – and a disheveled youngish man appeared. Surrounded by the college aged students, he yelled out: "No cancelations on today's ferry, maybe tomorrow."

The students, all with great tans and some with beards and shoulder length hair, moaned and groaned, "Hey buddy, we've got to get back to our schools. Can't you do something?" Apparently, sun worshippers flocked to Ios with one way tickets – and late August was the ferry company's busiest time.

The master of the ferry merely shrugged.

Then it was our turn. I showed him the four first class tickets and asked if I could get the mid-afternoon ferry to Athens?

"Are you crazy, mister? We're fully booked until September 9, and things are only getting worse. There are hundreds of these young people who will do anything to get to Athens" – and then the ferry master leaned forward and whispered. "Mister, I wouldn't wave those tickets around cause they're lots of desperate young people!"

I tried once again.

"Do you have a waiting list? After all, our tickets aren't good for eight days and you might get a cancellation," I was pleading.

Now growing impatient, the ferry master raised both his hands in frustration: "We might get one – or sometimes even two cancellations, but NEVER four on the same day. So relax, you and your family are here in Ios for another eight days!"

End of conversation.

Courtney looked up and saw that I was really upset. "Dad, don't worry, Christine and I will be ok. We may even teach the little girl English."

Courtney and Christine had met the chef's daughter in the kitchen the night before. Shy and no more than five, little Olympia would be their challenge.

"Okay Court," I sighed. "You and Christine are real troopers – and we'll make this adventure fun."

The walk back to the villa was reminiscent of the Coast Guard's August boot camp noontime marches with a full pack on the wide sandy beaches of Cape May, New Jersey. The cans got heavier and heavier with each step; the prickles were relentless, and the 11:00 am sun was literally scorching little Courtney and me on the 70-minute march back to the villa. We were so hot that we barely noticed the now jam packed beaches of nudes we had previously passed.

Back at the villa, everyone but Theresa and Christine had left for a hike and picnic. When I told them the bad news – namely eight more days at this hellhole, Theresa took control as she did with every family crisis.

"Girls, this clearly is not what we expected and now we're stuck here for another eight days. So let's make the best of it. Okay?"

Both girls thought for a long minute.

Then, with mini smiles, they both agreed that they would handle it.

Courtney spoke first: "Mom, we'll do fine but promise that this will be our last experimental trip."

Then Christine piped in "The water is nice – and even though the donkeys have messed the beach with their doo doo, we'll swim a lot and teach Olympia English."

And that's what these flexible, world class travelers did. They swam for hours each day - avoided the plentiful donkey droppings, and taught little Olympia how to greet people in English. And oh yes, they started each day with a tall glass of Pinot Grigio.

In the summer of 1972 on my first visit to the Oval Office, former Texas Governor and Nixon's Treasury Secretary, John B. Connally (left) introduces me (right) to the 37th President, Richard M. Nixon (center). Connally would later run for the Presidency in the 1980 campaign, and designate me to serve as his campaign's General Counsel.

Theresa and I (center) at the September 1972 Texas Hoedown with former Texas Governor Connally (far right) and his wife Nellie (far left) and President Nixon (immediately next to Theresa) and his wife Pat (to my left).

President Gerald Ford (far right with his back to the camera) holds a briefing in the Cabinet Room for members of the President's Committee on the Mental Retardation (PCMR). I am seated third from the left with long hair.

In honor of
The Right Honorable
The Prime Minister of the
United Kingdom of Great Britain
and Northern Ireland
and Mrs. Wilson

THE WHITE HOUSE
Thursday, January 30, 1975

The official program from the post-Watergate State Dinner hosted by President Gerald Ford and Betty Ford – a State Dinner where Theresa was "matched up" with the elegant actor Cary Grant.

Dressed in Safari gear, the Gardner family, Courtney (left), Christine (center), prepare for the harrowing nine-hour drive from Nairobi to the Saltlick Game Preserve. Kenya's first attempted coup would break out less than 24 hours later, leaving "Ambassador Gardner" and his family stranded for several days in a hotel on the Indian Ocean.

The Gardner family on a visit with President Reagan in the Oval Office to share stories of the family adventures in Kenya.

President Reagan (left) greets Theresa at a dinner hosted by the President's close friend Director of the USIA Charlie Wick (center).

Theresa and I visiting former President Reagan in his Los Angeles office where we presented the President a green graffiti painted chunk of the Berlin Wall. The President described this memento as "an Irish piece of the Berlin Wall."

Jim Brady (center) gives his trademark "thumbs up" as he and I (left) join Naval officers and former appointees of President Reagan in Newport News, Virginia at the March 4, 2001 christening of the aircraft carrier USS Ronald Reagan.

Theresa, dressed for her meeting at Hampton Court with the then HRH Princess Diana.

The Times
1785 - 1985

Guest List
and
Table Plan

Hampton Court Palace
Thursday 11 July 1985

The official guest book from Rupert Murdoch's 200th Anniversary Gala for his *London Times* in Henry VIII's Hampton Court.

Father Bob Lawton, S. J. (center) poses with Theresa (in white) after a fun day in the Bermuda sun.

Theresa and I pause after our private tour of Harry and Bess Truman's post-White House home at 219 North Delaware Street in Independence, Missouri.

Hampton Court, Rupert and the Mikimoto Pearls

For a four year period during the mid-80s, I had the pleasure of representing Rupert Murdoch in his efforts to become an FCC-licensed U.S. broadcaster. While journalism was his great love, Murdoch had determined that broadcasting was a must business; he also envisioned the impossible, a fourth network to compete with the then three powerful U.S. broadcast networks – CBS, ABC and NBC.

Once the Aussie-born Murdoch accepted my advice that holding a green card was not enough and that he had to become a U.S. citizen, my work was relatively easy. After all, a fourth network would promote competition and the FCC was dominated by Reagan appointees – appointees I had worked closely with in my capacity as President-elect Reagan's FCC Transition Chairman.

Murdoch was an ideal client, focused on the goal of getting licensed to run the Metromedia TV Stations he wanted to buy and passionate about bringing much needed competition to the three networks (an intoxicating concept for pro-competition Reaganites). Murdoch was also a very decent man to deal with; intensely focused and 24/7, Rupert didn't hesitate to ring you at home during weekends, but unlike other high maintenance clients, he always apologized for the off-duty interruption.

And he was frugal in the mid-80s before he was "Hollywoodized" by my favorite all time client-mentor Lew Wasserman. In fact, in those days before Murdoch bought the Fox Studio and Jules Stein's Hollywood mansion, he lived a very simple life-style, taking cabs instead of limos and arriving solo for meetings with the FCC's 8th floor officials.

One example of Murdoch's frugality occurred during a one-on-one lunch I had with him in his modest office in the shabby old New York Post Building overlooking the Brooklyn Bridge. After his trusted assistant Dot placed our sandwiches on a small table near the window, I spotted the River Café docked on the Brooklyn Heights side of the East River, a place Theresa and I always visited with our daughters on our annual Easter visit to New York.

"Hey Rupert," I innocently volunteered, "You can see the River Café from your office."

Somewhat bemused, Murdoch asked, "You've been there?"

"Oh, yes, we go there every time we're in New York; we even take the girls there during our Easter visit," I enthusiastically responded.

"Oh really, I, I…Anna and I don't go there often. It's too expensive."

So you can imagine my surprise some months later to get a call from Dot saying that Rupert wanted "me and my wife" to be his guests in London at the 200th Anniversary Party for Murdoch's journalistic jewel, the London Times. Dot went on to explain that in a rare show of deference to the historical stature of the London Times, the Royal Family had made Henry VIII's famous hunting lodge, Hampton Court, available for the bash. And while Dot did not think the Queen would attend, she was pretty sure that Princess Diana and Prince Charles would be on hand.

Initially, I thanked Dot but said that I thought we'd pass on it, but I greatly appreciated the gesture – an obvious thank you from Murdoch for our earlier success in getting him promptly licensed by the FCC.

Later that day, I casually mentioned the "thoughtful invitation from Rupert" to Theresa, who rarely enjoyed doing client-related events.

"What did you say?" Theresa asked.

"Of course, I said no. You hate client outings."

"Do you mean you passed up an opportunity for us to meet Princess Diana? What's the matter with you? For God's sake, call Dot back and accept!"

Three weeks later, Theresa and I boarded BA's Concord at Dulles for three days at London's Savoy Hotel, all thanks to the frugal Rupert Murdoch.

But meeting Princess Di wasn't going to be so easy. Theresa received several calls and written instructions from the British Embassy in Washington as well as staffers from the London Times outlining the rules of the night at Henry's VIII's Hampton Court:

"No one approaches the Royals unless invited to do so by a Lady in Waiting or a male protocol official."

"No sleeveless dresses, only floor length gowns should be worn <u>with</u> gloves."

"Do not extend your hand to the Royals"

"No cameras at all-anywhere, anytime etc, etc."

For Theresa, this meant she needed immediately to have a special black mid-calf length dress made with a slit in the front. Best of all, she would replicate Princess Di's trademark necklace by hanging her large mini-pear surrounded amethyst brooch on the double strand of Mikimoto pearls I had brought back from Hong Kong five years earlier.

"Carriages promptly at 7:00 in the evening at the King's entrance at Hampton Court, England" was the formal embossed invitation waiting for us as we checked into our favorite London getaway, the Savoy. And no sooner were we in our room, when the phone rang, and a very stern lady from the protocol office reiterated the dos and don'ts of the next night's bash at Hampton Court.

"Thank you, thank you...yes, I understand." Theresa assured the female drill sergeant.

Hanging up the phone, Theresa repeated her plan: "I will meet Prince Diana, no matter what."

"Theresa, please don't embarrass me with my client," I pleaded.

"Don't worry. Just keep your distance. And they won't know I'm your wife," was her disconcerting reply.

Walking up the front steps of Hampton Court, any chance for anonymity was immediately lost when a 6 foot-6 inch Beefeater asked to see our invitation. Without missing a beat, he ushered us to the top of the stairs, hit his large gold-flag draped pole firmly on the hardwood floor, and loudly announced:

"Ambassador Michael Gardner and Mrs. Gardner."

Surprised – and quite frankly a bit startled at the loud, formal introduction – we descended the stairs, to go through a small receiving line of Hampton Court curators.

I suddenly noticed that Theresa's amethyst broach was slightly off center.

"Here let me straighten it."

And then it happened.

The amethyst oval was suddenly in my hand and two strands of the precious Mikimoto pearls were cascading onto the hardwood floor of Henry VIII's favorite hunting lodge.

Theresa was cool. "Just give me my broach and leave me alone," she whispered through smiling but gritting teeth.

I, however, was distraught. The sound of those pearls bouncing on the hardwood floor was deafening. Every one of those pearls was sacred – I had gone way overboard in Hong Kong, and I was determined to retrieve every last one.

So, in desperation, I looked around expecting some help. All I saw were scowls, snickers and some bemusement.

So down I went on my knees for a good ten minutes, pocketing errant pearl after errant pearl. Guests moved this way and that, allowing me to crisscross the room, but not one person reached down to help or to hand me a pearl that had bounced off a shoe.

When my mission ended, both pockets of my tuxedo jacket were bulging with pearls (I would later learn that only three pearls were missing.)

As I stood up, a waiter appeared with a tray of champagne flutes. I grabbed two and looked frantically for Theresa. And there she was – standing gracefully by a huge ancient fireplace. As I walked over, she smiled and said: "Well, that was a sight these people won't forget."

While I had been on my knees collecting pearls, Theresa had attached her beautiful amethyst broach to her gold choker necklace; it wasn't Princess Di's exact look, but it was pretty spectacular.

So off we went to the adjacent room where a smallish, familiar lady with smiling eyes greeted us: "You're Americans, aren't you?" she asked with a twinkle. "That was quite a feat, retrieving all those pearls." I suddenly realized that we were talking to Prime Minister Lady Margaret Thatcher.

After introducing ourselves, Lady Thatcher told Theresa she looked "lovely" and wished us a "carefree evening."

The night was just beginning, and Theresa was still determined to shake hands with Princess Di.

After our brief exchange with Lady Thatcher, we ambled through four or five museum – type rooms that led to a large and crowded drawing room. Just inside the broad doorway stood Rupert and Anna Murdoch. Rupert was all smiles as he greeted us.

While making small talk with the Murdochs, a side door not far from us opened, and almost like magic, the entire room pushed back to create a pathway. On cue, the Royal entourage led by Prince Charles and Princess Diana walked through the side door and straight up to the Murdochs. A hush fell over the room. Then Charles, awkwardly fidgeting with his cufflinks, greeted Rupert and Anna with barely a smile. To Charles' left stood the radiant and elegant Princess Di – and yes, she was wearing her trademark multi-strand pearl necklace with the huge sapphire bauble right in the middle of the necklace.

After an awkward pause, Rupert introduced "Ambassador Gardner and his wife, Theresa Gardner" to the Royals. While Charles merely nodded, his taller Bride put her gloved hand out to Theresa and softly said "Hello" as they shook hands.

As soon as dinner in the Great Hall ended, guests were led outside for an Elizabethan Circus, and a spectacular fireworks display that Henry VIII would have loved. But knowing that "the mission was accomplished" in the Princess Di department, it was time to find our driver and take our "Carriage" back to the Savoy.

We laughed all the way back to the Strand and topped the evening off with room service: scones and two big bowls of the Savoy's world class porridge!

Carpe Diem and Michelangelo's Sistine Chapel

After the vacation debacle on Ios, I determined that the three Gardner Girls - Theresa, Courtney, and Christine - deserved a real vacation.

The next spring break provided the ideal opportunity. Having painfully learned from my lack of due diligence when taking the photo at Nairobi's International Airport as well as agreeing to go to Ios, I worked carefully with Theresa to plan a multi-country European trip that started in Paris, then Luxembourg, through the Swiss Alps and then to Venice, Florence and finally ending up in Rome.

Due to the thoughtful planning, the trip went spectacularly well until our last afternoon in Rome. We had planned so many things to do on our last, beastly hot day in Rome – so many things that our guide didn't get us to St. Peter's Basilica until 4:10 PM – a real problem since this enormous Vatican Church closed to tourists at 5:00 PM.

Making the most of the fifty-minute window, Theresa, Courtney, Christine and I rushed through St. Peter's doors. I particularly wanted to see Michelangelo's Pietà and the Sistine Chapel. As we hurried into the church, I heard a persistent buzzing, a hissing that I suddenly realized was directed at me. The hissing, which apparently meant "no, no, no" was coming from a youngish priest dressed all in black except for his white

Roman Collar. And this priest wasn't just hissing, he was racing towards me pointing frantically at my beige cotton Bermuda shorts.

"Mister, mister, you no go in! No shorts, no shorts," was his stern message. I was incredulous. No shorts when it was 90° plus?

Realizing that this agitated Vatican protector was uncompromising, I urged the three Gardner Girls to go into the Basilica which housed the Sistine Chapel.

"I'll be alright. You all shouldn't miss this opportunity. I'll see you out here in 45 minutes." What else could I do?

Well, my non-bureaucratic angels were on my side. No sooner had I stepped out into St. Peter's Square when I spotted a young couple guzzling some bottled water. They were obviously tourists from Europe and the tall young man, at least 6'3" was wearing sweatpants, not illicit shorts. So I decided to see if a marketplace approach to a 45 minutes lease of sweatpants would work if a $10 bill was the payoff.

When I approached the young couple, they were uneasy. Who wouldn't be when a Bermuda shorts clad Yank walked over to you with a $10 bill in his hand?

"Do you speak English?" I said with a smile.

The young woman was quick to respond with caution, "A little bit."

"Good. I need to get into the Basilica but it closes in 45 minutes. The problem is they wouldn't let me in unless I am wearing long pants." Pointing to my Bermuda shorts, I explained, "These are no good. I couldn't go in with my family who are already in the Basilica."

The young couple looked puzzled.

"I need to borrow your sweatpants." I explained as I pointed to the 6'3" man's well-worn sweatpants. "I'll pay you $10 U.S. if I can borrow them for 45 minutes."

While the tall young man still appeared confused, his girlfriend was an entrepreneur.

"$20 U.S. and you have a deal," she blurted out.

After some exchanges in their native tongue (Dutch), the tall young tourist stepped out of his sweatpants. Fortunately he was wearing navy blue briefs.

I immediately added another $10 bill to the one I was already holding, handed the $20 to the young woman and dashed into St. Peters. The bewildered priest, who previously had blocked me, stared in disbelief as I rushed by him; he had apparently watched the whole transaction. As I passed him, the priest didn't hiss this time. He merely shook his head and repeated, "not good, not good."

I entered the huge St. Peter's Basilica and checked my watch; I had 38 minutes left. But it was a magical 38 minutes as I briefly saw the Sistine Chapel and enjoyed a good, long look at the Pietà where I found the three Gardner Girls in the crowd huddled in front of the spectacular statue. Awesome was the right description. Michelangelo had done his magic, rivaling his own David which we had viewed earlier in the week in Florence.

Promptly at 5:00 PM, the ushers standing guard at St. Peter's Basilica made it clear that tourists should leave. It was then that Theresa and the girls got their first unrestricted view of me in my extra large borrowed sweatpants. They laughed together as we found the young tourists from Holland. In a split second, the transfer was done; the sweatpants were back on the 6'3" young man and I was dressed in my Bermuda shorts – ideal for Rome's hot afternoon weather.

While I had suffered through four long years of Latin at Gonzaga decades earlier, the Latin term "Carpe Diem" had new meaning for me. I had "seized the moment" and had gotten to see firsthand some of Michelangelo's greatest works.

Getting to Know Harry

From my earliest days as a D.C. kid, I had a great attraction to presidential politics; as I previously noted, that may have been due to the fact that the presidency was often the subject of heated discourse around our dining room table – especially on Sunday nights when one or two of the visiting Jesuits debated presidential ethics with my father. A committed Republican, my father despised FDR for trying to pack the Supreme Court; he was equally disdainful of the 33rd President, high-school educated Harry Truman from Missouri. Harry, in my father's view, was a political hack who got his start as a member of Kansas City's notorious Pendergast machine.

But I would discover over the next 40 years, as I studied and observed up close most of the modern American Presidents, my father was wrong about Harry Truman. He was the first cold war President and he brilliantly laid out the foundation for the country's cold war policy. Harry Truman would also be appropriately validated as our pioneering civil rights President.

My interest in Truman motivated me to teach a course on the Modern American Presidents at Georgetown University. My goal was to rigorously, and with no frills, examine two threads of presidential history: how the Cold War presidents (Harry Truman being the first cold war Commander in Chief in the White House) shaped their foreign policies, and secondly, how the presidents since Truman handled civil rights – rights largely ignored by presidents (except pro-abolitionist Ulysses S. Grant and racist Woodrow Wilson) since President Lincoln issued the Emancipation Proclamation in 1863.

Fortunately for me, my friend, the gifted Jesuit, Rev. Bob Lawton, was dean of the College at Georgetown University. Bob and I had countless discussions over the years about the modern American presidents; and when I proposed my course on the Modern American Presidents, Dean Lawton, SJ concluded that a seminar focusing on the Cold War presidents as well as presidential actions – or lack of actions – on civil rights would be worthwhile.

During my initial research on Harry Truman, I was increasingly curious why Truman would integrate the vast U.S. military in 1948 when the country was largely segregated, and Americans were relatively free of the violent racial turmoil of the late 1950's and early 1960's. I knew that the Washington D.C. of my youth was an apartheid city, just as rigidly segregated as Atlanta, Richmond or even Cape Town. I saw firsthand Black Americans who were forced to stand at the crowded end of white's only lunch counters, sit in the back of buses, use separate drinking fountains and restrooms in federal office buildings.

Based on my own observations as a D.C. kid during Harry Truman's seven-year presidency from April 12, 1945 until January 20, 1953, I was determined to find out what motivated Truman to become the pioneering civil rights president. What made this grandson of slave owners from a racist Missouri family send a comprehensive, first-ever 10-point civil rights proposal to Congress in February of election year 1948 – a proposal that was vigorously opposed by 82% of voters polled by Gallup in March of

1948. Surely, Harry must have had some political goal in mind; otherwise, why would he put his election to the White House in 1948 at such risk with 82% of the country's voters who opposed his vision of federally enforced civil rights?

As I intensified my search for the "true" Harry Truman vis-a-vis civil rights, I enjoyed teaching 20 Georgetown students each year who shared my interest in the modern American presidents. In addition to my two hour lectures each week, I included occasional guest lecturers who would give my students a personal sense of the various presidents based on their own extensive dealings with the modern American presidents. Among my guest lecturers were:

- LBJ's faithful assistant, Jack Valenti;
- New Yorker, Susan Thomases who not only headed the successful advance effort for Bill Clinton when he beat Bush 41, but also was an intimate friend and adviser to then First Lady Hilary Clinton;
- White House Curator, Rex Scouten who started his career as a trusted Secret Service Agent for Harry Truman and then Vice President Richard Nixon;
- Truman historian, author David McCullough;
- Witty and irreverent Jim Brady who served as press secretary for presidential candidate Governor Reagan and ultimately as President Reagan's press secretary.

But while the adjunct teaching gig at Georgetown University was extremely rewarding, after eight years, I realized that I had to devote extra time to telling that factual story that I had uncovered on Harry Truman's civil rights crusade.

As I started to actually write my Truman civil rights book, Father Lawton, SJ, cautioned me about the high academic standards expected in a nonfiction work that would challenge the widespread conventional wisdom held by most people that President Kennedy and/or President Johnson were the pioneering civil rights presidents. Mindful of Father Lawton's admonition to be meticulously accurate with hard supporting documentation, my Truman book would contain over 600 footnotes that collectively supported that fact that on numerous federal fronts, including his dealing with the U.S. Supreme Court, Harry Truman was the largely unrecognized pioneer of the federal civil rights movement in 20th century America. The fact that the Society for History in the Federal Government awarded my book <u>Harry Truman and Civil Rights: Moral Courage and Political Risks,</u> its prestigious Henry Adams Prize in 2003 was very significant because it confirmed that the society's federal archivists and historians agreed that high school-educated Harry Truman, not JFK or LBJ, was the president who was the relentless catalyst for the massive civil rights reforms of the 20th century.

While I would learn much about Harry Truman through seven-years of research at the Truman Library, Howard University and press archives across the country, I also had the invaluable good fortune to interview such firsthand observers of Harry Truman as Truman White House senior aide George Elsey, Rex Scouten, the White House curator who as noted above began his work for 10 U.S. presidents by serving as one of Truman's favorite Secret Service agents, and Dr. Dorothy Height, the president of National Council of Negro Women and one of the most important forces in this country's civil rights movement. These witnesses to history helped me understand that of all the modern American presidents, it was Harry Truman who took a series of unequivocal executive branch actions – without Congressional support – that put the United States on a public policy course that greatly hastened the ability of a General Colin Powell to serve as a president's ranking military commander, and for a young black U.S. senator from Illinois to become the 44th President of the United States.

Harry Truman's personal commitment to civil rights reform is unequivocally clear in an August 18, 1948 letter from Truman to his life-long racist friend Ernie Roberts. In this private election year letter from the president that was never released by the Truman White House, Harry writes that he would rather lose the White House than abandon his pioneering civil rights crusade:

"Dear Ernie:

"I appreciated very much your letter of last Saturday night from Hotel Temple Square in the Mormon Capital.

> *I am going to send you a copy of the report of my Commission on Civil Rights and then if you still have that antebellum proslavery outlook, I'll be thoroughly disappointed in you.*
>
> *The main difficulty with the South is that they are living eighty years behind the times and the sooner they come out of it the better it will be for the country and themselves...*
>
> *When a Mayor and a City Marshal can take a negro Sergeant off a bus in South Carolina, beat him up and put out one of his eyes, and nothing is done about it by the State Authorities, something is radically wrong with the system.*
>
> *...I can't approve of such goings on and I shall never approve it, as long as I am here, as I told you before. I am going to try to remedy it and if that ends up in my failure to be reelected, that failure will be in a good cause..."*
>
> Sincerely yours,
Harry S. Truman

Talk about moral guts. I learned that my dear father was wrong; Harry Truman was not a political hack but, instead, a president who put all Americans ahead of his political goals.

CONCLUSION

From that hot August afternoon in 1946 when I was first crowned King of Sprinkler Lane at the public Chevy Chase, D.C. playground, it has been a charmed life.

Sure there have been some bumps in the road, but my life has been remarkably blessed and interesting. For a barely literate grade schooler at Blessed Sacrament, to my "intellectual boot camp" under the Jesuits at Gonzaga High School, to Georgetown law school at night, my path has been extraordinarily lucky and unorthodox. And for someone who was hooked on presidential politics in my teen years, what a unique bi-partisan career path I followed: enjoying a bird's eye view of the Kennedy-Shriver families; knowing the real LBJ based on the insights of his lifelong friend Governor John B. Connally; also watching, firsthand, President Nixon and the Nixon White House both before and during the travails of Watergate; being named to four presidential Commissions by Presidents Nixon, Ford and Reagan; and finally having the opportunity to serve President Reagan in several capacities including his Ambassador to a U.N. Treaty Conference.

Given where I started – in that little row house on Military Road in Northwest Washington, it has been an extraordinary journey. And it's all thanks to my wife and soulmate Theresa, my two incredible daughters, Courtney and Christine, my loving parents and relatives, generous mentors, and loyal friends – people who never gave up on me even when I was a nearly hopeless case.

EPILOGUE

In the spring of 2007, I was diagnosed with Parkinson's disease. At that point, my only exposure to the disease was observing the husband of a close friend of 30 years. While my friend never complained as she provided steadfast support to her husband, I, nonetheless, knew of her deep concern as her husband deteriorated further.

When I first learned that I had this progressive disease, I was terrified. I dreaded ending up like my friend's husband, who, by his last years, was severely disabled due to his Parkinson's.

And that's when my wife Theresa and I determined that my life would not be defined by Parkinson's. I would do whatever I could to continue to live a productive and joyful life. With Theresa as my inspiration due to her own severe nerve disorder, I sought out the best medical care. Thanks to Jim Brady's miracle worker Dr. Art Kobrine, I found a young neurologist named Dr. Rhanni Herzfeld. Rhanni was and is a cutting edge, with-it doctor who prescribes the least amount of medication possible. She also advises her Parkinson's patients to relentlessly exercise – something I have been doing for 50 years plus.

But the critical ingredient in my addressing the challenge of Parkinson's was my Father's frequent admonishment; "attitude is 90% of the ballgame. And with a good attitude, anything is possible." For the past seven years, my father's advise has been validated. Aside from the routine, minor frustrations faced by people with Parkinson's, I have flourished.

I go to work every day, ready to represent my law firm clients in the most professional and creative way possible. And I still provide the pro-bono management for the USTTI - the nonprofit telecommunications-internet training institute that has over the last 32 years, provided its tuition-free training to 9,186 women and men who are bringing modern, affordable communications to their fellow country-men and women in 171 developing countries.

So it's still a charmed life for me and my loyal wife. We are blessed with two beautiful daughters who married good, respectful men of integrity; we are also blessed as the grandparents of Gardner and her sister Bennett living in Denver and Mackey, in nearby Bethesda. We have rich memories and have enormous gratitude for the adventures shared to date, and for those that await us.

ACKNOWLEDGEMENT

For any author, discipline is a much needed virtue. For authors who are writing stories about their own lives, discipline is especially critical. And that's where Dr. Lori Shpunt came in with the precision of a brain surgeon and the tenacity of a butcher; she edited *King of Sprinkler Lane* without mercy as she eliminated any extra words. I thank her sincerely for her unstinting efforts.

The veteran Washington journalist Chuck Lewis also deserves my sincere thanks for his keen editor's pen and helpful suggestions.

There are no words that can adequately express my gratitude to my loyal assistant Esther Gabriel who typed and retyped *King of Sprinkler Lane* so often that she no doubt has it memorized.

And finally many thanks to my wife Theresa and my daughters Courtney and Christine for their encouragement – and downright insistence that I memorialize some of our shared adventures. Without their relentless lobbying, *King of Sprinkler Lane* would not have been published.

Made in the USA
Middletown, DE
08 September 2015